OFFBEAT HISTORY

OFFBEAT
HISTORY

A COMPENDIUM OF LIVELY AMERICANA

EDITED BY

BULKLEY S. GRIFFIN

THE WORLD PUBLISHING COMPANY
CLEVELAND AND NEW YORK

Published by The World Publishing Company
2231 West 110th Street, Cleveland, Ohio 44102

Published simultaneously in Canada by Nelson, Foster & Scott Ltd.

First World Printing 1967

Library of Congress Catalog Card Number: 67–10450

PRINTED IN THE UNITED STATES OF AMERICA

TO BENNA

FOREWORD

BULKLEY GRIFFIN has many service stripes for news coverage of Washington, D.C. Over the years he has collected bits of Americana from various media, this volume being the product. The individual items may seem like trivia in the vast design of history. But each is a tiny facet of the America we love, and their total effect is luminous. I found this to be a constantly entertaining volume, as it has no real beginning or end, each page marking a fresh start.

WILLIAM O. DOUGLAS

INTRODUCTION

> "When an eye-witness sets down in narra-
> tive form some extraordinary occurrence
> which he has witnessed, that is news—that
> is the news form, and its interest is abso-
> lutely indestructible; time can have no de-
> teriorating effect upon that episode."
> —*Mark Twain in his* Autobiography

THIS compilation is history composed of little-known incidents, customs and reactions during the ongoing of the United States in the period 1775–1915.

Just about every aspect of our nation's life finds depiction, and generally from an uncommon point of view. Many of the happenings and their narrators are forgotten today; certainly no event or author is included on the ground of being well-known.

About ninety per cent of the accounts are first-person; the writers saw or experienced what they tell about. Nobody bears witness at a distance, so to speak.

No formal or programmed search led to this book. It is the product of a journeying through thousands of secondhand volumes purchased by the editor over the years for his own library. The clarifying notes that preface each selection are the yield of extended and illumining research.

The editor hopes these informal narratives will summon for the reader the same fresh and prompt interest—striking chords of memory and curiosity, making yesterday newly real—as they did for him in their discovery.

BULKLEY S. GRIFFIN

ACKNOWLEDGMENTS

A *Great Illustrator's Drawings Offend*. From HARDLY A MAN IS NOW ALIVE by Dan Beard. Copyright 1939 by Doubleday & Company, Inc. Reprinted by permission of the publisher, Doubleday & Company, Inc.

A *Shocking Picture of Stevenson's Last Years*. From LETTERS OF HENRY ADAMS, edited by Worthington C. Ford. Copyright 1930 by W. C. Ford. Copyright renewed 1958 by Emily E. F. Lowes. Reprinted by permission of the publisher, Houghton Mifflin Company.

Emigrants to a City that Wasn't There. Reprinted by permission of Appleton-Century, from A-RAFTING ON THE MISSISSIPP' by Charles Edward Russell. Copyright 1928 by Charles Edward Russell. Copyright renewed 1956 by Theresa H. Russell.

Julian Street—an Author and a Red-Light District. By permission of Margot Street, from ABROAD AT HOME by Julian Street. Copyright 1914 by Century Co. Copyright renewed 1942 by Julian Street.

When the Settlers Fleeced the Eastern Financiers. From FOLLOWING THE PRAIRIE FRONTIER by Seth King Humphrey. Copyright 1931 by the University of Minnesota. Copyright renewed 1958 by the Merchants Bank of Boston. Reprinted by permission of New England Merchants National Bank.

Why Lincoln Pardoned So Many. From GROVER CLEVELAND: A RECORD OF FRIENDSHIP by Richard Watson Gilder. Copyright 1910 by Century Co. Copyright renewed 1938 by Rosamond Gilder. Reprinted by permission of Rosamond Gilder.

CONTENTS

THE REVOLUTION

WAR OF 1812

THE CIVIL WAR

FOOD, FASHION AND MANNERS

TRAVEL AND HARDSHIPS

ASPECTS OF RELIGION

UNCOMMON GLIMPSES OF AUTHORS

A VARIETY OF HAPPENINGS

OFFBEAT HISTORY

PRESIDENTS
SEEN INFORMALLY

PRESIDENT WASHINGTON THROUGH CANDID EYES

SENATOR WILLIAM MACLAY of Pennsylvania (1734–1804) was one of those men, needful to any profitable society, who instinctively dislike pomp and most occupants of high office. His character was sturdy, independent, raspy and barren of reverence but not of courage.

Maclay served in the Senate of our first Congress (1789–91), which met behind closed doors, and his journal furnishes the best information on that historic body.

In that era of the Federalist party, Maclay, six-feet-three, muscular, and wearing his hair tied behind or "clubbed," emerged as the pioneer Jeffersonian Democrat. "Pennsylvania may be called the home of the first Jeffersonian Democrat. Jefferson did not reach the seat of government until eleven months after Congress commenced to work and dur-that time Maclay was at the democratic helm," wrote historian Mary R. Beard. Maclay failed of reelection.

His journal reveals Maclay as standing unbowed and critical before President George Washington, Vice-President John Adams and the rest of them. He successfully fought the wish of Adams, who presided over the Senate, to confer a royal-sounding title upon Washington, and to label "most gracious" Washington's first inaugural address to Congress.

Below, are two passages from his journal. The first tells of the going of the senators to Washington's residence to present the Senate's reply to the inaugural address, and how the President conducted himself. In that first session of the first Congress Washington had delivered his inaugural to a joint session. Each house of Congress then separately tendered a reply, and to each such reply Washington himself read a response. The second extract—also from the first session—details a dinner party given by Washington that Maclay attended, on an invitation that Maclay considered long overdue.

The first two sessions of the first Congress were held in New York, the third in Philadelphia.

Sketches of Debate in the First Senate of the United States, in 1789–90–91. *By William Maclay. Edited by George W. Harris.*

Monday 18th.[1] Senate met. The Address (to the President) was read over, and we proceeded in carriages to the President's to present it. Having no part to act but that of a mute, I had nothing to embarrass me. We were received in an antechamber. Had some little difficulty about seats, as there were several wanting; from whence may be inferred that the President's *major domo* is not the most provident, as our numbers were well enough known. We had not been seated more than three minutes, when it was signified to us to wait on the President in his levee room. Our President[2] went foremost, and the Senators followed, without any particular order. We made our bows as we entered; and our President, having made a bow, began to read an address. He was much confused. The paper trembled in his hand, though he had the aid of both by resting it on his hat, which he held in his left hand. He read very badly all that was on the front pages. The turning of the page seemed to restore him, and he read the rest with more propriety. This agitation was the more remarkable as there were but twenty-two persons present, and none of them strangers.

The President took his reply out of his pocket. He had his spectacles in his jacket pocket; having his hat in his left hand and the paper in his right. He had too many objects for his hands. He shifted his hat between his forearm and the left side of his breast. But taking his spectacles from the case embarrassed him. He got rid of this small distress by laying the spectacle case on the chimney-

[1] May 18, 1789.
[2] The president of the Senate, Vice-President John Adams.

*New York's Federal Hall, partly hidden by the large house
on the right, as it appeared in 1797. Here President Washington was
inaugurated in 1789.*

piece. Colonel Humphreys stood on his right, Mr. Lear on his left.[3]
Having adjusted his spectacles, which was not very easy, considering
the engagements on his hands, he read the reply with tolerable ex-
actness, and without much emotion.

I thought he should have received us with his spectacles on, which
would have saved the making of some uncouth motions. Yet, on the
whole, he did nearly as well as anybody else could have done the
same motions. Could the laws of etiquette have permitted him to
have been disencumbered of his hat, it would have relieved him
much.

After having read his reply, he delivered the paper to our
President with an easy inclination, bowed round to the company,

[3] Lt. Col. David Humphreys, distinguished soldier, poet and diplomat, was
then living with his friend George Washington. Tobias Lear was private secretary
to Washington.

and desired them to be seated. This politeness seems founded in reason, for men, after standing quite still some time, want to sit, if it were only a minute or two. Our President did not comply, nor did he refuse, but stood so long that the President repeated the request. He declined it by a low bow, and retired. We made our bows, came out to the door, and waited till our carriages took us up. Colonel Humphreys waited on us to the door. Returned.

Senate adjourned early [August 27]. At a little after four, I called on Mr. Bassett, of the Delaware State. We went to the President's to dinner.

The company were: President and Mrs. Washington, Vice-President and Mrs. Adams, the Governor and his wife, Mr. Jay and wife, Mr. Langdon and wife, Mr. Dalton and a lady, perhaps his wife, and Mr. Smith, Bassett,⁴ myself, Lear and Lewis, the President's two secretaries. The President and Mrs. Washington sat opposite each other, in the middle of the table. The two secretaries, one at each end. It was a great dinner, and the best of the kind ever I was at. The room, however, was disagreeably warm. *First*, was soup; fish, roasted and boiled; meats—gammon, fowls, &c. This was the dinner. The middle of the table was garnished in the usual tasty way, with small images, flowers (artificial), &c.

The desert was *first* apple pies, puddings, &c.; then iced creams, jellies, &c.; then water-melons, musk-melons, apples, peaches, nuts.

It was the most solemn dinner ever I sat at. Not an health drank—scarce a word said, until the cloth was taken away. Then the President, taking a glass of wine, with great formality, drank to the health of every individual, by name, round the table. Everybody imitated him—charged glasses; and such a buzz of health, sir, and health, madam, and thank you, sir, and thank you, madam, never had I heard before. Indeed, I had like to have been thrown out in the hurry; but I got a little wine in my glass, and passed the ceremony.

The ladies sat a good while, and the bottles passed about—but there was a dead silence almost. Mrs. Washington at last withdrew with the ladies. I expected the men would now begin, but the same

⁴ To further identify these guests: George Clinton was then governor of New York; John Jay was chief justice of the U.S. Supreme Court; John Langdon, senator from New Hampshire; Tristram Dalton, senator from Massachusetts; Richard Bassett, senator from Delaware; the unfortunate Mr. Smith, who was later to tell his anecdote, remains unidentified.

stillness remained. The President told of a New England clergyman, who had lost a hat and wig in passing a river called the Brunks. He *smiled*, and everybody else laughed. He now and then said a sentence or two on some common subject, and what he said was not amiss. Mr. Jay tried to make a laugh by mentioning the circumstance of the Duchess of Devonshire leaving no stone unturned to carry Fox's election.[5] There was a Mr. Smith, who mentioned how *Homer* described Aeneas leaving *his wife* and carrying *his father* out of flaming Troy. He had heard somebody (I suppose) witty on the occasion; but if he had ever *read* it he would have said *Virgil*. The President kept a fork in his hand, when the cloth was taken away, I thought for the purpose of picking nuts. He eat no nuts, but played with the fork, striking on the edge of the table with it. We did not sit long after the ladies retired. The President rose, went up stairs to drink coffee—the company followed. I took my hat, and came home.

A PRESIDENT RECREATES IN THE POTOMAC

THE YEARS have a habit of doing away with simplicity. The era when President John Quincy Adams (1767–1848) went down to the Potomac from the White House, left his clothes on a rock and swam for an hour or more in the river, attended at most only by a servant in a boat, has permanently departed.

These extracts from his diaries summon attention to an impressive physical prowess that we do not commonly associate with the scholarly John Quincy Adams, holder of a long line of official positions. Not only is fresh water less buoyant than salt, but the Potomac, which Adams often swam across, was broader at Washington then than now. It was a mile and three-quarters across when Adams was president, Congressman Ogle (Pennsylvania Whig), referring to these swims, told the House a dozen years later.

The age of the swimmer should be noted. The diary items start when Adams, secretary of state, was 57. They continue through his

---

[5] This sentence was omitted in the first edition of Maclay's journal, which is otherwise followed here.

presidency, 1825–29, and include a swim when Adams, then a member of the House, was 77.

From Memoirs of John Quincy Adams,
Comprising Portions of His Diary from 1795
to 1848. *Edited by Charles Francis Adams.*

July 11 [1823]—And I commence upon my fifty-seventh year. Swam with Antoine[1] an hour in the Potomac. We started for the bridge, but after swimming about half an hour, I perceived by reference to a house upon the shore, beyond which we were to pass, that we had ascended very little above where we had left our clothes, and that the current of the tide was insensibly carrying us into the middle of the river. We continued struggling against the tide about twenty minutes longer, without apparently gaining a foot upon the tide. I then turned back, and in fifteen minutes landed at the rock where I had left my clothes, upon which, in the interval, the tide has so much encroached that it began to wet them, and in another half-hour would have soaked them through or floated them away. We had been an hour and five minutes in the water, without touching ground, and before turning back I began to find myself weary.

Aug. 9—Swam in the Potomac to the bridge against the tide, and returned with it. One hour and fifty minutes in the water, Antoine being still at hand with the canoe. I was about an hour and a half in going, and not more than twenty minutes in returning.

Aug. 5 [1824]—Swam an hour in the Potomac alone; but the morning was cool, and the remonstrances of my friends against the continuance of this practice will induce me to abandon it perhaps altogether.

June 13 [1825]—I attempted to cross the river with Antoine in a small canoe, with a view to swim across it to come back. He took

---

[1] A servant, obtained in Amsterdam, 1814, who became Adams' steward and butler; he and his wife remained in the White House when Jackson succeeded Adams.

a small boat in which we had crossed it last summer without accident. The boat was at the shore near Van Ness's poplars; but in crossing the Tiber to the point, my son John, who was with us, thought the boat dangerous, and, instead of going with us, went and undressed at the rock, to swim and meet us in midway of the river as we should be returning. I thought the boat safe enough, or rather persisted carelessly in going without paying due attention to its condition; gave my watch to my son; made a bundle of my coat and waist-coat to take in the boat with me; put off my shoes, and was paddled by Antoine, who had stripped himself entirely naked. Before we had got half across the river, the boat had leaked itself half full, and then we found there was nothing on board to scoop up the water and throw it over. Just at that critical moment a fresh breeze from the northwest blew down the river as from the nose of a bellows. In five minutes' time it made a little tempest, and set the boat to dancing till the river came in at the sides. I jumped overboard, and Antoine did the same, and lost hold of the boat, which filled with water and drifted away. We were as near as possible to the middle of the river, and swam to the opposite shore. Antoine, who was naked, reached it with little difficulty. I had much more, and, while struggling for life and gasping for breath, had ample leisure to reflect upon my own indiscretion. My principal difficulty was in the loose sleeves of my shirt, which filled with water and hung like two fifty-six-pound weights upon my arms. I had also my hat, which I soon gave, however, to Antoine. After reaching the shore, I took off my shirt and pantaloons, wrung them out, and gave them to Antoine to go and look out for our clothes, or for a person to send to the house for others, and for the carriage to come and fetch me. Soon after he had gone, my son John joined me, having swum wholly across the river, expecting to meet us returning with the boat. Antoine crossed the bridge, sent a man to my house for the carriage, made some search for the drifted boat and bundles, and found his own hat with his shirt and braces in it, and one of my shoes. He also brought over the bridge my son's clothes with my watch and umbrella, which I had left with him.

While Antoine was gone, John and I were wading and swimming up and down on the other shore, or sitting naked basking on the bank at the margin of the river, John walked over the bridge home. The carriage came, and took me and Antoine home, half

*John Quincy Adams photographed by
Mathew Brady about 1847.*

dressed. I lost an old summer coat, white waistcoat, two napkins, two white handkerchiefs, and one shoe. Antoine lost his watch, jacket, waistcoat, pantaloons, and shoes. The boat was also lost. By the mercy of God our lives were spared, and no injury befell our persons.

July 27 [1828]—With my son John, my nephew, and Antoine, I crossed the river in our canoe, and swam a quarter of an hour on the other side; but the shore is so deceptive that after diving from the boat, as I supposed, within a ten minutes' swim of the shore, before reaching half the distance I found myself so fatigued that I called the boat to me, and clung to her till she was rowed to the shore. We had crossed nearly opposite the Tiber point, and were annoyed with leeches and ticks at the landing. The decline of my health is in nothing so closely brought to my conviction as in my inability to swim more than fifteen or twenty minutes without tiring. This was the day of most overpowering heat that we have had this season.

June 27 [1844]—This day set in the extreme heat of the summer; the trial of climate to my constitution. A burning sun; the thermometers in my chamber at ninety and a light breeze from the southwest—a fan delicious to the face, but parching instead of cooling the skin. I have been a full month longing for a river bath without daring to take it. This morning at five I went in the barouche to my old favorite spot, found the tide unusually high; all my station rocks occupied by young men, except one, and that surrounded by the tide, already upon the ebb. I had some difficulty to dress and undress, but got my bath, swam about five minutes, and came out washed and refreshed. It was my exercise for the day. After returning home I did not again pass the sill of the street door.

SLEDGE-HAMMER POLITICS—1840 CAMPAIGN

This House speech of Congressman Charles Ogle of Pennsylvania, (1798–1841), delivered April 14, 1840, lights up the pile-driver type of political attack of that time. Ogle was a Whig and the Whigs were trying to wrest the White House from the Democrats, who had held it for a dozen years under Andrew Jackson and Martin Van Buren. The latter was now a candidate for reelection, opposed by General William Henry Harrison, Whig.

The Ogle address, dealing in the main with the alleged regal extravagance of the White House under Van Buren—a follow-up speech was delivered the next day—also gives a glimpse of the rough-handed newspaper humor of that hot campaign. The first two quoted paragraphs of the Ogle assault refer to an editorial in the Democratic *Washington Globe*, which had elaborated in uncourtly fashion on the allegation that General Harrison's friends had shut him up in a cage to prevent his repetition of politically indiscreet remarks. Representative Ogle, without misquoting but with judicious omissions, invested this Democratic editorial with additional sinister aspect to all loyal Whigs.

Ogle was a lawyer who served in the House for four years without discernible distinction, save for these two speeches. He died in 1841. The addresses of Ogle—whose father and a nephew were also House members—were pamphleted and spread through the land. We get a description of Ogle in August 1840, from Anne Royall, author and editor: "Hon. C. Ogle is likewise conspicuous in the House and though he has lost much of the fullness and bloom of his fine manly face, yet his appearance is still striking."

From Speech of Mr. Ogle of Pennsylvania, The Regal Splendor of The President's Palace. *Delivered in the House of Representatives, April 14, 1840.*

I will not, assuredly, be restrained from the fullest exercise of the freedom of speech by the licentious course of the accredited "organ" of Martin Van Buren. I refer to the "Globe"—a newspaper which receives its pabulum, not "from the crumbs which fall from the rich man's table," but from enormous largesses and profitable contracts, voted for its sustenance from the treasury of the people— a paper that holds its existence by the sole tenure of Martin Van Buren's sovereign good pleasure, and which promulges daily, through its broad pages, not the thoughts and motives of the miserable scavenger whose name it ostensibly wears, but the wishes and designs of his despotic master—a paper, sir, that is published ''BY AU-THORITY.'' What honest man has read, without feelings of burning indignation, in the recent lucubrations of this "Official Organ," the foul, not to say beastly, assaults against the character and patriotism of the venerable and heroic defender[1] of the violated honor and invaded rights of his country? Who has not been fired with anger at beholding in Martin Van Buren's organ the false and malignant representations of the hero of Tippecanoe—as "a superannuated old woman"—a "pitiable dotard"—a "granny"—a "red petticoat general"—as the "hero of forty defeats"—as delivering "inaugural addresses to pigs and poultry"—as "shut up in an iron cage, and compelled to wear an iron mask, and drink hard cidar?" "No other person (says the "Globe" of April 13, 1840,) is permitted to come near him but an old servant waiter, who brings his meals,

[1] Gen. Harrison, Whig presidential candidate, who defeated the Indians at Tippecanoe.

and performs THE NECESSARY DUTIES OF THE CAGE. None of the domestic animals are allowed to come near the cage; and a favorite dog, WHO RAN AWAY WITH HIM IN ALL HIS BATTLES, having been observed to bark very significantly, after an interview with his master, was forthwith knocked in the head, and thrown into the Ohio."

I ask you, Mr. Chairman,[2] whether Martin Van Buren manifests a "decent respect" for the opinions and intelligence of the American People, when he vilifies, through the agency of his official organ, an old soldier, who, to rescue "thousands of women and children from the scalping knife of the ruthless savage," freely abandoned all the endearments of home and family, endured the icy and piercing blasts of north-western winters, wading through the deep and cold waters and black swamps of Michigan and upper Canada, sustaining, at times, an almost famished nature upon "raw beef, without salt," and often perilling life on the field of battle? . . .

. . . With your permission, Mr. Chairman, I will now again conduct you to the first story of the palace,[3] where we shall enter the great "Court Banqueting room," in which I can promise you a sight that will be "good for sore eyes." It is a genuine locofoco's[4] dinner table—set out, arranged in order, and duly prepared to receive the Court guests. In the first place, however, I must inform you that this table is not provided with those old and unfashionable dishes, *"hog and hominy," "fried meat and gravy," "schnitz, knep, and sourcrout,"* with a mug of *"hard cider."* No, sir, no. All these substantial preparations are looked upon by *gourmands, French cooks,* and *locofoco Presidents* as exceedingly vulgar, and fit only to set before "Bank Whigs,"[5] and men (as the "Globe" eloquently expresses it) *"who adopt the maxims and principles* of COBBLERS and TINKERS." But the true orthodox, democratic viands, with which a genuine locofoco furnishes his dinner table, consists in *massive gold plate and French sterling silver services, blue and gold*

[2] The House was in Committee of the Whole House, where the Speaker is, by rule, absent, and a designated member presides as Chairman.

[3] White House.

[4] A term applied to Democrats.

[5] Whigs who voted for the second Bank of the United States, which Jackson put out of business.

*French tambours, compotiers on feet, stands for bonbons, with
three stages, gilded French plateaus, garnished with mirrors and
garlands, and gaudy artificial flowers.*

Albeit, sir, there is no food for the palate placed upon this
locofoco's table, there is a feast of gold for the eye that would have
satiated King Midas himself. And although the wood of several large
forests was not cut down to dress the victuals for this Tamerlane
banquet, yet it required the enormous sum of ELEVEN
THOUSAND ONE HUNDRED AND NINETY-
ONE DOLLARS AND THIRTY-TWO CENTS OF
THE PEOPLE'S CASH TO BUY THE TABLE
"FURNITURE."

You seem amazed, Mr. Chairman. Do not believe that I speak
not the "words of truth and soberness." I have now in my hands,
sir, the *"official vouchers,"* which show the expenditure of every
dollar of that large sum, and that the whole amount thereof, with
the exception of $1,125, was expended since the days of the *plain,
frugal, economical, republican, retrenching reformation* of Jackson
and Van Buren commenced. And I here, in my place, demand, in
the name of my constituents, that the Committee on the Expenditures on the Public Buildings make a report to this House, and
communicate copies, not only of the vouchers on this subject, but
all the vouchers in relation to expenditures for the President's
House, furniture, and grounds; that they may be all spread before
the people in an *"official form."* This everlasting leakage from the
people's strong box must be stanched.

But I will exhibit to the committee the various bills which form
the aggregate of $11,191.32 for the table service of the democratic
President.

I will, in the first place, bring to the notice of the committee
the bill for the French STERLING SILVER PLATE and GILT
DESSERT SET, bought from a RUSSIAN NOBLEMAN, DE M.
LE GENERAL BARON DE TUYLL, *resident minister of his*
MAJESTY the EMPEROR of RUSSIA *at Lisbon,* for the sum of
four thousand three hundred and eight dollars and eighty-two cents.

The silver plate consists of SOUP TUREENS, SAUCE BOATS,
PLATES, *diverses* grandeurs, BOTTLE STANDS, SOUP LADLES,
ET CETERA ET CETERA ET CETERA, *three hundred and
thirty-eight pieces.*

This laudatory, illustrated political biography ran to almost 100 pages, demonstrating that in 1840 the opposing parties—Democratic (President Van Buren) vs. Whig (General Harrison)—anticipated today's copious output of political literature.

The gilt dessert set is composed of TABLE SPOONS, SWEET-MEAT SPOONS, TEA OR COFFEE SPOONS, KNIVES, FORKS, ET CETERA ET CETERA, *one hundred and forty pieces.*

It may be proper to remark that *pure* gold is generally considered too ductile and soft to manufacture into knives, forks, and other utensils, which require some degree of firmness or want of pliability. The gilt or gold service, therefore, used in the palaces of kings and at the castles of wealthy noblemen in Europe, is composed of a slight substratum of silver, thickly plated or overlaid with pure gold. And hence, I presume, the gilt service of the President was manufactured after the same manner. No honest democrat, however, by taking up the various articles of which it consists, would be led to doubt a moment that they are made of gold, without any alloy. They *may be pure gold,* though I am inclined to believe otherwise, inasmuch as they were procured from one of the great nobles of the Russian Empire.

Mr. Chairman, in my opinion, it is time the people of the United States should know that their money goes to buy for their plain hard-handed democratic President, knives, forks, and spoons of gold, that he may dine in the style of the monarchs of Europe.

I do not know that the rich gold and silver service is shown on all occasions; probably it is only when the *elite* are invited. But let any gentleman go to the palace when our *now* well-beloved cousin from South Carolina, whom the "Official Organ" *formerly* delighted to call John *Catiline* Calhoun,[6] is at the banquet, and then the gold service in all its democratic lustre will be presented to his admiring eyes! Oh! sir, how delightful it must be to a real genuine locofoco to eat his *paté de foie gras, dinde desossé,* and *salade à la volaile* from a SILVER PLATE with a GOLDEN KNIFE AND FORK. And how exquisite to sip with a GOLDEN SPOON his *soupe a la Reine* from a SILVER TUREEN. It almost "makes my mouth water" to talk about it.

I will in the next place call the attention of the committee to the bill for the *splendid French China for dinner service, and the elegant dessert set of blue and gold, with eagle;* ALL MADE TO ORDER in France, and imported by Lewis Veron & Co., celebrated dealers in Fancy China, et cetera, Philadelphia.

[6] John Caldwell Calhoun, South Carolina statesman, who broke with Jackson but supported Van Buren.

This ornate punch bowl, thought to be
from President Andrew Jackson's service,
is considered one of the choicest pieces in the
White House china collection.

The SET OF FRENCH CHINA for dinner service has *four hundred and forty pieces*, consisting of *olive boats, octagon salad bowls, pickle shells, long fish dishes*, et cetera et cetera, and cost one thousand dollars.

The DESSERT SET, *blue and gold, with eagle*, composed of *four hundred and twelve pieces*, including six stands for BONBONS, with three stages; EIGHT TAMBOURS, with three stages; TWELVE SWEETMEAT COMPOTIERS, on feet; EIGHT COMPOTIERS, on feet; SIX LARGE FRUIT BASKETS, on feet; FOUR ICE-CREAM VASES and Covers, with inside Bowls; FIVE DOZEN GREEK-FORM CUPS and SAUCERS, et cetera et cetera, cost one thousand five hundred dollars.

Mr. Chairman, don't you think that one of your plain republican "*Suckers*" would feel "kinder queer like" to be placed at the President's table, before these democratic "Tambours with three stages," and "Compotiers on feet?" Why, sir, he would almost imagine that he had suddenly been translated to the *salle a festin en maison royale* of Louis Philippe, King of the French. I have no doubt that some of my constituents would much rather face the grizzly bear, on the Appalachian mountains, than sit down before these "Tambours with three stages," and "Compotiers on feet," for *five consecutive hours* —the period usually required by Kings and democratic Presidents to masticate a state dinner.

BOSTON MADE PRESIDENT TYLER SNEAK HIS BRANDY

PRESIDENT TYLER and members of his cabinet came up to Boston for the dedication of the Bunker Hill Monument on June 17, 1843. A few days later, George Bancroft (1800–1891), the historian and public servant, penned some account of the day's events to former President Van Buren.

From The Life and Letters of George Bancroft. *By* M. A. DeWolfe Howe.

The dinner was a cold water one,—teetotal—but Tyler must have his brandy and water, and it was amusing to see him hold his tumbler below the table, to get a stiff glass of it, and then duck himself down to swallow it unseen. Quite a jest for the Washingtonians.

THE CROWD TOLERATED
LINCOLN'S GETTYSBURG ADDRESS

JOHN RUSSELL YOUNG, Civil War correspondent for the *Philadelphia Press*, sat a few feet from Lincoln during the delivery of the Gettysburg address. At its conclusion—it was so short—he leaned over and asked the President if that was all. Yes, replied Lincoln, he did not think he could say any more.

This is an eloquent eye-witness account, not only of the address but also of the rest of the ceremony, and of that day in Gettysburg and of the night before when the Presidential party arrived.

Mr. Young (1841–99) also wrote for the New York *Tribune* and the New York *Herald*. In 1877, he went around the world with former President Grant and wrote a book about the trip. He was minister to China (1882–85), and librarian of the Congressional Library from 1897 to his death.

From Men and Memories: Personal Reminiscences. *By John Russell Young. Edited
by May D. Russell Young.*

The celebration of Gettysburg took place on Thursday, the 19th of November, 1863, a little more than four months after the famous battle was fought.

When we arrived the rainy afternoon settled into a soggy November night. Gettysburg was in chaos over the new invasion, and a corner in a tavern was a crowning mercy. The Presidential party came in about sunset, and we were all on hand to do them honor. They were a straggled, hungry set. Lincoln, with that weary smile, which a poet might have read as a forecast of destiny; Seward, with an essentially bad hat; John Hay, in attendance upon the President, and much to be troubled by the correspondents, handsome as a peach, the countenance of extreme youth; Usher, Secretary of the Interior, if I remember, with heavy, reserved features, and a capacity for silence; Dennison, of Ohio, smiling and courteous; gruff Tod, from Ohio; Pierpont, of Virginia; Montgomery Blair,[1] with his face in which fanaticism was tempered by enthusiasm; John W. Forney, in the flush of his winning manhood, Secretary of the Senate and rather in the lead of the Washington party. Lincoln became invisible to us, and could not be enticed even by serenading parties, who were bewildering the night with music. Seward was more amenable, and as he came to the door I recall my trouble in reporting him. Nothing better than the note book and a stone step.

I think I was indebted to John Hay, assuredly to some kind friend, for a special audience with Edward Everett. We of this generation do not realize the space which Edward Everett filled, at least in the imagination of the younger men. He was the embodiment of a noble and stainless fame. Webster, Clay, Calhoun gone, he was the last of the orators. No more great men left to us, only Everett. He had welcomed Lafayette; his scholarship was our envy and admiration; he had been the friend of Byron, the guest of Walter Scott, Minister to England, Secretary of State, and we, even we were permitted to see him.

The procession from the town was a ragged affair, we all seeming to get there as best we could. A regiment of cavalry, a regiment of infantry, a couple of batteries clattering about, added to the confusion, and not much to the dignity of the day. Everett had been carefully conveyed in sheltered fashion. He was prudently not exposed to the vicissitudes of a crowd, and that oration impending and the sore task for a raw November day. We gathered about the house where Lincoln resided, and waited—led horses restlessly in attendance. The President came to the door, a fine flush and smile coming over his face at the rude welcome. "Three cheers for Old Abe," "Hurrah for Lincoln," most heartily given, as he mounted the saddle, sitting there to appearances a perfect horseman, his tall form tower-

---

[1] In further identification of the party: William H. Seward, Secretary of State; John Hay, Assistant Secretary to Lincoln, and future author and Secretary of State; John P. Usher, Secretary of Interior; William Dennison, Ohio Governor 1860–62, named Postmaster General 1864; David Tod, Ohio Governor 1862–64; Francis H. Pierpont, Union leader in Western Virginia and (Union) Governor of Virginia 1864–68; Montgomery Blair, Postmaster General.

ing above the escort. As he rode away Seward half mounted, went scurrying after to find his place. Many of the distinguished guests, Curtin[2] leading, Simon Cameron[3] among the number, walked off, a brisk tramp over the country road, the most conducive to comfort on this cold wintry morning.

It was about 11, as I recall it, when we got under way—cavalry, soldiers, statesmen, governors from other States, wounded soldiers, country folks who knew all about the battle, and teeming with narratives of its horror and glory; Horatio Seymour, then Governor of New York; Schenck, a good deal of a hero from his wound—all streamed along, and reached the cemetery in time. We journalists of the party, who had work in hand, forged ahead and were in place before the procession arrived. A rude platform looked out over the battlefield. On one side sat the journalists, John C. New, our Consul-General in London, among others. The eminent people had the other side, the President coming late. There was some little trouble over a Democratic reporter who did not admire Lincoln, and insisted upon standing near the front with his hat on and smoking a cigar, and jeering now and then at the ceremonies. No judicious remonstrance had effect, the reporter claiming his rights in a free country; even the right to stand around with his hat on and smoke whenever and wherever he pleased. A summary proposition to treat him after the manner of Daniel, and throw him over the rails among the lions, adjusted that incident, and there was nothing unseemly to disturb the President's reception. As he slowly came up the steps with his famous company we arose, and as he took his seat there were loud voices of welcome. He sat between Seward and Everett, near him the venerable chaplain of the day. It was an illustrious company, men of national, world-wide glory; others then unknown who were to have in time their own renown.

There was none who made a deeper impression than the clergyman as he arose in prayer,—Thomas H. Stockton, the chaplain of the House. Stockton was celebrated as an ecclesiastical orator; had a fame as wide as that of Everett, but which like Everett's was to pass into obscuration.

Everett spoke for two hours and was heard with the deepest attention. There was little applause—no invitation to applause. I felt

[2] Andrew G. Curtin was governor of Pennsylvania 1861–67.
[3] Former secretary of war and former and future senator from Pennsylvania.

*The draft of the address from which Lincoln read
at Gettysburg.*

as I looked at the orator as if he was some antique Greek statue, so finished, so beautiful, so chaste, so cold, the lines so perfect, the exquisite tracery of the divine manhood—all there—all evolved and rescued from stone—the masterful art, something that you ever dwell upon with freshening wonder at the capacity of human genius. But so cold! If it were only alive!

But if the voice that might have spoken did not come from the silver lips of Everett it yet was to be spoken, and here and now upon the hallowed ground of Gettysburg. When Everett ceased, exhausted, excited, the two hours' talk telling on him, there was a moment of rustle, hands extended in congratulation, the President and Secretary of State among the first, then loving hands carefully enfolding and wrapping him up in shelter from the insidious purposes of the cold November air. The music ran on a bit and the President arose. Deliberate, hesitating, awkward, "like a telescope drawing out," as I heard some one say, the large, bundled up figure untwisting and adjusting itself into reasonable conditions. I do not recall Lincoln as in appearance an imposing man—but impressive. You would turn and look at him a second time on the street. And there was that in his face when you looked closely that might well give one pause—a deep, unfathomable sense of power. He stood an instant waiting for the cheers to cease and the music to exhaust its echoes, slowly adjusted his glasses, and took from his pocket what seemed to be a page of ordinary foolscap paper, quietly unfolded it, looked for the place, and began to read.

My own personal anxieties at the moment were as to whether he would or would not make a speech. Coloney Forney had promised me a ride over the battlefield in the afternoon, along with Senator Cole, of California, and an army officer who had been in the engagement, and we were to have the story of Gettysburg. I had an easy time with Stockton and Everett; prayer and oration in type. But what would the President do? My outing was in the hands of Lincoln. Would he speak an hour? Would he speak from notes and memory or read his address? An extempore effort meant a long evening transcribing notes and no Gettysburg battlefield, no useful afternoon of the solemn study of a mighty drama—aught else, for that matter, but close work in a dingy tavern. I am afraid I pestered Hay on the subject for an advance sight of the manuscript, were there one; but Hay, ever generous and helpful, as I remember, either knew no more than I did or would not tell me. So when the President arose there was my uncertainty. I took up the pencil and began to take him in shorthand. The sight of the single sheet of paper was not reassuring. It could only hold the heads or threads of a discourse —a text as it were—and the outing over the battlefield dissolved into the gray wintry skies. Therefore the emotions with which I took down this immortal address were entirely selfish. To my surprise, almost it seemed before Mr. Lincoln had begun to speak, he turned and sat down. Surely these five or six lines of shorthand were not all. Hurriedly bending over the aisle I asked if that was all. "Yes, for the present," he answered. He did not think he could say any more.

Lincoln, as I was saying, when he arose, adjusted his glasses, and, taking out the single sheet of paper, held it close to his face. He began at once in a high key, voice archaic, strident, almost in a shriek. He spoke slowly, with deliberation, reading straight on. I did not write the report which appeared in the *Press,* as the manuscript had been given to the Associated Press, and the transcription of my notes was unnecessary. This report was studded with "applause," but I do not remember the applause, and am afraid the appreciative reporter was more than generous—may have put in the applause himself as a personal expression of opinion. Nor in fact was there any distinct emotion among those around me on the platform after the prayer, and when Lincoln was speaking, but one of sympathy for the forlorn photographer who failed to take his picture. This enterprising artist, by dint of persuasion and making interest with the crowd, had managed to place his camera in front of the President. And as he began to speak the workman began his work, peeping through his lenses, adjusting them, dodging his head to catch a favorable position, fooling with the cloth that covered the lens, staring wistfully at the President, in the hope to make him "look pleasant" in true photographic fashion. But the President was not a good subject. Whether conscious or not of the honor thus impending, he drove on with his speech, ever holding the paper before the face, the dismayed photographer vainly hoping for one glimpse of the face. And as the President summarily turned to sit down, he desperately uncovered the camera, but too late! The flash of sunshine brought him nothing. There was a general ripple of laughter at his dismay.

I have read many narratives of the scenes, of the emotions produced by the President's address, the transcendent awe that fell upon every one who heard those most mighty and ever living words, to be remembered with pride through the ages. I have read of the tears that fell and the solemn hush, as though in a cathedral solemnity in the most holy moment of the sacrifice. Nor am I insensible to the power of oratory, nor to the rapture that came from hearing Gladstone and Phillips and Castelar.[4] There was nothing of this, to the writer at least, in the Gettysburg address. Nor were the conditions such as to invite it. Mr. Lincoln was an orator. Even as I remember him, there were no flights of oratory to which he did

---

[4] Gladstone, four times prime minister of England; Wendell Phillips, American orator and reformer; Castelar, Spanish orator and republican leader.

not and might not ascend. But he needed to warm up to his subject.
This impression was confirmed by what was said to me in later years
by a very dear friend, who had followed Lincoln and Douglas in
their famous debate of 1858, hearing and reporting the speeches.
"Lincoln," he said, "never began to be an orator until he had been
talking a half hour, and then he was great, especially if any one
interrupted him." At Gettysburg he only spoke three or four minutes.
The long oration of Everett had made people restless. Bits of the
crowd had broken away and were wandering off toward the battle
scenes. We were tired and chilly, and even the November sun did not
take the place of the heavy wraps. Lincoln, as I said, began at once
in a high, strident key, as one who had little to say, and would say
it so as to be heard and seen. The two emotions of that memorable
scene were first the wonderful prayer as chanted by the chaplain,
the rich Hebrew phrases and intonations reverberating like organ
music, and the dismay of the poor artist, who failing to outline the
President's picture, was fain to bundle up his tools and take his
barren journey home.

WHY LINCOLN PARDONED SO MANY

RICHARD WATSON GILDER (1844–1909), poet and *Century* magazine
editor, had this conversation with former President Grover Cleveland in
1906.

From Grover Cleveland: A Record of
Friendship. *By Richard Watson Gilder.*

Mr. Cleveland got to talking about the genuineness of Lincoln's
devotion to the country. The reason, said Mr. Cleveland, that
Lincoln was able to do his work so successfully was because he was
absolutely disinterested, absolutely patriotic; he had real patriotism.
He went on talking about Lincoln with increasing earnestness.

He referred to the objections of the military authorities to his sympathetic attitude toward individual delinquents, and his frequent pardons. "Notwithstanding all that might be objectionable in these," said Cleveland, "what was he doing? *He was fortifying his own heart!* And that," said he, with intense feeling, "that was his strength, his own heart; *that* is a man's strength!"

THREE CONTROVERSIAL VIEWS OF ANDREW JOHNSON

THE FOLLOWING three extracts supply widely diverse views of Andrew Johnson, Lincoln's second Vice-President, who was President from April 1865 to March 1869. The rough, untactful Johnson warred with Congress, which sought, in a trial lasting almost three months, to impeach him, the openly stressed charge being that he endeavored to remove Secretary of War Stanton. The Senate voted for impeachment 35 to 19, but one short of the necessary two-thirds majority.

Both Senator William M. Stewart of Nevada and Secretary of the Treasury Hugh McCulloch were Washington eye-witnesses of Johnson, and each uncompromisingly contradicts the other as to whether, to cite the example presented below, Johnson was a drunkard. Each, by the way, asserts he was present at Johnson's taking of the oath after Lincoln's assassination.

Julius Chambers, New York newspaperman, was in the press gallery when, in March 1875, Johnson entered the room of his judges of seven years earlier, a senator-elect from Tennessee. Andrew Johnson didn't live long to enjoy this measure of vindication. He made one speech in the session that lasted only nineteen days. He died July 31, and on the following January 11 the Senate paid eulogy to its late member, the praise dwelling much on Johnson's blunt integrity of character.

STEWART SAW A BESOTTED JOHNSON

Senator Stewart (1827–1909) was a miner and a mining-claims lawyer, who was senator from Nevada for about thirty years, 1864–75 and 1887–1905. Mark Twain, after his return in 1867 from the voyage that produced his *Innocents Abroad*, was briefly private secretary to Stewart in Washington.

Later the two were less than good friends, Twain ribbing the Senator in *Roughing It* and the latter lambasting Twain in his reminiscences.

From Reminiscences of Senator William M. Stewart of Nevada. *Edited by George Rothwell Brown.*

The election of Andrew Johnson to the office of Vice-President of the United States was a calamity. It was caused by the desire of Northern Republicans and Union men to have a representative from the South on the ticket in 1864.

Johnson was very bitter in his language against the Southern leaders, and the Northern people supposed he was really patriotic. He came to Washington in January or February, 1865, and for some weeks previous to the inauguration of President Lincoln on the 4th of March, 1865, his general condition was a half-drunken stupor. When he entered the Senate Chamber to take the oath of office as Vice-President, and to call that body to order, he was very drunk. He was assisted to the chair by the Sergeant-at-Arms and two door-keepers, and was unable to stand without assistance. I do not believe he was conscious when he took the oath of office. He appeared as a man who did not realize what he was doing.

Immediately after the oath had been administered, he grasped the desk before him with an unsteady hand, and, swaying about so that he threatened to tumble down at any moment, he began an incoherent tirade.

There was no particular point or sense in what he attempted to say. "The people are everything," he bawled, "the people are everything"; and this seemed to be the sole idea he possessed. He lurched around, and pointed to Mr. Seward,[1] who was seated directly in front of the rostrum.

"You are nothing, you are nothing, Mr. Seward," he said. "I tell you, the people are everything."

This drunken jargon continued for some time. Several Senators

[1] Secretary of State William H. Seward.

endeavored to persuade him to leave the stand. Finally he was re-moved, not without some force, by the Sergeant-at-Arms to the Vice-President's room, where he was detained until the ceremony was concluded. All persons present were shocked and amazed, and there was a universal appeal to the representatives of the press to refrain from publishing anything about the disagreeable scene. The news-papers of the country which alluded to it at all did so in vague and obscure language.

After the inauguration of President Lincoln, Vice-President Johnson continued to drink at low groggeries and to associate with toughs and rowdies, both black and white. He was not choice in the selection of his company. Almost anybody was good enough for Johnson, apparently.

One evening, not long after Mr. Lincoln's second term began, I was passing through Judiciary Square. A great crowd of street hoodlums and darkies was congregated about the City Hall steps, listening to the Vice-President. He was intoxicated. His face was very red, and he was excited. I listened. He was contending before the rabble that all the Rebels must be hanged. Johnson didn't make any distinction. He put the whole South in one class. He said it was treason to fight against the Government and that he was in favor of hanging every traitor.

It was quite common for Mr. Johnson to make these open-air speeches; and as he delivered them whenever he had been drinking, naturally he became the most persistent orator in the capital.

Mr. Lincoln died shortly after daylight, and within ten minutes of the time I met Senator Foot,[2] the grand old gray-haired statesman from Vermont, who was chairman of the Republican caucus and master of ceremonies in the Senate. He was hailing a dilapidated wagon, which had seen better days as a carriage, in front of the Willard Hotel. He put his hand on my shoulder as the news of the President's death reached us, wafted on a thousand excited tongues, and said:

"We must get the Chief Justice at once and swear in the Vice-President. It will not do in times like these to be without a Presi-dent."

[2] Senator Solomon Foot of Vermont.

We directed the driver of the hack to take us to the residence of Mr. Chase,[3] who lived in what was then known as the Sprague mansion, at the corner of Sixth and E Streets. Mr. Chase was in his library, pacing back and forth, in deep thought. We explained our business, and he got into the vehicle with us, and went to the old Kirkwood House, on Pennsylvania Avenue.

I sprang out, went to the desk, and asked the clerk what room the Vice-President occupied.

"I will send up your card," he said.

"No, you won't," I said; "I'll go up myself. We want to see him on important business. Send a boy to show the way."

"It is on the third floor," the clerk then said. "Turn to the right at the head of the stairs."

There were no elevators in the hotels at that time, and we climbed the stairs laboriously. A negro boy showed us the room, and I rapped on the door. There was no answer. I rapped again and again. Finally I kicked the door, and made a very loud noise. Then a voice growled:

"Who's there?"

"Senator Stewart," said I, "and the Chief Justice and Senator Foot are with me. We must see you immediately."

After some little delay Johnson opened the door and we entered. The Vice-President was in his bare feet, and only partially dressed, as though he had hurriedly drawn on a pair of trousers and a shirt. He was occupying two little rooms about ten feet square, and we entered one of them, a sitting-room, while he finished his toilet in the other.

In a few minutes Johnson came in, putting on a very rumpled coat, and presenting the appearance of a drunken man. He was dirty, shabby, and his hair was matted, as though with mud from the gutter, while he blinked at us through squinting eyes, and lurched around unsteadily. He had been on a "bender" for a month. As he came into the room we were all standing. Johnson felt for a chair and sat down. Chief Justice Chase said very solemnly:

"The President has been assassinated. He died this morning. I have come to administer the oath of office to you."

Johnson seemed dazed at first. Then he jumped up, thrust his right arm up as far as he could reach, and said in a thick, gruff, hoarse voice:

[3] Salmon P. Chase, chief justice of the U.S.

"I'm ready."

The Chief Justice administered the oath. Johnson—President Johnson—went back to his bedroom, and we retired.

There were only three persons present besides Johnson when he was sworn in—Chief Justice Chase, Senator Foot, and myself. All statements to the contrary are absolutely false. Although he took the oath between seven and eight o'clock in the morning, Johnson pretended not to have heard of the assassination. So far as I am aware nobody knows where he spent the night, although his appearance at daylight indicated clearly what he had been doing.

The Kirkwood House was said by the clerks on the morning after the assassination to have been the headquarters of several of the conspirators. The clerks also told me that Johnson was friendly with them, and it seems strange to me that he did not learn of the assassination until informed by the Chief Justice and myself.

After leaving Johnson I went to Stanton's house.[4] As I arrived his carriage was being driven to his door, and presently he came down the steps. I told him of the condition of Johnson, and said that he must be taken care of—the man who had just taken the oath of office as President of the United States. Stanton and I were driven back to the Kirkwood House, and, accompanied by the coachman, we went directly to Johnson's room. He was lying down. We aroused him, dressed him as well as we could, led him down stairs, and put him in Stanton's carriage. We took him to the White House, and Stanton sent for a tailor, a barber, and a doctor. He had a dose administered, and the President was bathed and shaved, his hair was cut, and a new suit of clothes was fitted him. He did not, however, get into a condition to be visible until late in the afternoon, when a few persons were permitted to see him to satisfy themselves that there was a President in the White House.

"ANDY AIN'T A DRUNKARD"—LINCOLN

Hugh McCulloch (1808–95) was comptroller of the currency in 1863 and secretary of the treasury 1865–69—appointed by Lincoln and retained by Johnson. He served in the latter capacity again in 1884–85. He was also a banker, engaging in that profession both in this country and in England.

[4] Secretary of War Edwin M. Stanton.

From Men and Manners of Half A Century: Sketches and Comments. *By Hugh McCulloch.*

I was not present when Mr. Johnson took the oath of Vice-President in the Senate chamber, but the reports of his speech on that occasion amazed me. It was so different from what had been expected of him, so incoherent, so rambling, that those who listened to it thought that he was intoxicated. "It was not," said a senator to me the next morning, "the speech of Andrew Johnson, but the speech of a drunken man"; and such it undoubtedly was. He had been ill for some days before he left home, and on his way to Washington had taken brandy as an astringent. On the day of his inauguration as Vice-President he was really ill, and was so unwise as to resort to a stimulant before he went to the Senate chamber. His appearance and speech on that occasion made a most unfavorable impression upon the crowded assembly, and fears were excited that, at the time when wise and sober counsels were especially required, an intemperate man had been elected Vice-President. These fears were groundless, but the report of his apparance and speech made an impression upon minds suspicious of all Southern men that was never entirely removed. I had then no personal acquaintance with him, and I shared in the distrust which generally prevailed. Meeting Mr. Lincoln a day or two after, I said to him that the country, in view of the Vice-President's appearance on the 4th, had a deeper stake than ever in his life. He hesitated for a moment, and then remarked with unusual seriousness: "I have known Andy Johnson for many years; he made a bad slip the other day, but you need not be scared; Andy ain't a drunkard."

This remark of Mr. Lincoln came home to me when, a few weeks afterwards, I heard Mr. Johnson take the oath as President. Mr. Lincoln was right. Mr. Johnson was especially intemperate as a speaker when defending his policy and replying to the severe criticism to which he was subjected, but not in the use of liquor. I had good opportunities for observing his habits, and my fears made me watchful. For six weeks after he became President, he occupied a room adjoining mine, and communicating with it, in the Treasury De-

*President Andrew Johnson holds his first cabinet meeting at
the Treasury Building, April 16, 1865.*

partment. He was there every morning before nine o'clock, and he
rarely left before five. There was no liquor in his room. It was open
to everybody. His luncheon, when he had one, was, like mine, a cup
of tea and a cracker. It was in that room that he received the delega-
tions that waited upon him, and the personal and political friends
who called to pay their respects. It was there that he made the
speeches which startled the country by the bitterness of their tone—
their almost savage denunciations of secessionists as traitors who
merited the traitor's doom. So intemperate were some of these
speeches, that I should have attributed them to the use of stimulants
if I had not known them to be the speeches of a sober man, who

Andrew Johnson caught by Brady's camera in a somber mood.

could not overcome the habit of denunciatory declamation which he had formed in his bitter contests in Tennessee. They were, like all of his subsequent offhand addresses, quite unsuited to his position as President. If he had been smitten with dumbness when he was elected Vice-President, he would have escaped a world of trouble. From that time onward he never made an offhand public speech by which he did not suffer in public estimation, but none of them could be charged to the account of strong drink. For nearly four years I had daily intercourse with him, frequently at night, and I never saw him when under the influence of liquor. I have no hesitation in saying that whatever may have been his faults, intemperance was not among them. There was a marked difference between his carefully-prepared papers and his offhand speeches. The former were well written and dignified; the latter were inconsiderate, retaliatory, and in a style which could only be tolerated in the heat of a political campaign—hence the opinion that they were made when he was under the influence of liquor.

It was at his hotel, on the morning of the 14th of April, that the oath of office as President was administered to Mr. Johnson by Chief-Justice Chase, in the presence of the members of the Lincoln Cabinet (except Mr. Seward) and two or three senators who happened to be in the city.

The conduct of Mr. Johnson favorably impressed those who were present when the oath was administered to him. He was grief-stricken like the rest, and he seemed to be oppressed by the suddenness of the call upon him to become President of the great nation which had been deprived by an assassin of its tried and honored chief; but he was, nevertheless, calm and self-possessed. He requested the members of the Cabinet to remain with him after the Chief Justice and the other witnesses of the ceremony had retired, and he expressed to each and all of us his desire that we should stand by him in his difficult and responsible position. This desire was expressed in the language of entreaty, and he appeared to be relieved when he was assured that while we felt it to be our duty to him to place our resignations in his hands, he should have the benefit of such services as we could render until he saw fit to dispense with them. Our conference with him was short, but when we left him, the unfavorable impression which had been made upon us by the reports of his unfortunate speech when he took the Vice-President's chair had undergone a considerable change. We all felt as we left him, not entirely relieved of apprehensions, but at least hopeful that he would prove to be a popular and judicious President. The hopes of none of us were fully realized as time went on and controversies arose between him and Congress; but his first year's administration was cordially supported by every member of his Cabinet.

It is not my purpose to review Mr. Johnson's administration, but there were some things about which he was misunderstood or misrepresented, to which I must briefly refer. Mr. Johnson was a man of unblemished personal integrity. He was an honest man, and his administration was an honest and clean administration. In this respect it will bear comparison with any that preceded or has followed it.

JOHNSON'S DRAMATIC RETURN TO SENATE

Julius Chambers (1850–1920) was newspaperman and author in a field covering this country and Europe. He was in Washington in 1875 as representative of the New York *Herald*; was managing editor of that paper (1886–89) and first editor of its Paris edition; managing editor of the New York *World* (1889–91). He lectured on journalism, but never completely relinquished newspaper work. His books include *The Mississippi River and Its Wonderful Valley*.

Chambers' memory apparently misplaces by one day Johnson's official swearing-in as senator. Records state that this was noon, March 5, 1875, opening day of the special session of the 44th Congress. The 43rd Congress had ended at noon, March 4.

From The Book of New York. *By Julius Chambers.*

The last hours of the Forty-third Congress (March, 1875) were approaching—a session made historic by the enactment of the Civil Rights bill. Senators, as well as Members of the House, were chiefly intent upon the final passage of bills in which they were personally interested. Under such conditions, a short, broad-shouldered and aged man entered the main door of the Senate Chamber one afternoon, alone. He gazed about the room; then, with a sneer upon his shaven face, he walked to a sofa at the rear. Nobody appeared to know this stranger. Obviously, he had a right to the floor. I had seen him for the first time on the preceding night at his hotel. Therefore, I recognized the Senator-elect from Tennessee—a man who had sat in the Lower House in the forties, had presided over the Upper House and as President of the United States had been arraigned before the bar of this same Senate, charged with high crimes and misdemeanors! By the narrow margin of one vote, he had escaped becoming the victim of a political persecution as vindictive as any since the time of Warren Hastings.

Here was the small, stoop-shouldered man who had the nation by the ears in 1868, Andrew Johnson!

A hurried glance about the Chamber discovered Senators[1] who had voted to degrade this man, types of unbending will or slaves to party. How many, many things had happened in seven years!

While thinking of all these things, I had been watching the old man on the sofa whose mind probably had been following a similar channel. He beckoned to a page and sent the boy to the only Senator present among the nineteen who had voted "Not Guilty!" The moment Mr. McCreery[2] was aware of Senator-elect Johnson's presence, he hastened to welcome him. The fine Kentucky gentleman was arrayed in immaculate linen and a swallow-tail coat of perfect fit. The greeting was frank and hearty. By this time, people in the gallery "took notice," and the incident became the dominating one in the Chamber. The big Kentuckian towered head and shoulders over the stocky, stooping, tailorman from Tennessee. Still clasping hands, they turned and overlooked the Senators between them and the rostrum upon which Vice-President Wilson was enthroned. And Wilson [Massachusetts][3] had voted "Guilty!"

An eye-stroke of the Chamber showed Johnson that of the thirty-five who had condemned him, thirteen were still there! Senator Brownlow [Tennessee] whom Johnson was to succeed, kept out of sight; the Senator-elect was not on speaking terms with his prospective colleague, Mr. Cooper [Tennessee][4] because of alleged duplicity in the legislative election at which Johnson had been defeated two years previously.

Johnson tried to appear unconscious of the glances directed upon him from all parts of the Chamber. Morton, of Indiana, had a front seat on the main aisle. A look of defiance blazed in his face; lame as he was, he thought himself Sir Brian de Bois-Guilbert of the Senate, always ready for the lists of oratory. His long black

[1] Names of the states represented by the various senators named have been added.
[2] Thomas C. McCreery of Kentucky.
[3] Wilson was a senator in 1868.
[4] Brownlow and Cooper were not senators in 1868.

hair crackled with magnetism: but the man near the door took no notice of the menace of the "War Governor."[5]

Mr. Anthony's [Rhode Island][6] face assumed a far-away look. Simon Cameron [Pennsylvania],[7] just returned from the glamour of Russian court life, began to totter about, affecting to be unusually busy. Mr. Cragin [New Hampshire] kept his eyes on the floor. Mr. Edmunds, [Vermont], known as "St. Jerome" in the press gallery, was making an objection to a ruling; but when he caught sight of a group of Democratic Senators gathering about the former President, he abruptly sat down. In his abstraction, like the barber's brother in the Arabian tale, he kicked over a row of law books on shelves at the front of his desk. His colleague, Mr. Morrill [Vermont],[8] of the "moral tariff" was traveling afar on a train of thought! Senator Morton glanced at Morrill and sneered. When I asked him, days after, why he had done so, the Indianian answered: "Because Morrill thinks he looks like Charles Sumner,[9] but he doesn't."

Roscoe Conkling's [New York] figure was one that never could remain out of a picture. His desk was on the left side of the main aisle, in front of that occupied for so many years by Stewart, of Nevada. Conkling was aware of Johnson's presence, and taking up a letter pretended to read. In reality, he was watching from his left eye the attention bestowed upon the rehabilitated politician.

A deep hush fell upon the Senate Chamber. Mr. Johnson, on the arm of Mr. McCreery, began to move down the center aisle towards the high altar where sat Vice-President Wilson. Mr. Cooper appeared at the top of the centre aisle, bowed stiffly, and attended his colleague. Amid impressive silence, the three men walked down the broad steps. Johnson had grown much paler. Several of the younger members, memorably Carl Schurz, [Missouri][10] rose to do honor to Johnson's former greatness,—as the House of Commons uncovered to Warren Hastings on his final visit.

[5] Governor of Indiana during Civil War.
[6] Voting "Guilty" in 1868 and mentioned in the course of this quotation, were Morton, Anthony, Cameron, Cragin, Edmunds, Morrill (Vermont), Conkling, Frelinghuysen, Morrill (Maine), Ferry, Sherman.
[7] He was minister to Russia in 1862.
[8] Author of Tariff Act of 1862.
[9] Sumner (Massachusetts) voted "Guilty" in 1868.
[10] Schurz was not in the Senate in 1868.

Mr. Frelinghuysen, [New Jersey] one of "the thirteen apostles of reform," was on his knees, seeking a book or—a hatchet? Morrill, of Maine, and Ferry, of Connecticut, pretended to be chatting together and affected a sympathy for the man they had once condemned. John Sherman [Ohio] stared the newcomer frankly in the face! I was watching them closely from the front row of the press gallery. Their eyes met; in his glance, Johnson forgave Sherman. The two men afterwards became friends. Senator Hamlin, [Maine][11] who hadn't censured Johnson, nudged Boutwell [Massachusetts] and pointed to the ceiling. The Massachusetts man didn't appreciate this reference to his speech in the House,[12] during which he had described "a hole in the sky" through which alone the (then) President could escape punishment.

In a grave and sonorous voice, Henry Wilson read to the man before him the obligation of a United States Senator. Wilson was standing, an unusual thing for him. I wondered whether the act was a tribute to the candidate, or an atonement for wrong? On every side, recognition of irreparable injustice was shown. The scene suggested one in which a jury had condemned a man to death and afterward repented of its action.

Half an hour later, I met Senator Johnson in the corridor, still walking on the arm of the sturdy McCreery. There were tears in his eyes as I lifted my hat and greeted him and in the answer to my inquiry regarding his absent friends, he said with the frankness of a child:

"I feel very badly. I would wish to shake hands with Bayard (meaning the father of the then Senator from Delaware), Buckalew of Pennsylvania, Davis of Kentucky, Doolittle of Wisconsin, Dickson[13] of Connecticut, Fessenden of Maine, Grimes of Iowa, Fowler of Tennessee, Hendricks of Indiana, Johnson and Vickers of Maryland, Norton of Minnesota, Ross of Kansas, Saulsbury of Delaware, Trumble[14] of Illinois and Van Winkle of West Virginia. I cannot forget that they were steadfast when—when my own party had repudiated me and I needed friends."

[11] Hamlin was not a senator in 1868.
[12] In 1868 Boutwell was a member of the House when it voted articles of impeachment, 126 to 47.
[13] Correct spelling: Dixon
[14] Correct spelling: Trumbull

PATENT-MEDICINE TURNOUT CARRIES
GRANT IN INAUGURAL

THE FOLLOWING account of the freezing weather on the day of Grant's inaugural (1873) is also noteworthy for its offhand revelation that the President permitted a well-known seller of patent medicines to furnish his official transportation to and from the White House.

Dr. Henry T. Helmbold's sundry sure-fire cures were advertised extensively in the newspapers of the time. The Chicago *Tribune* in 1871 referred to Dr. Helmbold as widely known and added that he had expended "immense sums of money in advertizing his extracts and remedies." In the Library of Congress is a booklet, printed in 1877, titled: "Am I a Lunatic?, or, Dr. Henry T. Helmbold's Exposure of His Personal Experience in the Lunatic Asylums of Europe and America," by Henry T. Helmbold.

Mary Cunningham Logan (1838–1923), our observer of the inaugural scene, was not only the wife of an active and prominent husband, but a good deal of a person in her own right. Major General John A. Logan of Mexican and Civil War service, member of the Senate or House for almost twenty years, Republican Vice-Presidential nominee in 1884, an organizer of the G.A.R. and so on, found in her an able and devoted helpmate. After Logan's death in 1886, his widow kept active. She edited the *Home* magazine for a space, did work for the Hearst news syndicate, traveled much and wrote four books, including one of reminiscences and one about Washington.

From Reminiscences of a Soldier's Wife.
By Mrs. John A. Logan.

March 4, 1873, was probably the most inclement inauguration within the memory of any American. The thermometer had fallen below zero, a thing previously unknown in this climate. The militia from many States almost perished with the cold while they were en route, and they arrived in Washington to find inhospitable temperature and few preparations for their accommodation. The decorations of the city were frozen stiff and looked dismal with their coats of ice

*President Grant, in Dr. Helmbold's handsome equipage,
leaving the White House for the Capitol.*

and sleet, which had fallen the night before. The cadets from West
Point and Annapolis were nearly frozen in line, many dropping out
on account of their inability to stand on their feet, and, though they
were taken back to their academies as speedily as possible, they
left a number behind in the hospitals of Washington, while others
were borne to the hospital on their arrival at West Point and Annapolis, fatal pneumonia claiming several in each corps.

The Inauguration Ball, March 4, 1873.

The procession was the poorest display ever seen on such an occasion. Senators Logan, Cragin, and Bayard,[1] were the committee on the part of the Senate, supplemented by a large committee of distinguished men. Governors of many States with their staffs were present. The weather spoiled their splendor, their feathers and gold lace yielding to the frost in the air. Helmbold, of patent-medicine fame, was then in Washington with a famous four-in-hand mouse-colored team of horses which he drove attached to a superb landau with light lining. He insisted that the committee should allow him to use this turnout to convey President Grant and the committee to the Capitol for the inauguration, and back to the White House. The committee accepted his offer, and on inauguration day Grant, together with the Senate committee—Logan, Cragin, and Bayard—drove to the Capitol and thence to the White House in this beauti-

[1] Senators John A. Logan (Republican, Illinois), Aaron H. Cragin (American Party, New Hampshire), Thomas F. Bayard Sr. (Democrat, Delaware), Senate committee on inaugural arrangements.

AN UNWELCOME GUEST

MISS FLORA McFLIMSEY DECLARES SHE HAS NOTHING TO WEAR

—AND ABSOLUTELY WEARS NOTHING

—AND SUFFERS THE CONSEQUENCE

C.S. REINHART

THE INAUGURATION BALL—A LEAF FROM OUR ARTIST'S SKETCH-BOOK.

ful equipage. Another though less pretentious outfit conveyed Vice-President Wilson to the Capitol. A commendable but futile effort was made by the shivering throng on either side of Pennsylvania Avenue to cheer the President, Vice-President, and distinguished men whom they recognized in the procession. The crowd assembled in the park on the east side of the Capitol were packed close together in front of the rotunda steps, which were covered over to serve as the platform upon which the President takes the oath of office and delivers his inaugural address. These people were better able to resist the bitter blast that had been wildly blowing for forty-eight hours, beginning the day before the inauguration, than were those who held exposed positions on the avenue. Fortunately, the ceremonies were brief. The Vice-President proceeded to the Senate chamber to adjourn that body to wait for the President's message, while President Grant and the committee resumed their seats in the carriage to return to the White House.

The afternoon was spent by everybody in trying to get warm. The inaugural committee had made most extensive preparations for the inaugural ball. They had built a temporary marquee on Judiciary Square. It was magnificently decorated and extensive enough to have accommodated the thousands whom the committee expected would attend the ball. A superb banquet had been provided, and hundreds of waiters secured, and the committee on music had provided many bands. The weather abated not a bit or tittle, and, as night came on, it seemed to grow colder and colder, and yet every one felt they must carry out the inaugural programme.

The President and Mrs. Grant and Vice-President Wilson, who was a widower, arrived at about half past eleven o'clock. Mr. and Mrs. Fish, Secretary and Mrs. Boutwell, Secretary and Mrs. Belknap, Secretary Robeson, Postmaster-General and Mrs. Creswell, Attorney-General and Mrs. Williams, Secretary and Mrs. Delano,[2] accompanied by Mr. and Mrs. John Delano, were in the Presidential party, while the Diplomatic Corps, led by the Dean Blacque Bey of Turkey, Sir Edward Thornton, the Marquis de Naoville of France, Mr. and Madame Mori of Japan, and the Peruvian Minister,[3] all in full court dress—as on the occasion of all inaugural balls, the ladies wearing their most gorgeous gowns—attended the ball, and the grand promenade was given. The marquee not being heated, it became so cold that one lady was seized with congestive chill and died in the room. This sad event, in addition to the intensity of the cold, from which everybody was suffering, cut short the ceremonies of the evening. The food on the tables in the banquet hall was congealed, the coffee almost freezing into a *frappé*. Men and women in evening dress sought their heavy wraps to keep from perishing while they waited for their conveyances to take them to their abodes. Drivers of vehicles of all kinds were almost frozen, and great confusion reigned inside and outside the temporary building. Musicians were unable to play their instruments, the mouthpieces of some of the smaller instruments being frozen, and the festivities ended unceremoniously. The great crowd which had come to Washington

[2] Secretary of State Hamilton Fish, Secretary of Treasury George S. Boutwell, Secretary of War William W. Belknap, Secretary of Navy George M. Robeson, Postmaster General John A. J. Creswell, Attorney General George H. Williams, Secretary of Interior Columbus Delano.

[3] Colonel Don Manuel Freyre.

for the inaugural ceremonies left the city as rapidly as they could get trains to carry them away.

WAS LIQUOR SERVED IN HAYES' DRY WHITE HOUSE?

THE QUESTION whether strong drink was surreptitiously served in his dry White House was a touchy one with President Rutherford B. Hayes. Mr. Hayes, who was president 1877–81, and his wife were honest "drys" —although Hayes had not always been a teetotaler—and the congressmen and statesmen and diplomats who came to dinner did not get a drop of official liquor, thus causing the disillusioned and disgruntled remark that "water flowed like champagne."

Reports got around that, unknown to the host and hostess, waiters were serving the thirsty with "Roman punch" that was spiked with rum. Hayes resented these reports and did not think they were true. The following excerpts deal with one of the rumors.

The reminiscences of Ben: Perley Poore[1] were published in 1886 and soon read by Hayes. Poore (1820–87) was a newspaper editor and correspondent, with long and prominent service in Washington. He wrote three biographic volumes. His most solid work was a two-volume compilation of state constitutions and other organic laws of the U.S.

From Perley's Reminiscences of Sixty Years in the National Metropolis. *By Ben: Perley Poore.*

Mrs. Hayes brought with her from her rural home what was known as "the Ohio idea" of total abstinence from intoxicating drinks, and she enforced it at the White House, somewhat to the

[1] Almost a century ago, Poore compiled the official *Congressional Directory*, which appears with each session of Congress, and his name, with that unusual writing of "Ben:," is preserved today on the title pages of the volumes he edited.

Keeping liquor away from the White House was not the only problem facing President Hayes. The great electoral controversy as to whether Hayes or Samuel Tilden, the Democratic candidate, had really won, was kept alive for some time by the Democrat Washington Telegram.

annoyance of Mr. Evarts,[2] who, as Secretary of State, refused to permit the Diplomatic Corps to be invited to their customary annual dinner unless wine could be on the table. This Mrs. Hayes refused to allow, and all of the state dinners served while she presided over the hospitalities of the White House were ostensibly strictly temperance banquets, although the steward managed to gratify those fond of something stronger than lemonade. True, no wine glasses obtruded themselves, no popping of champagne corks was heard, no odor of liquor tainted the air fragrant with the perfume of innocent, beautiful flowers. The table groaned with delicacies; there were many devices of the confectioner which called forth admiration. Many wondered why oranges seemed to be altogether preferred, and the waiters were kept busy replenishing salvers upon which the tropical fruit lay. Glances telegraphed to one another that the missing link was found, and that, concealed within the oranges, was delicious frozen punch, a large ingredient of which was strong old Santa Croix rum. Thenceforth (without the knowledge of Mrs. Hayes, of course) Roman punch was served about the middle of the state dinners, care being taken to give the glasses containing the strongest mixture to those who were longing for some potent beverage. This phase of the dinner was named by those who enjoyed it "the Life-Saving Station."

From Diary and Letters of Rutherford B. Hayes. *Edited by* C. R. *Williams.*

Jan. 10, 1887. Also received, and read parts of, the second volume of Ben: Perley Poore's "Reminiscences." In the main, fair to Lucy and myself. The joke of the Roman punch oranges was not on us but on the drinking people. My orders were to flavor them *rather strongly* with the same flavor that is found in Jamaica rum, viz. ————[sic]. This took! There was not a drop of spirits in them! This was certainly the case after the facts alluded to reached our ears. It was refreshing to hear "the drinkers" say with a smack of the lips, "would they were hot!"

[2] William M. Evarts.

THE DANGEROUS RECREATION OF
WALKING WITH T.R.

THE STRENUOUS life, recommended by Theodore Roosevelt, was more than a tranquil aspiration to the enunciator thereof. He lived it, and enjoyed indoctrinating his friends; the circumscribed existence of a President of the United States never greatly thwarted him. Not all his companions were fervent worshipers of the exhaustive and apprehensive business of a walk or a horseback ride with the inexhaustible T. R.; there was danger in it for all hands. Here two of them bear warm witness of what a strenuous-life walk was like.

William Dudley Foulke (1848–1935) was an author and poet, civil service reformer and long admirer of Theodore Roosevelt. He was on the U.S. Civil Service Commission 1901–03, and later was a president of the National Civil Service Reform League. He went with the Roosevelt Bull Moose party in 1912.

George von Lengerke Meyer (1858–1918) was postmaster general the last two years of the Roosevelt reign, and then was Taft's secretary of the navy. Immediately before entering the cabinet he had been ambassador to Russia for a couple of years; this followed duty as ambassador to Italy.

From A Hoosier Autobiography. *By William Dudley Foulke, LL.D.*

We were lunching together one day, five of us, at the White House. Two of the party, we were told, were going to take a walk with the President that afternoon. He asked the rest of us the question: "Are you fond of walking? Wouldn't you like to join us?" We answered that we should be glad to go. Two carriages were ordered to take us to the starting-place. The first vague indication that there was trouble ahead came when the President stood by the door as we passed out of the dining-room, observed our apparel, and directed one of us, who was very well dressed, to go home and change his clothes. The carriages came, and we drove to the Chain Bridge, three miles above Georgetown, on the Potomac. There we crossed over to the Virginia side. Two of the party had brought

*T. R. prepared for exercise. Photographed here about 1901, just before
he became President.*

canes. The President noticed it. "You had better leave your canes in the carriage," he said, "you may not be able to keep them with you." This sounded ominous.

About a quarter of a mile below us, at the side of the river, there was a big stone quarry, and just as we were starting from the bridge there was a furious explosion, and rocks were seen flying like hailstones, some of them clear across the river, others splashing into the stream. The President's face was lit with glee. "Aha!" he exclaimed. "We are going right there." Somehow his joy was not contagious. Nobody answered. Soon we reached the quarry. Just beyond it there was what seemed to be an impassable barrier of rock overhanging the river, but before we came to this the President pointed out a place at the side, nearly perpendicular, about three or four hundred feet high, where it was possible, by scrambling over stones and bushes, to get up to the woods at the top of the bluff. He said, "If you can't pass the rocks, you can go up there," as if that were a great relief! When we came to the point of rocks it was evident enough why the canes had to be left behind. The President started ahead, followed by his son Theodore; he scrambled up a steep, smooth rock to a shoulder about fifty feet above the river, and then along a crack in a perpendicular cliff, holding on by another crack about seven or eight feet above the first one, and at last getting down—I don't know how. I quickly saw the thing was impossible for me. I had been up Popocatepetl and Toluca and other Mexican volcanoes, and had done a good deal of scrambling among the Alps, but this was too much. A negro close by pointed out a boat, and after much yelling the boat came and two of us ignominiously took passage and were rowed around, while young Roosevelt and two others succeeded in following the President. Then it was a furious tramp, up and down, round another ledge not quite so impossible, where we crawled on our hands and stomachs on and on, until all of us, except one thin Scotchman, were as red as boiled lobsters and as wet as if we had been in a Russian bath. After a while I gave out and had to stop and rest, and one of the party thanked me as we came home in the cars from Georgetown, because he said he could not have stood it five minutes longer. I believed that was true, for his face looked like raw beef. The man who had changed his clothes didn't change them quite enough, for he still had on a pair of new trousers, which were now covered with a fine plaster of mud nearly to the knees.

All this time the President was enjoying himself like a school-boy. He climbed another steep place, almost inaccessible, after wild flowers for Mrs. Roosevelt. The birds, the flowers, the still, shady places in the woods, the cascades that tumbled down the bluff, gave him the keenest delight. The rest of us would have enjoyed these things too if we had not been fagged out. One of us said to him, remembering the words of Dooley, "Do ye call this a walk, Mr. Prisident? Sure I thought it was capital punishment." After it was over and we had crossed the river to Georgetown, he told us to take the street-car back to Washington while he walked home with his son.

When I reached the door of my little house on New Hampshire Avenue, the servants were filled with consternation at my appearance. The cook showed the keenest sympathy; Miller, the coachman, charitably offered to rub me down. I declined the proffered assistance, however, and after a bath thought I would take a short nap before dinner. I did so and awoke next morning at half-past five!

From George von Lengerke Meyer: His Life and Public Services. *By M. A. DeWolfe Howe.*

November 24. (1907).—Take a three-hours' walk in the afternoon with the President and Robert Bacon. We climb cliffs and do all sorts of stunts, going along the banks of Rock Creek. If he had slipped, any one or all of us might have broken our legs or neck. I honestly think it is taking a foolish chance, as we are all within a year of 50.

January 11, 1908.—Have a long walk with the President. Jusserand,[1] the French Ambassador, was with us. We were taken over impossible places, climbing as best we could at considerable risk of falling. At one place, where we had to go along a narrow ledge with nothing to hold on to and every chance of falling into Rock Creek, the French Ambassador funked it, and I told him that now he had become the President of Mollycoddles, which quite depressed him the rest of the afternoon.

[1] Jules Jusserand, French Ambassador to the U.S. 1902–24.

CONGRESS
AND ITS CITY

OUR NATION'S CAPITAL IN THE WILDERNESS

WHEN THEY started from scratch to make the city of Washington, D.C., beginning the Capitol building in a space cleared from the woods and indicating the course of avenues by roughly cutting down trees to provide forest vistas, the unfinished result was observed by an English visitor, Thomas Twining. The Capitol's cornerstone had been laid by George Washington in 1793; it was the spring of 1795 when Twining started on horseback from nearby Georgetown and rode through the wilderness to the Capitol and beyond. Five more years would pass before the Congress, the President and the government moved to the new city.

Thomas Twining (1776–1861) made his American visit between tours of duty as an official with the East India Company in the Bengal region of India. This service, from 1792 to 1805, covered several responsible assignments, including charge of a district which, he said, embraced two million people. In comparison, the remainder of Twining's life—he returned to England when he was 29—was uneventful.

Twining's host in Washington, Thomas Law (1756–1834) was a former Indian official and one of Washington's earliest residents. He arrived with money, bought much real estate, married a granddaughter of Mrs. Washington and died comparatively poor. He was a forward-looking, eccentric and respected citizen.

From Travels in America 100 Years Ago;
Being Notes and Reminiscences. *By*
Thomas Twining.

27th[1]—When the landlord of the "Fountain" [in Georgetown]
found that I was going to Mr. Law's, he made every endeavor to
procure me a carriage, but without success. He this morning, however, procured me a horse, and had him brought to the door soon
after breakfast. Leaving, therefore, my portmanteau to be forwarded
in the course of the day, I set out for Washington, situated lower
down the Potomac, in the territory of Columbia, the name given
to a portion of land ceded by the contiguous states of Maryland
and Virginia for the construction and convenience of the new
metropolis.

Having crossed an extensive tract of level country somewhat
resembling an English heath, I entered a large wood through which
a very imperfect road had been made, principally by removing the
trees, or rather the upper parts of them, in the usual manner. After
some time this indistinct way assumed more the appearance of a
regular avenue, the trees here having been cut down in a straight
line. Although no habitation of any kind was visible, I had no doubt
but I was now riding along one of the streets of the metropolitan
city. I continued in this spacious avenue for half a mile, and then
came out upon a large spot, cleared of wood, in the center of which
I saw two buildings on an extensive scale, and some men at work on
one of them. Advancing and speaking to these workmen, they informed me that I was now in the center of the city, and that the
building before me was the Capitol, and the other destined to be a
tavern. As the greatest cities have a similar beginning, there was
really nothing surprising here, nor out of the usual order of things;
but still the scene which surrounded me—the metropolis of a great
nation in its first stage from a sylvan state—was strikingly singular.
I thought it the more so, as the accounts which I had received of
Washington while at Philadelphia, and the plan which I had seen
hung up in the dining-room at Bladensburg, had prepared me for
something rather more advanced. Looking from where I now stood I
saw on every side a thick wood pierced with avenues in a more or

[1] April 27, 1795.

less perfect state. These denoted the lines of the intended streets, which already appeared in the engraved plan with their future names. The Capitol promised to be a large and handsome building, judging from the part, about two thirds, already above the ground. I walked through several of the lower apartments, and saw the halls designed for the representatives and senate, now in an unfinished state, and encumbered with building materials. I did not go into the tavern. It was a large building of red brick, and in a much more advanced state than the Capitol, being roofed in.

The masons having answered all my questions with much civility, I rode on, following the avenue they pointed out to me. After going about three quarters of a mile through a silent wilderness, I found myself upon a trackless plain partially covered with trees and brushwood. I in vain looked about for Mr. Law's house or some one to guide me to it. I therefore rode on in the direction I judged the most likely to lead me out of this labyrinth. I knew that in case of my not succeeding, my retreat was always open to the Capitol, for while talking with the workmen I observed that all the avenues converged to that point. I continued therefore to explore my way through the thickets, keeping my horse's head rather towards the right, to gain, if necessary, the Potomac, whose bank I might then follow.

I had not proceeded far before I saw a carriage issue from the forest beyond the plain, and I soon perceived that it was making for a small bridge, which I now discovered for the first time, considerably to the right of the point for which I was making. I shaped my course accordingly, and hastened forward as fast as the nature of the ground would permit, that I might catch the carriage at the bridge, from which we were both at nearly the same distance. The carriage, however, was apparently trotting along upon a road, while my progress was almost stopped, and was soon likely to be quite so, by the bogginess of the land as I drew near a small stream that I found running along the bottom. Thus I saw the carriage pass the bridge, and escaping, while I was yet at some distance. It fortunately, however, turned afterwards rather to the right, making toward the wood I had left, and it seemed possible that I might still intercept it by regaining the high ground and getting to the road it was taking. I succeeded in this attempt, reaching the road just before it passed. As it approached the hope I had indulged was confirmed. It *was* Mr. Law's chariot, which, in the expectation of my arrival at Georgetown,

Washington, D. C., about 1794. This earliest known engraved view, taken from above Georgetown on the District side, shows Analostan Island and the city opposite.

Mr. Law had sent for me. The coachman tying my horse behind, we recrossed the small bridge, passed through the forest I had seen, and a second plain beyond it, and reached the banks of the Potomac. In a few minutes more we arrived at Mr. Law's where I had a most cordial reception.

In the afternoon Mr. Law took me about his new estate. His house, built by himself, was only a few yards from the steep bank of the Potomac, and commanded a fine view across that river, here half a mile wide. In the rear of the house Mr. Law was building a street, consisting of much smaller houses than his own, speculating upon a great increase in their value when the expected transfer of the seat of government should be effected. The position at least was favorable, being on a point of land between the Potomac and a tributary stream called "eastern branch," thus offering a double waterfront.

TREELESS CITY OF WASHINGTON—1816

IN EARLIER days this country's plenitude of trees blocked civilization, and our attitude toward clearing them was wont to be comprehensive. Compare Thomas Twining's experience in 1795, in finding his way through woods to and from the Capitol, to the spectacle of a treeless Washington—only former President Jefferson's young poplars along Pennsylvania Avenue breaking the monotony—beheld by Lieutenant Hall twenty-one years later.

Lieutenant Francis Hall (1789–1833), after writing a book on travels in France, identified himself with the Latin-American liberation movement, and for fourteen years, until his death, served the government of Colombia. In 1825 he published a book about that country— where he held the office of government hydrographer—urging English emigration to it. He died a colonel, leading his Colombian troops against the revolution that saw Ecuador break away from Colombia.

From Travels in Canada and the United States, in 1816 and 1817. *By Lieut. Francis Hall, 14th Light Dragoons, H.P.*[1]

From the foot of the Capitol Hill there runs a straight road, (intended to be a street,) planted with poplars, for about two miles, to the President's house, a handsome stone mansion, forming a conspicuous object from the Capitol Hill: near it are the publick offices, and some streets nearly filled up: about half a mile further is a pleasant row of houses, in one of which the President at present resides: there are a few tolerable houses still further on the road to Georgetown, and this is nearly the sum total of the City for 1816. It used to be a joke against Washington, that next door neighbours must go through a wood to make their visits; but the jest and forest have vanished together: there is now scarcely a tree betwixt Georgetown and the Navy Yard, two miles beyond the Capitol, except the

[1] Hall went on half-pay—"H.P."—in 1817 and severed all connection with the British Army in 1829.

poplars I have mentioned, which may be considered as the *locum tenentes* of future houses. I doubt the policy of such thorough clearing; clumps of trees are preferable objects to vacant spaces, and the city in its present state, being commenced from the extremities instead of the centre, has a disjointed and naked appearance.

THE PERILOUS WASHINGTON STREETS

FOR LONG years the condition of Washington streets constituted a topic of strong comment. The Treasury, where in April 1818 Secretary of State John Quincy Adams procured his life-saving lantern, stood approximately in its present location.

From Memoirs of John Quincy Adams, Comprising Portions of His Diary from 1795 to 1848. *Edited by Charles Francis Adams.*

We went and dined at Mr. Middleton's, at Georgetown. . . . The weather having been foul, the roads were bad. Our carriage in coming for us in the evening was overset, the harness broken, and the boy Philip took a sprain in the side, so that we were obliged to take him home in the carriage. We got home with difficulty being twice on the point of oversetting, and at the Treasury Office corner we were both obliged to get out of the carriage in the mud. I called out the guard of the Treasury Office and borrowed a lantern, with which we came home. We immediately sent for the surgeon nearest at hand, who came and bled Philip. It was a mercy that we all got home with whole bones.

SUPREME COURT LAWYERS FACE ASPHYXIA

GEORGE COMBE (1788–1858) was the famous Scot phrenologist, an amiable and serious-minded man, who toured the United States 1838–40. He penned phrenological studies of the heads of several of our political leaders.

Combe always relished fresh air and when, on February 20, 1839, he explored the Capitol building in Washington, D.C. (where the Supreme Court sat then and for long after), he gleaned arresting intelligence.

From Notes on the United States of North America during a Phrenological Visit in 1838–39–40. *By George Combe.*

The hall of the Supreme Court, in which the meeting was held, was destitute of ventilation, and I suffered severely for several hours after leaving it from the effects of bad air. On mentioning this next day, I was told that several lawyers have fallen down dead on the spot while engaged in the most animated pleadings in this hall, and that, although apoplexy was assigned as the cause, some medical men, who knew the state of the atmosphere, had expressed an opinion that the catastrophes were probably hastened, if not caused by asphyxia.

The grand vestibule[1] is under the dome, and has no opening upwards to allow of the escape of air. The consequence is, that the effluvia of human bodies and of tobacco-juice greet the nostrils and afflict the lungs the moment it is entered. We found also that the Senate Chamber and House of Representatives are, in this weather, hermetically sealed; except at the doors and chimneys. Although these may provide some change of air for the members, who are all

[1] The Capitol Rotunda.

accommodated on the floor, the unhappy visitors in the galleries receive all the vitiated air from below, render it worse by their own breathing, and are nearly doomed to suffocation. The ladies are accommodated with the front seat, and occasionally faint from the impurity of the atmosphere. I sat three hours in the gallery of the senate chamber today, and afterwards experienced those debilitating, irritable, and unpleasant sensations which are generated by imperfectly decarbonized blood.

TOBACCO JUICE DECORATES SENATE FLOOR

TOBACCO-SPITTING presented a distinguishing aspect of American life long before and long after 1842, when Charles Dickens visited this country. The custom flourished with a prodigality that amazed, and a matter-of-fact carelessness that disgusted, pilgrims from other lands.

Examples line the years. In 1828, Mrs. Basil Hall, wife of the British naval captain who wrote a controversial book on this nation, reported that "the gallery of the House of Representatives was an inch thick with dirt; the floor where the members sat was actually flooded with their horrible spitting."

Dickens (1812–70) remained here less than three months (compared with a more than three-year sojourn by Mrs. Trollope, another English visitor), but in that time he acquired an amplitude of exasperations and criticisms which he delivered in *American Notes*. The irritated mood of this favorite author, who possessed both good humor and liberal leanings, may have been traceable to two facts: his wife was in poor health during a good part of the visit in America, and both were forced to undergo the constant and unaccustomed affliction of shaking hands with dozens or hundreds of people at a time. Twenty-six years later, when Dickens was in America again, he attempted an apology for his earlier condemnations.

Following Dickens' appraisal of the American custom of chewing tobacco is the pronouncement of Harriet Martineau, written seven years earlier.

The House Chamber. From a water color made by August Kollner in the 1840's. The artist appears to have overlooked the ubiquitous spittoons.

From American Notes. *By Charles Dickens.*

The Senate is a dignified and decorous body, and its proceedings are conducted with much gravity and order. Both Houses are handsomely carpeted; but the state to which these carpets are reduced by the universal disregard of the spittoon with which every honorable member is accommodated, and the extraordinary improvements on the pattern which are squirted and dabbled upon it in every direction, do not admit of being described. I will merely observe, that I strongly recommend all strangers not to look at the floor; and if they happen to drop anything, though it be their purse, not to pick it up with an ungloved hand on any account.

It is somewhat remarkable too, at first, to say the least, to see so

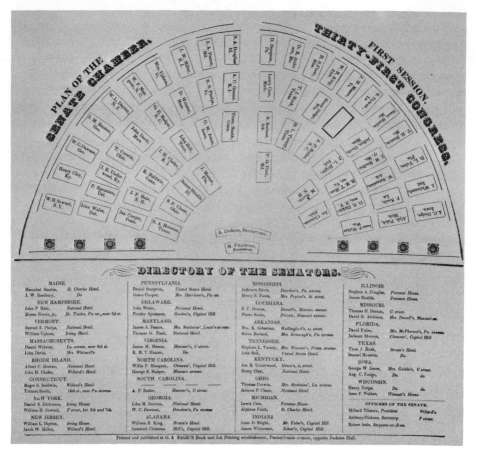

Seating plan and home addresses of the Senators in the first session of the 31st Congress, which met December 13, 1849, and adjourned September 30, 1850.

many honorable members with swelled faces; and it is scarcely less remarkable to discover that this appearance is caused by the quantity of tobacco they contrive to stow within the hollow of the cheek. It is strange enough, too, to see an honorable gentleman leaning back in his tilted chair, with his legs on the desk before him, shaping a convenient "plug" with his penknife, and when it is quite ready for use, shooting the old one from his mouth as from a pop-gun, and clapping the new one in its place.

I was surprised to observe that even steady old chewers of great experience are not always good marksmen, which has rather inclined me to doubt that general proficiency with the rifle, of which we have heard so much in England. Several gentlemen called upon me who, in the course of conversation, frequently missed the spittoon at five paces; and one (but he was certainly shortsighted) mistook the closed sash for the open window at three. On another occasion, when I dined out, and was sitting with two ladies and some gentlemen round a fire before dinner, one of the company fell short of the fireplace six distinct times. I am disposed to think, however, that this was occasioned by his not aiming at that object; as there was a white marble hearth before the fender, which was more convenient and may have suited his purpose better.

MISS MARTINEAU SUMS UP

HARRIET MARTINEAU (1802–76) was one of those valuable English writers who did much to bring knowledge, clothed in her liberal thought, to the poor and badly-educated mass of her own people. Her books, several in the shape of simple tales bearing upon common circumstances, covered a wide scope.

Deaf from childhood on, she traveled with an ear-trumpet. Her visit to America in 1834 resulted in two books, *Society in America* and *Retrospect of Western Travel*, both of which show she was neither ill-natured nor superior in her attitude.

From Society In America. *By Harriet Martineau.*

Of the tobacco and its consequences, I will say nothing but that the practice is at too bad a pass to leave hope that anything that could be said in books would work a cure. If the floors of boarding-houses, and the decks of steam-boats, and the carpets of the Capitol, do not sicken the Americans into a reform; if the warnings of physicians are of no avail, what remains to be said? I dismiss the nauseous subject.

MORSE'S TELEGRAPH MAKES HOUSE LAUGH

CONGRESSMEN AWARDED the invention of the telegraph the human race's usual cold reception to something new. In this selection, Washington correspondent Nathan Sargent relates the skeptical and merry House debate, in February 1843, on the bill to allow Morse $30,000 to construct an experimental line from Washington to Baltimore. After House passage of the bill by a narrow margin, it was put through the Senate, without debate, on the final night of the session, March 3, 1843.

The Democratic National Convention met in Baltimore, May 27, 1844, and Sargent pictures how the telegraph reported that convention to Washington. Today Capitol visitors view a tablet, honoring the inventor, on the wall outside the room where the news was received.

It should be mentioned in passing, however, that this was not the first political employment of the invention—not by almost a month. As the Whig National Convention convened in Baltimore, May 1, 1844, the line was but halfway completed. After Clay's nomination, when the first train from Baltimore passed the first outpost of the advancing line, the intelligence was shouted to the operator. The operator flashed the news on to Morse in the Capitol and the information beat the train into Washington by an hour. Similar procedure was followed for the Vice-Presidential nomination.

Nathan Sargent (1794–1875), who signed his dispatches "Oliver Oldschool," became Washington correspondent for the *U.S. Gazette*, Philadelphia, in January 1842. He was House sergeant-at-arms, 1847–51; register general of the U.S. Land Office, 1851–55; and commissioner of customs, 1861–71.

From Public Men and Events, from the Commencement of Mr. Monroe's Administration in 1817, to the Close of Mr. Fillmore's Administration in 1853. *By Nathan Sargent.*

On the opening of the third session of the Twenty-seventh Congress,[1] Mr. Morse, of telegraphic celebrity, obtained leave to set

[1] December 1842.

up his telegraph in the lower rooms of the Capitol, in order to exhibit to Senators and members its operation, he being an applicant for an appropriation of thirty thousand dollars with which to establish an experimental line from Washington to Baltimore.

The rooms in which were the termini of this temporary illustrative telegraph were almost constantly filled by Senators, members of the House, and others, and the two operators were often kept busy for hours transmitting messages to and from those in the different rooms, to the great wonder of those who sent and those who received them. They could hardly credit their senses. Members in the different rooms would carry on for some time a jocose conversation, full of wit, point, and repartee, to the great amusement of others in the rooms, apparently with as much ease as if they stood face to face. Still, it was no easy matter to convince many that this telegraph could be made practically useful to the world. It was considered by some as a sort of Redhelfer's perpetual-motion machine,—might do for short distances, but impracticable for long ones. However, there were others who, if they did not foresee all the great results to be wrought by this invention, or discovery,—and who could at that time?—were satisfied that it was destined to effect great results.

Mr. Morse asked for an appropriation of thirty thousand dollars; and a bill was introduced authorizing the Secretary of the Treasury to make an experiment, by erecting a line of telegraph—of a single wire—from Washington to Baltimore, and making an appropriation for that purpose.

The bill came up, and was considered in committee of the whole on the 21st of February.[2] It met with most decided opposition, its opponents, not numerous, endeavoring to kill it by ridicule. Mr. Cave Johnson, who, a little more than a year after this, was Postmaster-General, moved that one-half of the appropriation be expended in making experiments in mesmerism, which was sustained by twenty votes. Another member moved that the Secretary use the appropriation in trying an experiment to construct a railroad to the moon. Other ridiculous propositions were made, some of them creating much merriment and pleasant badinage among members. Prominent among the opponents of the bill were Cave Johnson and George

---

[2] 1843. Under House procedure most major bills are first considered in Committee of the Whole House, and then by the House itself, with the Speaker present. The House can reverse an affirmative vote taken in Committee of the Whole.

W. Jones, of Tennessee; Edmund Burke, of New Hampshire, Commissioner of Patents under Mr. Polk; George S. Houston and William W. Payne, of Alabama; William Pettit and Andrew Kennedy, of Indiana; and Samuel Gordon, of New York. Mr. Pettit, of Indiana, afterwards a Democratic Senator, opposed it, and looked upon all magnetic telegraphs as miserable chimeras, fit for nothing. Nobody who did not understand the Pottawattomie or some other outlandish jargon could know what the telegraph reported.

Governor Wallace of Indiana, who voted for the appropriation, was superceded by William J. Brown, one of the leaders of the Democratic party, who made the vote of Governor Wallace the great theme in his electioneering canvass.

But, finally, the opposition gave up, and the bill was reported to the House, and passed by a small majority.

While the bill was undergoing the ordeal of ridicule in the committee of the whole, Mr. Morse stood leaning on the bar of the House, or railing, in a state of intense excitement and anxiety. Seeing him thus, I went to him, remarking that he appeared to be much excited. He turned and said, "I have an awful headache," putting his hand to his forehead. I said, "You are anxious." "I have reason to be," he replied; "and if you knew how important this is to me, you would not wonder. I have spent seven years in perfecting this invention, and all that I had: if it succeeds, I am a made man; if it fails, I am ruined. I have a large family, and not money enough to pay my board bill when I leave the city." I assured him he need not feel so anxious, as the bill would pass. "Are you sure of it?" he asked. "Yes, perfectly; all this ridicule goes for nothing." He was soon relieved by the vote, first in the committee, and then in the House. I seldom met him in after-years that he did not recall the conversation between us, and remark how much relief my assurance gave him. . . .

. . . Mr. Morse had completed his telegraph line from Washington to Baltimore just previous to the sitting of the Democratic convention, and was ready to report its proceedings every fifteen minutes. The terminus of the line in Washington was in a room adjoining the Supreme Court room, under the Senate-chamber, now the Supreme Court room. Here he received and communicated dispatches during the sitting of the convention, and read them to the large crowd assembled around the window, manifesting the most intense

27th CONGRESS, Rep. No. 17. HO. OF REPS.
3d *Session.*

ELECTRO-MAGNETIC TELEGRAPHS.
[To accompany bill H. R. No. 641.]

DECEMBER 30, 1842.
Five thousand extra copies ordered to be printed.

Mr. FERRIS, from the Committee on Commerce, made the following

REPORT:

That they regard the question, as to the general utility of the telegraphic system, settled by its adoption by the most civilized nations ; and experience has fully demonstrated the great advantages which may be derived from its use. Its capability of speedily transmitting intelligence to great distances, for national defence, and for other purposes, where celerity is desirable, is decidedly superior to any of the ordinary modes of communication in use. By it, the first warning of approaching danger, and the appearance of hostile fleets and armies on our coasts and borders, may be announced simultaneously at the most distant points of our widely-extended empire, thus affording time and opportunity for concentrating the military force of the country, for facilitating military and naval movements, and for transmitting orders suitable to the emergency.

In the commercial and social affairs of the community, occasions frequently arise, in which the speedy transmission of intelligence may be of the highest importance for the regulation of business transactions, and in relieving the anxious solicitude of friends, as to the health and condition of those in whose fortunes they feel an interest.

The practicability of establishing telegraphs on the electric principle is no longer a question. Wheatstone, of London, and his associates, have been more fortunate than our American inventor, in procuring the means to put his ingenious system into practical use for two or three hundred miles, in Great Britain ; and the movements of the cars on the Blackwall railroad are at this time directed with great economy, and perfect safety to life and property, by means of his magnetic needle telegraph. If a system more complicated and less efficient than the American telegraph is operated for great distances in England, with such eminent success and advantage, there can be no reasonable doubt that, if the means be furnished for putting in operation the system of Professor Samuel F. B. Morse, of New York, the original inventor of the electro-magnetic telegraph, the same, if not greater success, will be the result. Your committee are of opinion that it is but justice to Professor Morse, who is alike distinguished for his attainments in science and excellence in the arts of design, and who has patiently devoted many years of unremitting study, and freely spent his private fortune, in inventing and bringing to perfection a system of telegraphs which is calculated to advance the scientific reputation of the country, and to be emi-

First page of the report to the House of its Commerce Committee, urging passage of the bill that caused all the merriment.

interest in the proceedings at Baltimore, as they were from time to time received and read aloud.

It was a novelty. Every few minutes it would be reported that Mr. So-and-so had made such a motion, and in a minute or two, "the motion has failed," or, "has carried," as the case might be. Again, "A ballot is being taken," etc. "Mr. Polk has been proposed, and a vote is being taken; such a State has voted for Mr. Polk,—such and such and such States have voted for him; he has received two-thirds, and is nominated."

This talking with Baltimore was something so novel, so strange, so extraordinary, and upon a matter of such intense interest, that we could hardly realize the fact. It seemed like enchantment, or a delusion, or a dream.

When the telegraph announced that a vote was being taken for James K. Polk for President, and he had been nominated, the Democrats received the intelligence in silence, not knowing what to make of it.

The next important dispatch sent over the wire was, that the convention had nominated Silas Wright as Vice-President; and in a few minutes a dispatch was sent to him, informing him of his nomination. Mr. Wright was then in the Senate-chamber just above, and telegraphed back that he respectfully declined the nomination. Another dispatch was immediately received asking him to reconsider the matter,—that a committee had just started in the cars to wait on him, and would call upon him that evening. The committee came, but he persisted in declining the nomination.

SOLDIERS BIVOUAC IN HOUSE AND SENATE CHAMBERS

In 1861 the United States Capitol, accustomed to historic scenes, housed unique tenants: Northern Soldiers come to the defense of panicky Washington at the outbreak of the Civil War. All the Capitol building was filled; the House and Senate chambers constituted some of the barracks, while bread was baked in the basement and reveille sounded under the unfinished dome.

Theodore Winthrop, traveler and writer, author of this sketch, came to Washington in May 1861 as a member of the 7th New York Regiment, the second regiment to enter the city. Quickly transferred to Fortress Monroe, as a major and military secretary to General Benjamin F. Butler, he left the 7th in Washington and died in action the next month at Great Bethel, Virginia, at the age of thirty-three.

In his brief career Winthrop had traveled in Europe and the Pacific Coast and spent two years in Panama with the Pacific Steamship Co. After his death his writings were published and ran through many editions, particularly the novels, *Cecil Dreeme* and *John Brent*.

The congressman mentioned as franking soldiers' letters was Representative Henry Van Wyck (Republican, New York), who was to appear at the Capitol twenty years later as senator from Nebraska. Representatives whose desks Winthrop says he used in writing were Covode (Republican, Pennsylvania), Cochrane (States Rights Democrat, New York) and Burlingame (Republican, Massachusetts); the last two had already been defeated for reelection. Burlingame, a future friend of Mark Twain, later became minister to China.

From Life In The Open Air, And Other Papers. *By Theodore Winthrop.*

We marched up to the White House, showed ourselves to the President, made our bow to him as our host, and then marched up to the Capitol, our grand lodgings.

There we are now, quartered in the Representatives Chamber.

Some of our companies were marched up-stairs into the galleries. The sofas were to be their beds. With their white cross-belts and bright breast-plates, they made a very picturesque body of spectators for whatever happened in the Hall, and never failed to applaud in the right or the wrong place at will.

Most of us were bestowed in the amphitheatre. Each desk received its man. He was to scribble on it by day, and sleep under it by

Civil War troops quartered in the House of Representatives.
These are the New York Fire Zouaves, who followed the Seventh New
York into the Capitol.

night. When the desks were all taken, the companies overflowed
into the corners and into the lobbies. The staff took committee-
rooms. The Colonel reigned in the Speaker's parlor.

Once in, firstly, we washed.

Such a wash merits a special paragraph. I compliment the
M.C.s, our hosts, upon their water-privileges. How we welcomed
this chief luxury after our march! And thenceforth how we prized
it! For the clean face is an institution which requires perpetual
renovation at Washington. "Constant vigilance is the price" of neatness. When the sky here is not travelling earthward in rain, earth is
mounting skyward in dust. So much dirt must have an immoral effect.

After the wash we showed ourselves to the eyes of Washington, marching by companies, each to a different hotel, to dinner. This
became one of the ceremonies of our barrack-life. We liked it. The
Washingtonians were amused and encouraged by it. Three times

a day, with marked punctuality, our lines formed and tramped down the hill to scuffle with awkward squads of waiters for fare more or less tolerable. In these little marches we encountered by and by the other regiments, and, most soldierly of all, the Rhode Island men, in blue flannel blouses and *bersaglière* hats. But of them hereafter.

It was a most attractive post of ours at the Capitol. Spring was at its freshest and fairest. Every day was more exquisite than its forerunner. We drilled morning, noon, and evening, almost hourly, in the pretty square east of the building.

But the best of the entertainment was within the Capitol. Some three thousand or more of us were now quartered there. The Massachusetts Eighth were under the dome. No fear of want of air for them. The Massachusetts Sixth were eloquent for their State in the Senate Chamber. It was singularly fitting, among the many coincidences in the history of this regiment, that they should be there, tacitly avenging the assault upon Sumner[1] and the attempts to bully the impregnable Wilson.[2]

In the recesses, caves, and crypts of the Capitol what other legions were bestowed I do not know. I daily lost myself, and sometimes when out of my reckoning was put on the way by sentries of strange corps, a Reading Light Infantry man,[3] or some other. We all fraternized. There was a fine enthusiasm among us: not the soldierly rivalry in discipline that may grow up in future between men of different States acting together, but the brotherhood of ardent fellows first in the field and earnest in the cause.

All our life in the Capitol was most dramatic and sensational.

Before it was fairly light in the dim interior of the Representatives' Chamber, the *réveilles* of the different regiments came rattling through the corridors. Every snorer's trumpet suddenly paused. The impressive sound of the hushed breathing of a thousand sleepers, marking off the fleet moments of the night, gave way to a most vociferous uproar. The boy element is large in the Seventh Regiment. Its slang dictionary is peculiar and unabridged. As soon as we woke,

[1] Senator Charles Sumner of Massachusetts, assaulted in Senate, 1856, by Representative Brooks of South Carolina.

[2] Senator Henry Wilson of Massachusetts.

[3] Probably of the Ringgold Light Artillery Co. of Reading, Pa., one of the first to be quartered in the Capitol.

the pit began to chaff the galleries, and the galleries the pit. We were allowed noise nearly *ad libitum*. Our riotous tendencies, if they existed, escaped by the safety-valve of the larynx. We joked, we shouted, we sang, we mounted the Speaker's desk and made speeches, —always to the point; for if any but a wit ventured to give tongue, he was coughed down without ceremony. Let the M.C.'s adopt this plan and silence their dunces.

Perhaps we should have served our country better by a little Vandalism. The decorations of the Capitol have a slight flavor of the Southwestern steamboat saloon. The pictures (now, by the way, carefully covered) would most of them be the better, if the figures were bayoneted and the backgrounds sabred out. Both—pictures and decorations—belong to that bygone epoch of our country when men shaved the moustache, dressed like parsons, said "Sir," and chewed tobacco,—a transition epoch, now become an historic blank.

The home-correspondence of our legion of young heroes was illimitable. Every one had his little tale of active service to relate. A decimation of the regiment, more or less, had profited by the tender moment of departure to pop the question and to receive the dulcet "Yes." These lucky fellows were of course writing to Dulcinea regularly, three meals of love a day. Mr. Van Wyck, M.C., and a brace of colleagues, were kept hard at work all day giving franks and saving three-pennies to the ardent scribes. Uncle Sam lost certainly three thousand cents a day in this manner.

What crypts and dens, caves and cellars, there are under that great structure! And barrels of flour in every one of them this month of May, 1861. Do civilians eat in this proportion? Or does long standing in the "Position of a Soldier" (*vide* "Tactics" for a view of that graceful *pose*) increase a man's capacity for bread and beef so enormously?

It was infinitely picturesque in these dim vaults by night. Sentries were posted at every turn. Their guns gleamed in the gaslight. Sleepers were lying in their blankets wherever the stones were softest. Then in the Guardroom the guard were waiting their turn. We have not had much of this scenery in America and the physiognomy of volunteer military life is quite distinct from anything one sees in European service. The People have never had occasion until now to occupy their Palace with armed men.

MOMENTOUS INTERNATIONAL SOCIETY WAR

WASHINGTON SOCIETY protocol is a grave matter, fired by the deathless human need for self-importance. Who shall be invited, who shall call first, who shall sit next to whom at table—this is an endless rivalry as grim and restless as the sea, though more entertaining to the newspapers.

Mrs. Garret A. Hobart, wife of McKinley's first Vice-President, illuminates a flare-up of this protocol, one with international reverberations. She was in the thick of the fight, being uncommonly prominent at the top rungs of the social ladder because of Mrs. McKinley's ill health.

Mrs. Hobart (1849–1941) was Fannie Tuttle of Paterson, New Jersey, and her husband-to-be studied law in the office of her father. They married in 1869. Her neighbors knew her as active in church and charity offices, a chief worker for the Old Ladies' Home, and in her own home, capable and hospitable. An old friend summed her up as "bright, cordial and womanly." She was a good conversationalist, with some gift of quick repartee, and she met her unceasing Washington social duties and opportunities undismayed and, one gathers, with efficiency and enjoyment. The death of her husband in November 1899 ended all this and, incidentally, opened the way for Theodore Roosevelt to become McKinley's second Vice-President and, later, President.

From Memories. *By Mrs. Garret A. Hobart.*

My entire life in Washington that first Spring[1] was colored by a social crisis which the English ambassador, Lord Pauncefote, precipitated. It involved the ticklish question of social precedence, of where one sat at the state dinner table—which always touches the most sensitive nerve in Washington's social body; therefore it called for a sense of humor as well as the utmost diplomacy.

It arose over so trivial an incident as a social call which, according to official etiquette, must be exchanged between the Vice-President and the British ambassador, Sir Julian Pauncefote.

[1] 1897.

Should the Pauncefotes call first on the Hobarts or the Hobarts call first on the Pauncefotes? This was the burning question with which Washington seethed for a season. It seemed literally a tempest in a teapot, ridiculous to the point of absurdity, but in reality it was far more than this, for whoever paid the first call acknowledged the superior rank of the other. Did the British ambassador outrank the Vice-President or the Vice-President outrank the ambassador?

This episode lives in tradition because it settled once and for all the fact that the Vice-President precedes all others except the President.

Sir Julian Pauncefote was a pompous man of faultless manners and grooming, who looked just as an English lord should look, even to the sideburns. He took himself and his position very seriously. Claiming that he represented "the Body of Queen Victoria," he felt he should be second to none but the Chief Executive himself, and in public ceremonies and social affairs should precede the Vice-President. The reason this same question had not arisen before was because, until the McKinley Administration, we had no ambassadors —merely ministers—as representatives of the foreign nations. But with our growing importance in foreign affairs, the United States was recognized as a world power and England elevated Lord Pauncefote from minister plenipotentiary to ambassador, representative of the sovereign. Being our first ambassador, he was dean of the diplomatic corps.

In monarchical countries ambassadors follow directly after the royal family. Hence Sir Julian claimed he should follow the President.

Now, no one was more indifferent to titles and ceremonies than were Mr. Hobart and myself. Personally we cared not a fig who paid the first call or who sat above whose salt at the state dinner table. But we did feel very strongly that the office of Vice-President outranked any foreign ambassadorship. The Vice-President, we felt, was heir apparent to the President, his successor in case of death, occupying the same position in the United States as the Prince of Wales in the United Kingdom. To uphold the dignity of our office, the Hobarts must precede the Pauncefotes.

We were the more confident of this because the three other ambassadors in Washington—the French, the German, and the Italian —had already called upon us, thus acknowledging our stand. Baron and Baroness Thielman of the German embassy had not only called

The Indomitable Mrs. Hobart.

upon us but had given a dinner in our honor, thereby showing their stand in the matter. They had made their own decision and had the courage to give expression to it. If these ambassadors had graciously granted us precedence, why should not the English ambassador do likewise? Should we yield to the Pauncefotes we would have to yield precedence to everyone of ambassadorial rank. This we quietly refused to do. The Pauncefotes must make the first call on us or no calls would be exchanged.

In the narrow circle that was official Washington then, it was inevitable that the Pauncefotes and the Hobarts should meet. It happened at a musicale at the Austrian embassy on the Baroness Hengelmüller's birthday. The stage was set with twin gold sofas, one on either side of the piano, reserved for the two official couples cast in the star parts. By a strange chance, the four of us entered together, and as we were presented to one another the spectators at this comedy of manners made the silence loud with expectancy. Later

Lord Pauncefote.

I told my husband I felt like end man in a minstrel show. But the hoped-for climax did not come. With Chesterfieldian courtesy, Sir Julian conducted me to one gold sofa on his side of the stage, while the Vice-President conducted Lady Pauncefote to the sofa on the opposite wing.

"The outside of your house is charming, madam," Sir Julian said to me.

"Oh, but you should see the inside, Sir Julian," I beamed.

Lady Pauncefote.

When supper was announced Sir Julian preceded the Vice-President to the dining room, but he had to take me on his arm to do it! Again the crisis was averted.

So our little social warfare for British or American supremacy continued, with much witty comment from the press. Fertile humorists gave it relish in cartoons and on the stage, and the country talked of it, tongue in cheek. In fact, the only people in America who did not discuss it were the Hobarts. The only remark I ever made on the subject was to President McKinley, in response to a joking question which he put to me concerning it.

Then I said: "I believe the ticket on which you were elected, Mr. President, read McKinley and Hobart, not McKinley and Pauncefote, did it not?"

Thenceforward, when he met my husband he would link arms with him and say: "Here comes the ticket!"

The winter passed with neither side granting an inch. At last, in May, Lady Pauncefote tried to force an issue by inviting us to a spring garden party to meet the delegates to the Postal Congress. I had my secretary acknowledge it with this reply:

> The Vice-President and Mrs. Hobart have received
> Lady Pauncefote's courteous invitation to meet the
> Postal Delegates on Thursday, May 20

To send either acceptance or regrets would have granted her the victory.

She parried with a personal note the morning of the party, asking me to bring my little son, whom she thought "it would amuse." Happily, I was out of town; on my re-return I answered with this letter:

21 Lafayette Square

Dear Lady Pauncefote:

Your very kind note of invitation for my little son did not reach me before my departure for my New Jersey home, or you should have received this note of thanks earlier. The Vice-President and I both appreciate the attention, and I assure you nothing would have given us greater pleasure than to have been with you last Thursday; but we felt that the invitation was only sent in an official way and, as we have received no visiting cards, that we could not be expected to attend the reception. Your very kind note, however, has made us feel that perhaps there has been some mistake about the cards. If so, no one could regret more than we that we have been deprived of so much pleasure.

Again with thanks for your kindness to our boy, believe me, dear Lady Pauncefote,

Very sincerely yours,

Jennie T. Hobart

May 26, 1897

The moot question still hung fire when the Pauncefotes left for the summer in England. There royal authorities, baffled by the deadlock, took matters into their own hands and advised their ambassador to yield honors to the Vice-President.

Thus it happened that early in the fall the ambassadorial carriage drew up to our door. Lord and Lady Pauncefote had come to pay their respects. Shortly after, Lord Pauncefote sent General Kasson to the President with this message: Now that he had paid the official call on the Vice-President, kindly advise him as to his social status.

This was the President's reply:

Make my regards to Sir Julian and tell him there has never been any question in my mind. The Vice-President comes after me.

On all sides we were deluged with congratulations for our manner of handling the matter. John Hay wrote[2] from London:

I congratulate you on the peaceful outcome of your battle for precedence. I have always heartily approved the position you assumed and think it was imposed by a proper sense of dignity of the great office you hold. . . .

Theodore Roosevelt, then Assistant Secretary of the Navy, wrote us:

My dear Mr. Hobart:

I must just write a line to tell you the great admiration and respect I felt for the way you have met this trying crisis. We are all under a debt to you.

Faithfully yours,

Theodore Roosevelt

So the cloud blew completely over. Not a feathery trace remained. The Hobarts and the Pauncefotes became the best of friends.

[2] Then Ambassador to Great Britain.

THE REVOLUTION

A COURAGEOUS PATRIOT LAWYER

JOSIAH QUINCY, JR. (1744–75) was a patriot who did not live for the fighting but who provided an example of that moral courage which was part of the American Revolution.

On March 5, 1770, seven British soldiers, commanded by a captain, fired upon a group of Boston citizens, with a result of five dead and five wounded. This was immediately called the Boston Massacre. Passions, cumulative over several years from restrictive acts of the British government, including the quartering of British troops on Boston, ran high.

In this situation, the British captain asked Quincy to defend him and his men at their trial. Quincy, placing law and his lawyer's oath above men and popularity, agreed. So also did John Adams (the same Adams who would one day become President of the nation still unborn), when faced with a similar request. Adams and Quincy succeeded in getting acquittals for the officer and five soldiers, the other two receiving sentences for manslaughter. Adams later wrote that his participation and the verdict lost him "over half my business at the bar."

Quincy, an outstanding patriot, had been prominent from the time of the Stamp Act (1765) in condemning British impositions and seeking to arouse his countrymen. Four years after his participation in the Boston Massacre trial, leaders of the American cause sent him to London to do some quiet propagandizing. He died on his return voyage, aged thirty-one.

Quincy's stately and moving eloquence—an authoritative article of time gone by—is displayed in reply to his father's letter of agitated concern; and in the opening two paragraphs of his court defense of the soldiers.

From Memoir of the Life of Josiah Quincy Jun. of Massachusetts: by his Son, Josiah Quincy.

[*From the Father of Josiah Quincy, Jr.*]

TO JOSIAH QUINCY JUN., BOSTON.

Braintree, March 22, 1770.

My Dear Son,

I am under great affliction, at hearing the bitterest reproaches uttered against you, for having become an advocate for those criminals who are charged with the murder of their fellow-citizens. Good God! Is it possible? I will not believe it.

Just before I returned home from Boston, I knew, indeed, that on the day those criminals were committed to prison, a sergeant had inquired for you at your brother's house,—but I had no apprehension that it was possible an application would be made to you to undertake their defence. Since then I have been told that you have actually engaged for Captain Preston;—and I have heard the severest reflections made upon the occasion, by men who had just before manifested the highest esteem for you, as one designed to be a saviour of your country.

I must own to you, it has filled the bosom of your aged and infirm parent with anxiety and distress, lest it should not only prove true, but destructive of your reputation and interest; and I repeat, I will not believe it, unless it be confirmed by your own mouth, or under your own hand.

Your anxious and distressed parent,

Josiah Quincy.

[*The Son's Reply to His Father*]

TO JOSIAH QUINCY, ESQ., BRAINTREE.

Boston, March 26, 1770.

Honoured Sir,

I have little leisure, and less inclination either to know, or to take notice, of those ignorant slanderers, who have dared to utter their "bitter reproaches" in your hearing against me, for having become an advocate for criminals charged with murder. But the sting of reproach when envenomed only by envy and falsehood, will never prove mortal. Before pouring their reproaches into the ear of the aged and infirm, if they had been friends, they would have surely spared a little reflection on the nature of an attorney's oath, and duty;—some trifling scrutiny into the business and discharge of his office, and some small portion of patience in viewing my past and future conduct.

Let such be told, Sir, that these criminals, charged with murder, are *not yet legally proved guilty,* and therefore, however criminal, are entitled, by the laws of God and man, to all legal counsel and aid; that my duty as a man obliged me to undertake; that my duty as a lawyer strengthened the obligation; that from abundant caution, I at first declined being engaged; that after the best advice, and most mature deliberation had determined my judgment, I waited on Captain Preston, and told him that I would afford him my assistance; but, prior to this, in presence of two of his friends, I made the most explicit declaration to him, of my real opinion, on the contests (as I expressed it to him) of the times, and that my heart and hand were indissolubly attached to the cause of my country; and finally, that I refused all engagement, until advised and urged to undertake it, by an Adams, a Hancock, a Molineux, a Cushing, a Henshaw, a Pemberton, a Warren, a Cooper, and a Phillips.[1] This and much more might be told with great truth, and I dare affirm, that you, and this whole people will one day REJOICE, that I became an advocate for the aforesaid "criminals," *charged* with the murder of our fellow-citizens.

I never harboured the expectation, nor any great desire, that all men should speak well of me. To inquire my duty, and to do

[1] Respected and prominent citizens of Boston, most of them active in the patriot cause.

it, is my aim. Being mortal, I am subject to error; and conscious of this, I wish to be diffident. Being a rational creature, I judge for myself, according to the light afforded me. When a plan of conduct is formed with an honest deliberation, neither murmuring, slander, nor reproaches move. For my single self, I consider, judge, and with reason hope to be immutable.

There are honest men in all sects,—I wish their approbation;—there are wicked bigots in all parties,—I abhor them.

I am, truly and affectionately,

your son,

Josiah Quincy Jun.

Josiah Quincy, Jr.'s Opening Remarks at the Trial of the British Soldiers.[1]

May it please your Honors, and you, Gentlemen of the Jury.

The prisoners at the bar stand indicted for the murder of five of his Majesty's liege subjects, as set forth in the several indictments, which have been read to you. The persons slain, those indictments set forth, as "being in the peace of God, and our lord the king," at the time of the mortal wounds given.

To these indictments, the prisoners have severally pleaded Not Guilty: and for their trial have put themselves on God and their country, which country you are. And by their pleas, thus severally pleaded, they are to stand, or fall, by the evidence which shall respectively apply to them.

TREASON IN THREE PARAGRAPHS

In these brief newspaper paragraphs from the Connecticut *Journal* the tragedy of Major General Benedict Arnold is compressed and spotlighted.

---

[1] Captain Preston had been acquitted; the trial of the soldiers followed.

In 1778, the daring and ambitious Arnold, having wrought a splendid and courageous war record, was paying a visit to his home city of New Haven.

Three years later, in November 1781, the traitor Arnold had been with the enemy over a year, and less than three months before had led the British force that burned New London and massacred the garrison in Fort Griswold.

From the Connecticut Journal.

[*Issue of Wednesday, May 6, 1778*]

Monday last came to town, Major General BENEDICT ARNOLD;— he was met on the road by several Continental and Militia Officers, the Cadet Company, and a Number of respectable Inhabitants, from this Place, to testify their Esteem for One who has, by his Bravery, rendered his Country many important Services. On his Arrival in Town, he was saluted by a Discharge of thirteen Cannon."

[*Issue of Thursday, December 6, 1781*]

We, the Subscribers being (by the Court of Probate for the District of New-Haven) appointed Commissioners to receive and examine the Claims of the several Creditors of Benedict Arnold, late of New-Haven, in New-Haven County, now joined with the Enemies of the United States of America, whose Estate hath been in due Form of Law confiscated; give Notice to all concerned, That we shall attend to the Business of our said Appointment, at the Dwelling-House of Pierpont Edwards, Esq; in said New-Haven, on the second Monday of December next, at two of the Clock Afternoon; on the second Monday of January next, at the same Time of Day; and on the third Monday of February next, also at the same Time of Day.

ISAAC JONES Commissioners
MICHAEL TODD

New-Haven, November 29, 1781.

The Tempter and the Traitor—the treason of Arnold on the night of September 21, 1780.

[*Issue of Thursday, December 6, 1781*]

All Persons that were indebted to said Arnold at the Time he joined said Enemies are requested, by the Subscriber, who is, by said Court of Probate appointed Administrator on said Arnold's Estate, to make immediate Payment of such Debts to said Administrator; And all Persons who are possessed of any personal Estate, that was the Property of said Arnold at the Time he joined as aforesaid, are requested to deliver the same to the Subscriber or account with him therefor.

PIERPONT EDWARDS

New-Haven, November 29, 1781.

A NAVAL BATTLE AT CLOSE QUARTERS

DURING THE Revolution, before the establishment of federal government, most of the separate colonies built their own warships to fight
the British. Massachusetts built several such vessels, among them one
called the *Protector*, which triumphed over a large enemy privateer in
its first engagement. An on-the-scene account of this Revolutionary
naval battle follows.

Ebenezer Fox (1763–1843), the chronicler, was a native of Roxbury, Massachusetts, and rose from humble beginnings to a measure of
remembrance for the story of his adventures during the Revolution. After
the war, he returned to Roxbury, where he opened a crockery-ware shop
which he kept till his retirement in 1837, and where he was postmaster
from 1831 to 1835.

After the *Protector*'s victory over the *Admiral Duff* in 1780, she
went on a second cruise, took five prizes and then was herself captured.
Fox and his companions were confined for a few months on the *Old
Jersey*, a British prison ship of evil memory, at New York. To end this
misery, Fox enlisted in the British army and was assigned to Jamaica.
Soon Fox and three companions escaped to Cuba, then to Santo Domingo
where, in the summer of 1782, Fox signed on an American frigate bound
for France. Peace came in 1783; Fox reached home that summer.

A letter-of-marque was a government license to a private ship to
prey upon the enemy; such a vessel was also called a letter-of-marque, or
a privateer. The business of falsifying one's identity was a custom of the
seas in those days.

From The Revolutionary Adventures of
Ebenezer Fox.

Our coast was lined with British cruisers, which had almost
annihilated our commerce; and the state of Massachusetts judged it
expedient to build a government vessel, rated as a twenty-gun ship
named the "Protector," commanded by Captain John Foster Williams. She was to be fitted for service as soon as possible, to protect
our commerce, and to annoy the enemy. A rendezvous was established
for recruits at the head of Hancock's wharf,[1] where the national

[1] In Boston.

flag, then bearing thirteen stripes and stars, was hoisted. All means were resorted to, which ingenuity could devise, to induce men to enlist. A recruiting officer, bearing a flag and attended by a band of martial music, paraded the streets, to excite a thirst for glory and a spirit of military ambition.

My excitable feelings were roused; I repaired to the rendezvous, signed the ship's papers, mounted a cockade, and was in my own estimation already more than a half of a sailor. The ship was as yet far from being supplied with her complement of men; and the recruiting business went on slowly. Appeals continued to be made to the patriotism of every young man to lend his aid, by his exertions on sea or land, to free his country from the common enemy. Promises of gain were held out, which set truth at defiance, and offers the most tempting that the impoverished state of the finances of government could promise. About the last of February the ship was ready to receive her crew, and was hauled off into the channel, that the sailors might have no opportunity to run away after they were got on board.

Upwards of three hundred and thirty men were carried, dragged, and driven on board, of all kinds, ages, and descriptions, in all the various stages of intoxication; from that of "sober tipsiness" to beastly drunkenness, with the uproar and clamor that may be more easily imagined than described. Such a motley group has never been seen since Falstaff's ragged regiment paraded the streets of Coventry.

The wind being fair, we weighed anchor and dropped down to Nantasket roads, where we lay till about the first of April; and then set sail for a cruise of six months.

On the morning of June 9th, 1780, the fog began to clear away; and the man at the mast head gave notice that he saw a ship to the westward of us. As the fog cleared up, we perceived her to be a large ship under English colours to the windward, standing athwart our starboard bow. Our relative position gave us an opportunity to escape, but our valiant captain did not see fit to avail himself of it.

As she came down upon us, she appeared as large as a seventy-four; and we were not deceived respecting her size, for it afterwards proved that she was an old East-Indiaman of eleven hundred tons burden, fitted out as a letter-of-marque for the West-India trade, mounted with thirty-two guns, and furnished with a complement of one hundred and fifty men. She was called the Admiral Duff, commanded by Richard Strang, from St. Christopher and St. Eustatia, laden with sugar and tobacco, and bound to London. I was standing near our first lieutenant, Mr. Little, who was calmly examining the enemy, as she approached, with his spy-glass, when Captain Williams stepped up and asked his opinion of her. The lieutenant applied the glass to his eye again and took a deliberate look in silence, and replied, "I think she is a heavy ship, and that we shall have some hard fighting; but of one thing I am certain, she is not a frigate; if she were, she would not keep yawing, and showing her broadsides as she does; she would show nothing but her head and stern: we shall have the advantage of her, and the quicker we get alongside the better." Our captain ordered English colours to be hoisted and the ship to be cleared for action. The shrill pipe of the boatswain summoned all hands to their duty. The bedding and hammocks of the sailors were brought up from between decks; the bedding placed in the hammocks, and lashed up in the nettings: our courses hauled up; the top-gallant sails clewed down; and every preparation was made, which a skilful officer could suggest, or active sailors perform.

The enemy approached till within musket shot of us. The two ships were so near to each other that we could distinguish the officers from the men; and I particularly noticed the captain, on the gangway, a noble looking man, having a large gold-laced cocked hat on his head, and a speaking trumpet in his hand. Lieutenant Little possessed a powerful voice, and he was directed to hail the enemy; at the same time the quarter-master was ordered to stand ready to haul down the English flag and to hoist up the American. Our lieutenant took his station on the after part of the starboard gangway, and, elevating the trumpet, exclaimed, "Hallo! whence come you?"—"From Jamaica, bound to London," was the answer. "What is the ship's name?" inquired the lieutenant. "The Admiral Duff," was the reply.

The English captain then thought it his turn to interrogate, and asked the name of our ship. Lieutenant Little, in order to gain time, put the trumpet to his ear, pretending not to hear the question. During the short interval, thus gained, Captain Williams called upon the gunner to ascertain how many guns could be brought to bear upon the enemy. "Five," was the answer. "Then fire, and shift the colours," were the orders. The cannons poured forth their deadly contents, and, with the first flash, the American flag took the place of the British ensign at our mast-head.

The complement was returned in the form of a full broadside, and the action commenced. I was stationed on the edge of the quarter-deck, to sponge and load a six-pounder: this position gave me a fine opportunity to see the whole action. Broadsides were exchanged with great rapidity for nearly an hour; our fire, as we afterwards ascertained, produced a terrible slaughter among the enemy, while our loss was as yet trifling.

I happened to be looking for a moment towards the main deck, when a large shot came through our ship's side and killed Mr. Benjamin Scollay, a very promising young man, who was, I think, a midshipman. At this moment a shot from one of our marines killed the man at the wheel of the enemy's ship, and, his place not being immediately supplied, she was brought alongside of us in such a manner as to bring her bowsprit directly across our forecastle. Not knowing the cause of this movement, we supposed it to be the intention of the enemy to board us. Our boarders were ordered to be ready with their pikes to resist any such attempt, while our guns on the main deck were sending death and destruction among the crew of the enemy. Their principal object now seemed to be to get liberated from us, and by cutting away some of their rigging, they were soon clear, and at the distance of a pistol shot.

The action was then renewed with additional fury; broadside for broadside continued with unabated vigor; at times so near to each other that the muzzles of our guns came almost in contact, then again at such a distance as to allow of taking deliberate aim. The contest was obstinately continued by the enemy, although we could perceive that great havock was made among them, and that it was with much difficulty that their men were compelled to remain at their quarters.

A charge of grape-shot came in at one of our port-holes, which dangerously wounded four or five of our men, among whom was our third lieutenant, Mr. Little, brother to the first. His life was despaired of, but by the kind attention he received from his brother, and the surgeon, he finally recovered, though he bore evidence of the severity of his wounds thro' life.

While Captain Williams was walking the quarter deck, which he did during the whole action, a shot from the enemy struck the

The battle between the Protector *and the* Admiral Duff *ended when an explosion blew off part of the latter's stern, as vividly depicted in this old painting.*

speaking trumpet from his hand, and sent it to a considerable distance from him. He picked it up with great calmness of manner, and resumed his walk, without appearing to have been at all disturbed by the circumstance.

The battle still continued with unabated vigor on both sides, till our marksmen had killed or wounded all the men in the fore, main, and mizen tops of the enemy. The action had now lasted about an hour and a half, and the fire from the enemy began to slacken, when we suddenly discovered that all the sails on her mainmast were enveloped in a blaze. The fire spread with rapidity, and, running down the after-rigging, it soon communicated with her magazine, when her whole stern was blown off, and her valuable cargo emptied into the sea. All feelings of hostility now ceased, and those of pity were excited in our breasts for the miserable crew that survived the castastrophe.

Our enemy's ship was now a complete wreck, though she still floated, and the survivors were endeavoring to save themselves in the only boat that had escaped the general destruction. The humanity of our captain urged him to make all possible exertion to save the miserable, wounded, and burnt wretches, who were struggling for their lives in the water.

We ascertained that the loss of the enemy was prodigious, compared with ours. This disparity however will not appear so remarkable, when it is considered that, although their ship was larger than ours, it was not so well supplied with men; having no marines to use the musket, they fought with their guns alone, and, as their ship lay much higher out of the water than ours, the greater part of their shot went over us, cutting our rigging and sails, without injuring our men. We had about seventy marines, who did great execution with their muskets, picking off the officers and men with a sure and deliberate aim.

AN UNCOMFORTED WARTIME NEUTRAL

THE LOT of the wartime neutral is seldom tranquil and often dangerous. This fact was accentuated in our Revolution, when the people were divided and the stakes were the limit—freedom.

James Allen, member of a rich and politically active Pennsylvania family, supported the American rebellion against England up to a point —the decision for independence. Then he became neutral, but with unvoiced pro-British sympathies, and his afflictions descended upon him.

Family precedent may have influenced him. His father, William Allen, who had been chief justice of Pennsylvania for twenty-four years, left the colonies for England in 1774. Three brothers who had held positions of trust in the colony went openly to the British side after the proclamation of independence. James himself was elected a member of the Pennsylvania Assembly in 1776 and served some months in that dying body of the colonial regime before it was superseded by a strongly pro-independence one.

In happier, pre-Revolutionary days, Chief Justice Allen had been holder of a land grant that included the site of the present city of Allentown, then called Northampton, in Northampton County. He deeded this Allentown tract to his son James in 1767, and one of the latter's early actions was to claim back 1,000 acres originally placed in trust for common use. In 1770, James built a home, Trout Hall, in Allentown, where he took up residence in 1776, and it was there that his neighbors demonstrated that the existence of a neutral is unhappy.

James Allen died in Philadelphia at the age of thirty-seven, less than a year after the last diary entry quoted here.

From the Diary of James Allen, Esq. of Philadelphia, Counsellor-at-Law, 1770– 1778.

Jany. 25, 1777—When Gen¹ Howe[1] was expected in Philadᵃ a persecution of Tories, (under which name, is included every one disinclined to Independance tho' ever so warm a friend to constitutional liberty and the old cause,) began; houses were broken open, people imprison'd without any colour of authority by private persons, & as, was said a list of 200 disaffected persons made out, who were to be siezed, imprisoned & sent off to North Carolina; in which list, it was said, our whole family was set down; My Brothers under this dreadful apprehension fled from Philadᵃ to the Union,[2] where I went over to them. Soon after, against my Judgmt, they all went to Trenton & claimed protection from Gen¹ Howe's army. From whence they went to N. York where they now are, unhappily separated from their families and like to be so for some time. I was informed of this by Gen¹ Gates at Bethlehem—& of course became alarmed for my own safety. Accordingly on Thursday 19 Decʳ 1776 at 7 o'clock A.M. my house was surrounded by a Guard of Soldiers with fixed Bayonets; I got up & when I came down stairs the officer who was at the front door produced a Warrant from the Council of Safety to seize me & bring me before them. I accordingly went to Philadᵃ & appeared before them, & opened the scene, by saying, that they had drawn me from my retirement unexpectedly; Mʳ Owen

[1] General William Howe, commander of the British troops in this country, was then in New York. The following September he occupied Philadelphia.

[2] Union Iron Works, Hunterdon County, New Jersey, where John Allen, a brother of James, had a home.

Biddle[3] then said, that they had received accounts of the unwilling-
ness of the Militia of Northampton County to march, that they
knew my influence and property there, & were afraid of my being
the cause of it, & added that my brothers being gone over to the
enemy the publick would expect that I should be put on my Parole
& hoped I wou'd have no Objection to stay within six miles of
Philad[a]. M[r] Matlack[4] said "at least M[r] Allen may chuse his place
of Residence." I told them that my political principles were well
known, to be unfriendly to the present views of Independance, which
I had strenuously opposed before it was declared, that since I had
not interfered in publick matters, further than in confidential con-
versations with my friends & I wished always to remain so during
the present unhappy war. I then produced some certificates which
I had the precaution to procure, testifying the truth of the above. . . .
In the afternoon, they produced a certificate, which they hoped
I would not object to; wherein they set forth, my brothers departure & the backwardness of our Militia as reasons for sending
for me, that I had given them satisfaction respecting my prudent
conduct, that my conduct did not appear unfriendly to the cause of
Liberty, nor inconsistent with the character of a Gentleman; & I in
return pledged my honor verbally not to say or do any thing injurious
to the present cause of America. So we parted amicably & as we
began, with great politeness on both sides. This disagreeable business over I spent five or six days in Philad[a] & near it with great
pleasure at being in company with my relations and friends after
so long absence. Philad[a] seemed almost deserted & resembled a
Sunday in service time. The Quakers are almost the only people
determined to remain there. They pressed all persons walking the
streets to work in trenches surrounding the Town; I was stopt &
with difficulty got off by walking on and taking no notice of 'em.
28th got home & continued quiet & happy for some time, amusing
myself with my family; having opened my poetic vein, which had
long been dormant by an Ode on the Birthday 4th Jan[y] 1777 of
my daughter Polly.

This happiness was unfortunately interrupted; by an unlooked
for accident. Being ignorant that any of the Militia were in the
Town M[rs] Allen with her daughter Peggy & Lyddy Duberry went

[3] Member of the Council of Safety.
[4] Member of the Council of Safety.

to visit Mrs Bond in the Chariot: entering the street a company of the Militia met them in front; Samson endeavoured to drive out of the Road, but was stopt by a hollow way. The soldiers beat him with their muskets, & pushed at him with their Bayonets, on which to defend himself he made use of his Whip. This so enraged them, that they pushed their Bayonets into the Chariot, broke the glass & pierced the chariot in 3 places; during the whole scene my wife begging to be let out & the children screaming; they also endeavoured to overset it, while they were within it. David Deshler[5] happening to be present prevented it & led the horses on, by which means they escaped. Their design was to destroy the Chariot. I having walked across the field saw nothing of this till it was over & the company had marched on. Soon after the Major Boehm & the Captn Buckhalter returned. —The former, a violent man, countenanced the attack, whereupon a recounter ensued between him & me, in which he attempted to draw his sword on me. . . .

Feby 17, 1777—My particular situation has been of late very uneasy, owing to the Battalion of Militia of this district, assembling in the Town of Northampton, to the number of 600 men, where they continued a fortnight & marched off the day before yesterday viz 15 Feby inst—They are generally disorderly, being under no discipline; & I was particularly obnoxious, on account of my political opinions, & the conduct of my brothers, but particularly for the late assault I made on the Lieut: Coll. when my chariot was attacked & which the whole Battalion highly resented. Eight or nine parties of 15 to 20 men each came to demand Blankets, one party of which, was very uncivil. But by prudence I escaped without any insult, having parted with 10 Blankets. The principal officers behaved with great civility & the Coll. Boehm whom I had the rencounter with, came to my house, to assure me he was innocent of the attack on my chariot & we buried the affair in Oblivion. He assured me, that the soldiers were ripe for doing some violence to my house, which he with difficulty prevented, & upon the whole I had great good fortune to escape without some injury from a riotous incensed soldiery, & am at present pretty easy on that head. Notwithstanding this I am uneasy & wish to be in Philad^a^. My wife is often alarmed;

---

[5] Commissioner of Army Supplies for Northampton County.

James Allen.

I am afraid to converse with persons here, or write to my friends in Philad^a; & a small matter, such as a letter intercepted or unguarded word, would plunge me into troubles. I never knew, how painful it is to be secluded from the free conversation of one's friends, the loss of which cannot be made up by any other expedients. I am considering whether I shall not leave this place in May & adjourn to Philad^a & am in that state of uncertainty, that has hitherto distressed me so much. I should prefer continuing here, were I not in so conspicuous a point of light. It is odd to reflect that I am taking as much pains to be in obscurity, as others are to blaze in the publick Eye & become of importance.

6 *June*, 1777—A great gap in my diary. Genl Howes army has remained since the Winter at Brunswick & Amboy, confined to their quarters & harassed by our Army. Contrary to the expectations of every one, he is still inactive; most unaccountably so, as our army does not at present exceed 7 or 8000 & till lately was not half so numerous. It is supposed that Howe's army, tho' large enough to drive our's before it, is insufficient for the garrisons he must have

& therefore, he waits for reinforcements from England & Canada, that are daily expected. Delaware Bay has a long time (been) & still is full of men of War & of course Trade is at an end & every article of importation enormous. Privateering is also almost over, as the men of War scour the Seas & nothing escapes 'em. Washington, will, in my opinion have but an indifferent army, recruiting goes on heavily; all over the continent. His present supplies are from the Southern provinces; very few from New-England; it is said those provinces, who were the most forward in Independance are sick of the war. America is more divided than ever, & tories increase.

October 15, 1777—It is painful to be so much at a loss as we are, about the truth of events; which is encreased since Gen¹ Howe is in Philadᵃ as all accounts come thro' the hands of the army, the only line of communication, & are delivered out as they please. Gen¹ Washington has issued orders to take the blankets, shoes, stockings &c of private families for the use of the army. This together with the licentiousness, plundering stealing & impressing of the military, will sink this country to perdition. Misery begins to wear her ghastliest form; it is impossible to endure it. Three fourths of my income arises from my estate in Philadᵃ, from which I am cut off. My rents are being paid in continental money, which is now depreciated as 6 to 1 & I obliged to pay in all articles four fold; in some, as butter, meat, cheese &c nine fold, ruin can't be very distant. The prevailing idea now is, that no man has any property in what the publick has use for, & it is seldom they ask the owner; so wanton is this species of oppression called pressing, that if they could by fair means get any thing by a little trouble, they chuse to take private property by violence if somewhat nearer at hand. This I have seen in many instances, & felt in my own case. When the hospital & publick works were erected in this little town, I offered to supply them with wood at a reasonable rate, to avoid being plundered; yet they have hitherto gone on cutting my timber, burning my fences & taking bricks from me, rather than employ some of the many idle men they have, in cutting wood. The militia who occasionally assembled here, & have now met for near a month plunder without ceremony, all who do not turn out in Militia; Horses, Waggons, Cows, Turkeys are daily brought into Town. Yesterday a farmer, sold me his whole brood of Turkeys & Fowls, on receiving information that a neighbor with whom he had a law suit 3 years ago, had informed the Militia, who were setting out to take them away. It is probable they will soon plunder me of them, as every night they steal my poultry. The officers of militia never think of punishing them, neither are they able or disposed to do it. It is a fine time to gratify low private revenge, & few opportunities are lost. My tenants whose rents are due in sterling, often pay off arrears of 6 or 7 years in continental money at the old Enchange, and yet I dare not object, tho' I am as much robbed of 5/6ths, of my property, as if it was taken out of my Drawer.

A BRITISH OFFICER DESPAIRS OF HIS CAUSE

BRITISH TROOPS here during the Revolution were charged with inhumanity by one of their own commanders. His letters also reveal low morale among the highest British officers on American soil.

Lieutenant Colonel Charles Stuart (1753–1801), commanding the 26th Regiment of Foot, the Cameronians—operating in the vicinity of New York City—was writing to his father, Lord Bute. The latter had been Prime Minister (1761–63), with a strong influence over George III, an influence which he claimed to have lost long before these letters were written. However, those who complained to Lieutenant Colonel Stuart probably had hopes that their plaints would reach high quarters in London.

After his service in America, Stuart went on to become a lieutenant general with a distinguished record in the Mediterranean during the early Napoleonic wars. He took the islands of Corsica and Minorca, was appointed governor of the latter, and seized the capital of Malta.

Among those mentioned in his letters are Admiral Marriot Arbuthnot (1711–94), who was in command of British naval activities in our waters in 1779; Sir Henry Clinton (1738–95), who in 1778 had succeeded Sir William Howe as commander-in-chief on American soil; and Lord Cornwallis (1738–1805), who surrendered at Yorktown in 1781.

All the locations here named were in the broad vicinity of New York City. "Old Japan" is apparently a manuscript misreading of Old Tappan, or Tappan.

From A Prime Minister and His Son. *By*
Mrs. E. Stuart Wortley.

[*Col. Stuart to Lord Bute*]

Laurel Hill Camp, King's Bridge, *Sept.* 16, 1778

We have no occasion to try whether acts of severity will cause
these people to submit—wherever our armies have marched, where-
ever they have been encamped during the last campaign, every species
of barbarity has been executed. We planted an irrecoverable hatred
wherever we went, which neither time nor measures will be able to
eradicate. What, then, are we to expect from it, conciliation or
submission?

Valentine Hill Camp, *Oct.* 7, 1778

A few days ago Ld. Cornwallis and General Grey marched with
two Columns to surprise a Rebel Post near Old Japan. To render it
effectual three Batts. marched from hence and crossed the N. River
to attack their rear at the same instant; but two deserters from one
of our Regts. acquainting the Enemy with our intention, the party,
which consisted of 300 men, retreated, but forgot to inform a hundred
and 10 of their number who were near them. General Grey had the
good fortune to surround their cantonment before they were
alarmed, by which means 60 were killed, including a Lt. Col. and
Major, and 50 taken, most of whom were wretchedly wounded with
Bayonets.

As they were in their beds, and fired not a shot in opposition,
the credit that might have been due to the Corps that effected the
surprise is entirely buried in the barbarity of their behaviour.

Staten Island, *Aug.* 1779

As he [Sir Henry Clinton] had always indulged me with a very
particular degree of his confidence, he opened his mind to me very
freely upon this occasion.

He stated how particularly cruel it was to be served so ill by
subordinate Officers, blamed Col. Johnson tho' with that delicacy

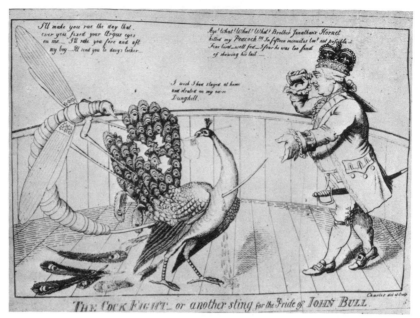

A Revolutionary War cartoon. The American hornet is killing the British peacock, while King George III, astonished and dismayed, laments that his fine bird was "too fond of showing his tail."

that it hardly bore the name of censure, he told me with tears in his eyes that he was quite an altered man—that business oppressed him, that he felt himself incapable of his station; "believe me," he said, "my dear Col. Stuart, I envy even that Grenadier who is passing the door, and would exchange with joy situations—no!" he added, "let me advise you never to take command of an army."

"I know I am hated, nay, detested in this Army, but I am indifferent about it, because I know it is without a cause, but I am determined to return home. The Minister has used me so ill that I can no longer bear with this life."

New York, *Sept.* 26, 1779.

The Ad. [Admiral Arbuthnot] took me into his Closet, and with tears in his eyes told me he was tired to death by the Gen. [Sir

Henry Clinton] and giving way to his passion, abused him for his want of candour and folly. He then shewed me a long letter which the Gen. had just sent him, remonstrating against his going to Halifax, with his own answer, wherein he said that he went to Halifax in consequence of the General's declaration that nothing was to be done to the Southward—that he came to America merely for the good of the service, and if the Gen. had any plan to propose, he would adopt it, but if not it was his duty to defend the first Post in America when so seriously threatened.

He, however, in some measure changed his mind, and ordered Com. Drake to go to Halifax, while he remained to forward any expeditions that might be on foot. I accordingly returned to the General, who, not being able to contain himself at the disappointment of his plans in regard to the Evacuation of Rhode Island,[1] abused the Ad. in the grossest terms, called him full of deceit and artifice, and declared that he never could agree with one who meant to mislead him.

Seeing matters in this situation with an entire want of confidence between them, I own I was happy to have this burden taken from me, and asked leave to go home, which was granted. Subsequently the Ad. saw the Gen., and the result of the interview was that no ships of the Line are to go to Halifax. This indecision seems to be the rule of those, from whose conduct the American conquest is expected.

[1] Newport, Rhode Island, was occupied by the British, 1776–79.

WAR OF 1812

ABOUT DR. BEANES AND
THE STAR-SPANGLED BANNER

HISTORY IS a matter of beginnings, whether the latter be early or recent. *The Star-Spangled Banner* was written by Francis Scott Key because Dr. William Beanes,[1] prominent citizen of Upper Marlborough, Maryland, had been seized by the British on their retreat from Washington, and Key, trying to secure Beanes' release, was detained near the British fleet while it attacked Fort McHenry. As he watched the assault Key conceived the verses which became our national anthem.

This was the obvious source of *The Star-Spangled Banner*; if Dr. Beanes hadn't been held captive, the song wouldn't have been born. The next historical question is, what factors made the doctor a British prisoner?

Conflicting answers are on record. One, by a relative of Key, indicates that Dr. Beanes was in his backyard when the lawlessness of some British soldiers forced Beanes to have them arrested. Another explanation, from a relative of the doctor's, is that the latter had partaken of much punch and in consequence exuberantly and needlessly jailed three unoffending British stragglers. The detention of the soldiers, from whatever cause, induced the British to send back a detachment to release them and take Dr. Beanes.

The version which follows comes from Key's brother-in-law, Roger Brooke Taney. Taney (1777–1864), pronounced Tawny, became chief

---

[1] The name of Dr. Beanes has been spelled variously. One can accept the version of two of his contemporaries as correct. Chief Justice Taney and Mrs. William Thornton, wife of the original designer of the Capitol, spell the name "Beanes."

justice of the United States in 1836, remaining in the post till his death. He wrote the controversial Dred Scott decision.

From Memoir of Roger Brooke Taney, LL.D. Chief Justice of The Supreme Court of The United States. *By Samuel Tyler, LL.D.*

Washington, D.C., March 12, 1856.

. . . On the evening of the day that the enemy[2] disappeared, Mr. Richard West arrived at Mr. Key's, and told him that after the British army passed through Upper Marlbro on their return to their ships, and had encamped some miles below the town, a detachment was sent back, which entered Dr. Beanes's house about midnight, compelled him to rise from his bed, and hurried him off to the British camp, hardly allowing him time to put his clothes on; that he was treated with great harshness, and closely guarded; and that as soon as his friends were apprised of his situation, they hastened to the head-quarters of the English army to solicit his release; but it was peremptorily refused, and they were not even permitted to see him; and that he had been carried as a prisoner on board the fleet. And finding their own efforts unavailing, and alarmed for his safety, his friends in and about Marlbro thought it advisable that Mr. West should hasten to George Town, and request Mr. Key to obtain the sanction of the Government to his going on board the admiral's ship, under a flag of truce, and endeavoring to procure the release of Dr. Beanes before the fleet sailed. It was then lying at the mouth of the Potomac, and its destination was not at that time known with certainty. Dr. Beanes, as perhaps you know, was the leading physician in Upper Marlbro, and an accomplished scholar and gentleman. He was highly respected by all who knew him; was the family physician of Mr. West, and the intimate friend of Mr. Key. He occupied one of the best houses in Upper Marlbro,

[2] The British fleet that had taken Alexandria, Virginia, in sight of Washington.

Upper Marlborough was about 17 miles from Washington.

and lived very handsomely; and his house was selected for the quarters of Admiral Cockburn, and some of the principal officers of the army, when the British troops encamped at Marlbro on their march to Washington. These officers were, of course, furnished with everything that the house could offer; and they, in turn, treated him with much courtesy, and placed guards around his grounds and out-houses, to prevent depredations by their troops.

But on the return of the army to the ships, after the main body had passed through the town, stragglers, who had left the ranks to plunder, or from some other motive, made their appearance from time to time, singly or in small squads; and Dr. Beanes put himself at the head of a small body of citizens to pursue and make prisoners of them. Information of this proceeding was, by some means or other, conveyed to the English camp; and the detachment of which I have spoken was sent back to release the prisoners and seize Dr. Beanes. They did not seem to regard him, and certainly did not treat him, as a prisoner of war, but as one who had deceived, and broken his faith to them.

Mr. Key readily agreed to undertake the mission in his favor, and the President promptly gave his sanction to it. Orders were immediately issued to the vessel usually employed as a cartel,[3] in the communications with the fleet in the Chesapeake, to be made ready without delay; and Mr. John S. Skinner, who was agent for the Government for flags of truce and exchange of prisoners, and who was well known as such to the officers of the fleet, was directed to accompany Mr. Key. And as soon as the arrangements were made, he hastened to Baltimore, where the vessel was to embark; and Mrs. Key and the children went with me to Frederick, and thence to his father's on Pipe Creek, where she remained until he returned.

We heard nothing from him until the enemy retreated from Baltimore, which, as well as I can now recollect, was a week or ten days after he left us; and we were becoming uneasy about him, when, to our great joy, he made his appearance at my house, on his way to join his family.

He told me that he found the British fleet at the mouth of the Potomac, preparing for the expedition against Baltimore. He was courteously received by Admiral Cochrane and the officers of the

3 A cartel ship was one used in the exchange of prisoners and communications between belligerents.

BOMBARDMENT OF FORT McHENRY.

The rockets all appear to be falling short of their mark in this illustration from The Naval Temple, *a book published in Boston in 1816.*

army, as well as of the navy. But when he made known his business, his application was received so coldly that he feared it would fail. General Ross[4] and Admiral Cockburn—who accompanied the expedition to Washington—particularly the latter, spoke of Dr. Beanes in very harsh terms, and seemed at first not disposed to release him. It however happened, fortunately, that Mr. Skinner carried letters from the wounded British officers left at Bladensburg; and in these letters to their friends on board the fleet they all spoke of the humanity and kindness with which they had been treated after they had fallen into our hands. And after a good deal of conversation, and strong representations from Mr. Key as to the character and standing of Dr. Beanes, and of the deep interest which the community in which he lived took in his fate, General Ross said that Dr. Beanes deserved much more punishment than he had received; but that he felt himself bound to make a return for the kindness which had been shown to his wounded officers, whom he had been compelled to leave at Bladensburg, and upon that ground, and that only, he would release him. But Mr. Key was at the same time informed that neither he nor any one else, would be permitted to leave the fleet for some days, and must be detained until the attack on Baltimore, which was

4 General Ross was killed in the attack on Baltimore.

then about to be made, was over. But he was assured that they would make him and Mr. Skinner as comfortable as possible while they detained them. Admiral Cochrane, with whom they dined on the day of their arrival, apologized for not accommodating them in his own ship, saying that it was crowded already with officers of the army; but that they would be well taken care of in the frigate *Surprise*, commanded by his son, Sir Thomas Cochrane. And to this frigate, they were accordingly transferred.

Mr. Key had an interview with Dr. Beanes before General Ross consented to release him. I do not recollect whether he was on board of the admiral's ship, or the *Surprise*, but I believe it was the former. He found him in the forward part of the ship, among the sailors and soldiers; he had not had a change of clothes from the time he was seized; was constantly treated with indignity by those around him, and no officer would speak to him. He was treated as a culprit, and not as a prisoner of war. And this harsh and humiliating treatment continued until he was placed on board of the cartel.

Something must have passed, when the officers were quartered at his house on the march to Washington, which, in the judgment of General Ross, bound him not to take up arms against the English forces until the troops had re-embarked. It is impossible, on any other grounds, to account for the manner in which he was spoken of and treated. But whatever General Ross and the other officers might have thought, I am quite sure that Dr. Beanes did not think he was in any way pledged to abstain from active hostilities against the public enemy. And when he made prisoners of the stragglers, he did not consider himself as a prisoner on parole, nor suppose himself to be violating any obligation he had incurred. For he was a gentleman of untainted character and a nice sense of honor, and incapable of doing anything that could have justified such treatment. Mr. Key imputed the ill usage he received to the influence of Admiral Cockburn, who, it is still remembered, while he commanded in the Chesapeake, carried on hostilities in a vindictive temper, assailing and plundering defenceless villages, or countenancing such proceedings by those under his command.

Mr. Key and Mr. Skinner continued on board of the *Surprise*, where they were very kindly treated by Sir Thomas Cochrane, until the fleet reached the Patapsco, and preparations were making for landing the troops. Admiral Cochrane then shifted his flag to the frigate in order that he might be able to move farther up the river and superintend in person the attack by water on the fort; and Mr. Key and Mr. Skinner were then sent on board their own vessel, with a guard of sailors or marines, to prevent them from landing. They were permitted to take Dr. Beanes with them; and they thought themselves fortunate in being anchored in a position which enabled them to see distinctly the flag of Fort McHenry from the deck of the vessel. He proceeded then, with much animation, to describe the scene on the night of the bombardment. He and Mr. Skinner remained on deck during the night, watching every shell from the moment it was fired until it fell, listening with breathless interest to hear if an explosion followed. While the bombardment continued, it was sufficient proof that the fort had not surrendered. But it suddenly ceased sometime before day, and, as they had no communication with any of the enemy's ships, they did not know whether the fort had surrendered or the attack had been abandoned. They paced the deck for the residue of the night in painful suspense, watching with intense anxiety for the return of day, and looking every few minutes at their watches to see how long they must wait for it; and as soon as it dawned, and before it was light enough to see objects at a distance, their glasses were turned to the fort, uncertain whether they should see the Stars and Stripes or the flag of the enemy. At length the light came, and they saw that "our flag was still there." And, as the day advanced, they discovered, from the movements of the boats between the shore and the fleet, that the troops had been roughly handled, and that many wounded men were carried to the ships. At length he was informed that the attack on Baltimore had failed, and the British army was re-embarking, and that he and Mr. Skinner and Dr. Beanes would be permitted to leave them, and go where they pleased, as soon as the troops were on board and the fleet ready to sail.

He then told me that, under the excitement of the time, he had written the song, and handed me a printed copy of "The Star-Spangled Banner." When I had read it, and expressed my admiration, I asked him how he found time, in the scenes he had been passing through, to compose such a song? He said he commenced it on the deck of their vessel, in the fervor of the moment, when he saw the enemy hastily retreating to their ships, and looked at the flag he had watched for so anxiously as the morning opened; that he had written some lines, or brief notes, that would aid him in calling them to mind, upon the back of a letter which he happened to have in his pocket; and for some of the lines, as he proceeded, he was obliged to rely altogether on his memory; and that he finished it in the boat on his way to the shore, and wrote it out, as it now stands, at the hotel on the night he reached Baltimore, and immediately after he arrived.

Another Version—Mrs. Dorsey's Mother Was There

Mrs. Anna Hanson Dorsey (1815–98) was the daughter of Rev. William McKenney, a navy chaplain, and Chloe Ann Lanigan. She married Lorenzo Dorsey in 1840, became a convert to the Catholic faith and for over half a century was a writer, especially of fiction. She pioneered "in light Catholic literature in the United States and was a leading writer for the young." Pope Leo XIII twice sent her his benediction and the University of Notre Dame conferred on her the Laetare medal. Most of her life was spent in Washington.

From an article in the Washington Chronicle, *May 12, 1861. By Mrs. Anna H. Dorsey.*

Chief Justice Taney, the brother-in-law of Francis Key, esq., the author of the song, wrote a very interesting account of it some years ago, in which, however, some of the lesser facts connected with the affair were omitted. These facts I have heard related hundreds of times by a dear mother, now at rest, who was a guest at the house of her uncle, Dr. William Beans, where the incidents which I shall describe occurred. Dr. Beans lived on his estate in Marlborough, where he dispensed his hospitalities after the liberal and hearty fashion of an old Maryland cavalier.

While Dr. Beans and several congenial spirits were sitting over their wine, a negro rushed in with the tidings that the British army was retreating from Washington and were within a few miles march of the place. Nothing authentic or particular had been heard of their operations, since their departure, the facilities for the transmission of news being of a most primitive kind, and constantly impeded, owing to the state of the country. The only inference that our party could draw from this sudden news was, that there had been a battle in which the English had been beaten and routed, and were now retreating in confusion to their ships, which lay off Annapolis, under the broad pennant of Admiral Cockburn. Filled with patriotic enthusiasm, the doctor proposed an adjournment to a romantic spring near the house, with lemons and other et ceteras, necessary to concoct the favorite libation, which they intended to pour out, to celebrate the news. This was forthwith agreed to: and in a short time the carousal was inaugurated and conducted with spirit. Patriotic speeches and toasts were the order of the day, and so well were the host and his guests occupied that they scarcely noticed that the slanting rays of the sun announced its setting. Suddenly three footsore, dusty and weary English soldiers made their appearance on the scene, in quest of water.

Truth must be told. Punch had made these old cavaliers, who had won laurels in the revolution, more than valiant, and they conceived the brilliant idea of making prisoners of war of the enemy, which, with the assistance of their servants, they succeeded in doing, and conveyed them to the court-house for safe keeping, locked them in, placed a guard over them, and returned home to sleep on their laurels. But lo! at midnight Dr. Beans was aroused from his slumbers by a furious knocking at his hall door, the sound of hoofs on the gravelled drive, and the barking and yelping of hounds. The mystery was soon explained. The English soldiers had been missed. The officer in command thought they had deserted, and a detachment were sent in pursuit.

WASHINGTON'S HAPPY-GO-LUCKY
PROTECTION OF 1813

A BRITISH fleet had appeared in Chesapeake Bay, but Washington, in the summer of 1813, took matters easily. Elbridge Gerry, Jr., of Massachusetts, son of the Vice-President, and Benjamin Lear, son of George

Washington's secretary, both aged twenty-one, were among the carefree volunteers patroling the city after sunset.

Through exuberance or nervousness this proved a noisy business. Congressman John Lovett (Federalist, New York), recently wounded in the war, wrote on July 17, 1813, that persons were troubled "*nights* by the yells and popping of our undisciplined Patrols." Part of the patroling was done in taverns.

Young Gerry, whose diary extracts follow, arrived in Washington on June 27 and departed the first of August. Hardly a year after these cheerful entries, he was suddenly faced with the glamorless responsibilities of life by the death of his father. The latter left his widow, three sons and six daughters unprovided for, and President Madison named Elbridge Gerry, Jr. to a position in the customs as an aid to the support of the family. Soon Gerry became surveyor of customs at Boston and held this office until displaced in 1830 by the regime of President Jackson. Then Gerry was elected to the Massachusetts House for a couple of years, after which he entered mercantile business. In his last years he followed "literary pursuits." At seventy-three, this man, so absorbed in 1813 in the pretty girls and social life of Washington, died a bachelor.

From The Diary of Elbridge Gerry, Jr.
With Preface and Footnotes by Claude G. Bowers.

At my lodgings I learned that the Capt. of the Guard had called on me, on Sunday eve, to patrole in my turn, but could not find me. I however agreed to turn out on Monday night and tho't myself fortunate to escape this last night, as it rained quite fast. This afternoon I spent with Mr. Lear and at home, and at ten commenced my nocturnal walk. We were divided into two parties, three in each, and our patrole was thro' one ward. Our duty was to hail every person, and if he could not give our countersign, or if he was not known to us, we must put him into the watch house until morn. We walked all over the ward on the first cruise, about 3 ms., and only met two persons. I had an encounter with two dogs, who attacked me, and when I had hailed them to no purpose, I charged bayonet, and combatted them with great presence of mind. I had not engaged them long before the master put his head out of the window, and joined in their barking, against me; I resolved to silence his guns, and in a loud tone hail'd him with "Who goes there?" He gave no answer and I added "Speak or I'll run you thro'." The poor fellow pulled in his head quite slyly, and after routing the dogs, who all this time were at my heels, I joined my comrades. When we reached the main street we heard talking in a house, and on approaching, was desired by a woman to take care of a drunken man, who had entered her house to repose. We took hold of him, and told him to come with us, when he exclaimed, "What! damn it, have you got me a second time?" We told him he must go with us, and asked where he came from. In a sleepy tone, he answered, "Why Gordamn-e, I deserted from the Queen Charlotte, at Anappolis." We asked who commanded her, and he said, "That damn scoundrel of admirable Warren." After he highly amused with his conversation, we left him to his peregrination, thro' the streets. By this time we were inclined to rest a short period, and came in sight of a grog shop. To support the system, we determined to go in and take a drop, and then to laugh at the other watch, at our advantage over them. When we came to the door, we were hailed by them and found that they had made a similar combination. When we had refreshed ourselves, we took a short cruise, and then awoke the morning watch. We could not muster enough by one, and I was chosen to supply his place. I joined Duval, an acquaintance of mine, and we set out on a secret expedition together. On the way we had an engagement with three dogs; the first I combatted and pricked his nose thro' the fence. The other two, Mr. D. chased and I cut off their retreat, and by that maneuver we conquered. As the city was very still, we pitched our tents in my lodgings and drank port wine and ate cake untill day light. On Tuesday morn, I awoke at my usual hour, and went to breakfast.

The City is still in arms, and the enemy are much in the same position. Should they come up, our company will join in the attack, which turns some cowards blue. As the militia are ordered off, I expect to patrole more frequently, and this is very necessary, for the blacks in some places refuse to work, and say they shall soon be free, and then the white people must look out. One negro woman went so far as to steal her mistress's keys, and refused to return them, saying she would soon pay her for old and new. This was in the city, and the negro was confined. Should we be attacked, there will be great danger of the blacks rising, and to prevent this, patroles are very necessary, to keep them in awe. One other preventative at present is, the want of a leader.

ADMIRAL COCKBURN ENJOYED HIMSELF IN WASHINGTON

MARGARET BAYARD SMITH returned to her Washington home on August 28, 1814, less than three days after the British had ended their destructive occupation. She saw the Capitol's smoking walls, and from her friends who had stayed behind heard the living details.

Mrs. Smith (1778–1844) was of the Bayard clan of Delaware, which has contributed five United States senators from that state. She came to Washington in 1800 with her husband, Samuel Harrison Smith (1772–1845), who, in that year, started the *National Intelligencer*. They remained in Washington the rest of their lives, with a house in the center of the city and a farm, Sidney, in the area where Catholic University now stands, making their home a social center which was often visited by many of the notables in Congress and the government.

A writer as well as an informed and attractive hostess, Mrs. Smith produced two novels, one, *A Winter in Washington*, containing anecdotes of Jefferson, a friend and hero, to both her and her husband. She wrote for *Godey's Lady's Book* and other magazines, but her fame justly rests on her day-by-day letters to members of her family, largely to her sister, the wife of Chief Justice Andrew Kirkpatrick of New Jersey.

Her husband gave up his newspaper, which continued to prosper long after him, in 1810, and for most of the next quarter-century was president of the Bank of Washington, before and after it became a branch of the Bank of the United States.

Sir George Cockburn (1772–1853), of whom Mrs. Smith paints a lively and informal portrait in this selection, was commander of the British fleet that landed the force which attacked Washington. He later carried Napoleon to St. Helena, where Cockburn remained as governor, 1815–16. He was knighted in 1815, was in Parliament several times, and became one of the Lords of the Admiralty.

General Ross, to whom Mrs. Smith refers, led the march on Wash-

The Capitol after burning by the British.

ington. It is stated that Cockburn persuaded Ross, after his destruction of an American flotilla up the Patuxent River, to continue on to Washington.

From The First Forty Years of Washington Society Portrayed by the Family Letters of Mrs. Samuel Harrison Smith (Margaret Bayard). *From the Collection of her Grandson, J. Henley Smith. Edited by Gaillard Hunt.*

TO MRS. KIRKPATRICK

Washington, August 30. (1814)

The poor capitol! Nothing but its blacken'd walls remained! 4 or 5 houses in the neighbourhood were likewise in ruins. Some men had got within these houses and fired on the English as they were quietly marching into the city, they killed 4 men and genl. Rosse's horse. I imagine Genl. R. thought that his life was particularly aim'd at, for while his troops remained in the city he never

The White House after burning by the British.

made his appearance, altho' Cockburn and the other officers often
rode through the avenue. It was on account of this outrage that
these houses were burnt. We afterwards look'd at the other public
buildings, but none were so thoroughly destroy'd as the House of
Representatives and the President's House. Those beautiful pillars
in that Representatives Hall were crack'd and broken, the roof,
that noble dome, painted and carved with such beauty and skill, lay
in ashes in the cellars beneath the smoldering ruins, were yet smoking. In the P. H.[1] not an inch, but its crack'd and blacken'd walls
remain'd. . . .

Aftcr this melancholy survey, Mr. Smith went to see the
President,[2] who was at Mr. Cutts' (his brother in law) where we
found Mrs. Madison and her sister Mrs. Cutts. Mrs. M. seem'd
much depress'd, she could scarcely speak without tears. She told
me she had remained in the city till a few hours before the English
enter'd. She was so confident of Victory that she was calmly listening
to the roar of cannon, and watching the rockets in the air, when she
perceived our troops rushing into the city, with the haste and dismay
of a routed force. The friends with her then hurried her away, (her
carriage being previously ready) and she with many other families,

1 President's House or White House.
2 President James Madison.

among whom was Mrs. Thornton and Mrs. Cutting with her, re-treated with the flying army. In George town they perceived some men before them carrying off the picture of Genl. Washington (the large one by Stewart) which with the plate, was all that was saved out of the President's house. Mrs. M. lost all her own property. The wine, of which there was a great quantity, was consumed by our own soldiers. Mrs. M. slept that night in the encampment, a guard being placed round her tent, the next day she cross'd into Virginia where she remained until Sunday, when she return'd to meet her husband. Men, soldiers, expresses were round the house, the Presi-dent was in a room with his cabinet, from whence he issued his orders. The English frigates were laying before Alexandria and as it was supposed only waiting for a wind to come up to the city. The belief was that about 700 or more sailors were to be let loose in the city for plunder, dreadful idea. A universal despondency seem'd to pervade the people,—we every where met them in scatter'd groups, relating or listening to their fears.

We drank tea at Mrs. Thornton's,[3] who described to us the manner in which they conflagrated the President's H. and other buildings,—50 men, sailors and marines, were marched by an officer, silently thro' the avenue, each carrying a long pole to which was fixed a ball about the circumference of a large plate,—when arrived at the building, each man was station'd at a window, with his pole and machine of wild-fire against it, at the word of command, at the same instant the windows were broken and this wild-fire thrown in, so that an instantaneous conflagration took place and the whole building was wrapt in flames and smoke. The spectators stood in awful silence, the city was light and the heavens redden'd with the blaze!

The day before Cockburn paid this house a visit and forced a young gentleman of our acquaintance to go with him,—on entering the dining room they found the table spread for dinner, left pre-cipitally by Mrs. M,—he insisted on young Weightman's sitting down and drinking Jemmy's health, which was the only epithet he used whenever he spoke of the President. After looking round, he told Mr. W. to take something to remember this day. Mr. W. wished for some valuable article. No, no said he, *that* I must give to the flames, but here, handing him some ornaments off the mantle-piece, these

---

[3] Wife of Dr. William Thornton, original designer of the Capitol and super-intendent of the Patent Office, 1802–27, who persuaded the British not to burn it.

will answer as a memento. I must take something too, and looking round, he seized an old hat a *chapeau de bras* of the President's, and a cushion of Mrs. M.'s chair, declaring these should be his trophies, adding pleasantries too vulgar for me to repeat. When he went to burn Mr. Gale's office,[4] whom he called his "dear Josey"; Mrs. Brush, Mrs. Stelle and a few citizens remonstrated with him, assuring him that it would occasion the loss of all the buildings in the row. "Well," said he, "good people I do not wish to injure you, but I am really afraid my friend Josey will be affronted with me, if after burning Jemmy's palace,[5] I do not pay him the same compliment,—so my lads, take your axes, pull down the house, and burn the papers in the street." This was accordingly done. He told Mrs. Brush and several others, that no houses should be injur'd but such as were shut and deserted. Mr. Cutting and Mrs. B. saved ours, by opening the windows.

Cockburn often rode down the avenue, on an old white mare with a long main and tail and followed by its fold to the dismay of the spectators. He, and all his officers and soldiers were perfectly polite to the citizens. He bade them complain of any soldier that committed the least disorder and had several severly punished, for very slight offenses. All provisions were paid for. He stop'd at a door, at which a young lady was standing and enter'd into familiar conversation. "Now did you expect to see me such a clever fellow," said he, "were you not prepared to see a savage, a ferocious creature, such as Josey represented me? But you see I am quite harmless, don't be afraid, I will take better care of you than Jemmy did!" Such was his manner,—that of a common sailor, not of a dignified commander. He however deserves praise and commendation for his good conduct and the discipline of his sailors and Marines, for these were the destroying agents. The land troops and officers were scarcely seen while in the city, but kept close qrs at the navy yard.

TO MRS. KIRKPATRICK

Sidney Sept. 11. (1814)

The battle was very near to us. In the next farm, there was skirmishing, and 10 dead bodies were found (of the enemy) some

[4] Joseph Gales, who bought the *National Intelligencer* from Smith in 1810.
[5] The White House.

only 4 or 5 days ago. I am persuaded the enemy lost many more than was at first supposed, as bodies are daily found, unburied, under bushes, in gulleys. Alas poor wretches, how many anxious hearts in England may be looking for your return! The wounded and prisoners who remain, all express themselves delighted with this country, many who have been in France and Spain, say they never saw so beautiful or so rich a country and wonder how so happy a people could go to war.

WASHINGTON BURNING—A BEAUTIFUL SPECTACLE

THE ANGLE of vision is responsible for contentions. The artistic aspect of the burning of Washington evoked the enthusiastic admiration of a young officer with the British troops. The spectacle was sublime, he repeated.

George Robert Gleig (1796–1888) was a lieutenant as he entered the Penninsula Campaigns of 1813–14 under Wellington; he earned an honorable fighting record there and, in 1814, in the battles for Washington, Baltimore and New Orleans. He was wounded six times, once at Bladensburg, that unepic prelude to the taking of Washington. Later, when he was chaplain at Chelsea Hospital (London), home for incapacitated English soldiers, "the flag, in capturing which he was wounded at Bladensburg, was always suspended from his pulpit in the hospital chapel," says the English Dictionary of National Biography.

Gleig went on to become inspector-general of military schools and —for thirty-one years—chaplain-general of The Forces (the army). He entered the Church of England in 1820 and in that same year wrote his account, quoted here, of the British campaigns in America; he had kept a daily journal during army life. His subsequent voluminous writings in history, biography and theology, with occasional fiction, brought him wide attention in his day.

From A Narrative of the Campaigns of the
British Army, at Washington, Baltimore &
New Orleans, under Generals Ross, Paken-
ham, & Lambert, in the Years 1814 and
1815; with some Account of the Countries
Visited. *By an Officer who Served in the
Expedition.*

While the third brigade[1] was thus employed, the rest of the
army, having recalled its stragglers, and removed the wounded into
Bladensburg, began its march towards Washington. Though the
battle was ended by four o'clock, the sun had set before the different
regiments were in a condition to move, consequently this short
journey was performed in the dark. The work of destruction had
also begun in the city, before they quitted their ground; and the
blazing of houses, ships, and stores, the report of exploding magazines, and the crash of falling roofs, informed them, as they proceeded, of what was going forward. You can conceive nothing finer
than the sight which met them as they drew near to the town. The
sky was brilliantly illumined by the different conflagrations; and a
dark red light was thrown upon the road, sufficient to permit each
man to view distinctly his comrade's face. Except the burning of
St. Sebastian's,[2] I do not recollect to have witnessed, at any period
of my life, a scene more striking or more sublime.

Having advanced as far as the plain, where the reserve had
previously paused, the first and second brigades halted; and, forming
into close column, passed the night in bivouack. At first, this was
agreeable enough, because the air was mild, and weariness made up
for what was wanting in comfort. But towards morning, a violent
storm of rain, accompanied with thunder and lightning, came on,
which disturbed the rest of all those who were exposed to it. Yet,
in spite of the disagreeableness of getting wet, I cannot say that I
felt disposed to grumble at the interruption, for it appeared that what
I had before considered as superlatively sublime, still wanted this
to render it complete. The flashes of lightning seemed to vie in

[1] The third brigade entered Washington ahead of the rest.
[2] Fortress and town in Spain, stormed by Wellington, 1813.

This print, published in London in 1814, dramatically portrays the burning of Washington.

brilliancy, with the flames which burst from the roofs of burning houses, while the thunder drowned the noise of crumbling walls, and was only interrupted by the occasional roar of cannon, and of large depots of gunpowder, as they one by one exploded.

I need scarcely observe, that the consternation of the inhabitants was complete, and that to them this was a night of terror. So confident had they been of the success of their troops, that few of them had dreamt of quitting their houses, or abandoning the city; nor was it till the fugitives from the battle began to rush in, filling every place as they came with dismay, that the President himself thought of providing for his safety. That gentleman, as I was credibly informed, had gone forth in the morning with the army, and had continued among his troops till the British forces began to make their appearance. Whether the sight of his enemies cooled his courage or not, I cannot say, but, according to my informer, no sooner was the glittering of our arms discernible, than he began to discover that his presence was more wanted in the senate than with the army; and having ridden through the ranks, and exhorted every man to do his duty, he hurried back to his own house, that he might prepare a feast for the entertainment of his officers, when they should return victorious. For the truth of these details, I will not be answerable; but this much I know, that the feast was actually prepared, though, instead of being devoured by American officers, it went to satisfy the less delicate appetites of a party of English soldiers. When the detachment, sent out to destroy Mr. Madison's house, entered his dining parlour, they found a dinner-table spread, and covers laid for forty guests. Several kinds of wine, in handsome cut-glass decanters, were cooling on the side-board; plate holders stood by the fire-place, filled with dishes and plates; knives, forks, and spoons, were arranged for immediate use; in short, every thing was ready for the entertainment of a ceremonious party. Such were the arrangements in the dining-room, whilst in the kitchen were others answerable to them in every respect. Spits, loaded with joints of various sorts, turned before the fire; pots, sauce-pans, and other culinary utensils, stood upon the grate; and all the other requisites for an elegant and substantial repast, were exactly in a state which indicated that they had been lately and precipitately abandoned.

You will readily imagine, that these preparations were beheld, by a party of hungry soldiers, with no indifferent eye. An elegant dinner, even though considerably over-dressed, was a luxury to which few of them, at least for some time back, had been accustomed; and which, after the dangers and fatigues of the day, appeared peculiarly inviting. They sat down to it, therefore, not indeed in the most orderly manner, but with countenances which would not have disgraced a party of aldermen at a civic feast; and having satisfied their appetites with fewer complaints than would have probably escaped their rival *gourmands*, and partaken pretty freely of the wines, they finished by setting fire to the house which had so liberally entertained them."

A GREAT EXPONENT OF PERSONAL JOURNALISM

AMERICAN JOURNALISM has never replaced Hesikiah Niles, an editor with intense convictions which he wholeheartedly conveyed to his readers. He edited *Niles' Weekly Register*, Baltimore, from 1811 to

1836, tincturing both editorial and news columns with his own indefatigable news coverage and articulate patriotism. The latter was not without occasion, anti-war incidents being in evidence, particularly in New England. The files of his paper have long been historians' source material.

A contemporary described Niles as "a short stout-built man, stooping as he walked, speaking in a high key, addicted to snuff, and with a keen grey eye that lighted up a plain face with shrewd expression."

The first paragraph below is from the issue of the *Register* after the British repulse from Baltimore. The manpower problem harassed Niles throughout the war. The next two extracts exhibit the editor's exultation over the victory at New Orleans, and include one of the early quotations from our national anthem, which was born during the Baltimore (Fort McHenry) battle.

Niles' *Register* was characterized with occasional depictions of a hand, with pointing finger to a paragraph to be carefully read; and, for example, a triumphant eagle over verification of the outcome at New Orleans.

From Niles' Weekly Register, *Baltimore,*
Saturday, September 24, 1814.

Being disturbed by the enemy, and having every person in the office, a small boy excepted, under arms, last Saturday passed without a publication of the WEEKLY REGISTER. We shall bring up the now *two* wanting numbers as fast as we can, without regard to particular days of publication, until we get into regularity of time, with our work. The pressure of important matter is a particular inducement to this mode of proceeding at this time; and the index for the 6th volume will be a little delayed for the purpose of speedily laying many documents and facts before our readers.

As the "events of the war" thicken, the utility of such a record as this becomes the more manifest. By copious details and methodical arrangement we shall exert ourselves to meet the expectation of our patrons and friends.

The present number contains an account of four glorious events —the defeat of the British at fort *Erie,* at *Plattsburg,* and *Baltimore,* and the capture of their *whole fleet* on *Champlain.* "*Te Deum laudamus!*"

NILES' WEEKLY REGISTER.

No. 25 of Vol. VII.]   BALTIMORE, SATURDAY, FEBRUARY 18, 1815.   [WHOLE NO. 181.

Hæc olim meminisse juvabit.—VIRGIL.

Printed and published by H. NILES, South-st. next door to the Merchants' Coffee House, at $5 per ann.

Glorious News!

Orleans saved and peace concluded.

"The star spangled banner in triumph shall wave
"O'er the land of the free and the home of the brave."

The matters detailed and recorded in the present number of the REGISTER, are of incalculable importance. The enemy has retired in disgrace from New Orleans, and peace was signed at *Ghent* on the 24th December, on honorable terms: At least, so we believe from the *dolefuls* of the British ministerialists. For particulars, see the several heads.

In our next paper, as we hope by that time to be a little more composed under those joyful tidings, we shall endeavor to arrange a great mass of interesting matter that lies over for insertion.

Who would not be an American? Long live the republic! All hail! last asylum of oppressed humanity! Peace is signed in the arms of victory!

☞The present number was held back on the hope of obtaining a copy of the TREATY. See page 397.

New Orleans preserved.

Copy of a letter from major-general Jackson to the secretary of war, dated

Head-quarters, 7th military district,
Camp 4 miles below New-Orleans, 19th Jan. 1815.

Last night at 12 o'clock, the enemy precipitately decamped and returned to their boats, leaving behind him, under medical attendance, eighty of his wounded including two officers, 14 pieces of his heavy artillery, and a quantity of shot, having destroyed much of his powder. Such was the situation of the ground which he abandoned, and of that through which he retired, protected by canals, redoubts, entrenchments and swamps on his right, and the river on his left, that I could not without encountering a risk, which true policy did not seem to require, or to authorize, attempt to annoy him much on his retreat. We took only eight prisoners. Whether it is the purpose of the enemy to abandon the expedition altogether, or renew his efforts at some other point, I do not pretend to determine with positiveness. In my own mind, however, there is but little doubt that his last exertions have been made in this quarter, at any rate for the present season, and by the *next* I hope we shall be fully prepared for him. In this belief I am strengthened not only by the prodigious loss he has sustained at the position he had just quitted, but by the failure of his fleet to pass fort St. Philip.

His loss on this ground, since the debarkation of his troops, as stated by the last prisoners and deserters, and as confirmed by many additional circumstances, must have exceeded four thousand; and was greater in the action of the 8th than was estimated, from the most correct data then in his possession, by the inspector-general, whose report has been forwarded to you. We succeeded, on the 8th, in getting from the enemy about 1000 stand of arms of various descriptions.

Since the action of the 8th, the enemy have been allowed very little respite—my artillery from both sides of the river being constantly employed, till the night, and indeed until the *hour* of their retreat, in annoying them. No doubt they thought it quite time to quit a position in which so little rest could be found.

I am advised by major Overton, who commands at fort St. Philip, in a letter of the 18th, that the enemy having bombarded his fort for 8 or 9 days from 13 inch mortars without effect, had, on the morning of that day, retired. I have little doubt that he would have been able to have sunk their vessels had they attempted to run by.

Giving the proper weight to all these considerations, I believe you will not think me too sanguine in the belief that *Louisiana* is now clear of its enemy. I hope, however, I need not assure you, that wherever I command, such a belief shall never occasion any relaxation in the measures for resistance. I am but too sensible that the moment when the enemy is opposing us, is not the most proper to provide for them.

I have the honor to be, &c.

ANDREW JACKSON,
Maj. gen. com'g.

P. S. On the 18th our prisoners on shore were delivered us, an exchange having been previously agreed to. Those who are on board the fleet will be delivered at Petit Coquille—after which I shall still have in my hands an excess of several hundred.

20th—Mr. Shields,* purser in the navy, has to-day taken 54 prisoners; among them are four officers.

A. J.

*I have the honor to claim the gallant *Shields* as one of my most respected friends. I have letters from him of the 16th and 17th ult. He says, "the day after the gun-boats were taken I was sent down, under a flag of truce to ascertain the fate of our officers and men, with power to negociate an exchange, especially for the wounded. But the enemy would make no terms—they treated the flag with contempt, and myself and the surgeon, who was with me, as prisoners, until the 14th inst. He has now lowered his tone, and begs the exchange that we offered. Defeat has humbled the arrogance of the enemy, WHO HAD PROMISED HIS SOLDIERS FOR TWENTY-EIGHT HOURS' PILLAGE AND RAPINE OF THE CITY OF NEW-ORLEANS!"

"Our beloved Jackson deserves immortality. He was always in the hottest and thickest of the fight, and although his health is much impaired he still sticks to his post. We pray the Almighty to spare him.

"Every movement of the enemy indicates a retreat. I am just starting on a secret business to avenge myself. If I succeed, the world will be creditable to me—if I fail, the world, at least, shall say "he suffered a man."

We have not yet the particulars of Mr. *Shields'* successful enterprise, but, I flatter myself when they come to hand, they will redound no little to the honor of my generous high-minded friend, and perhaps add a ray of glory to the blaze that encircles the American navy. Mr. S. was a volunteer.

He adds that our five gun-boats had a complement of 200 men—they were attacked by forty-five boats carrying 1000 men. The fight against such fearful odds lasted one hour and fifty minutes—we had only five killed and thirty wounded, the enemy acknowledge a loss of 400, but Mr. *Shields* adds "we may with perfect safety double that number."

[Ed. Reg.

VOL. VII   Z

From Niles' Weekly Register, *Baltimore,*
Saturday, February 11, 1815.

GLORIOUS FROM NEW-ORLEANS.

The leading facts contained in the following letters, independent of the high character that some of them bear as being *official*, are supported by such a host of testimony that the most sceptical cannot refuse entire belief to them, however extraordinary some of the parts may appear. Glory be to GOD, that the barbarians have been defeated, and that at *Orleans* the intended plunderers have found their grave!—Glory to *Jackson, Carroll* and *Coffee*, and the hardy and gallant *Tennesseeans, Kentuckians* and *Louisianians* who "seized opportunity by the forelock" to "*demonstrate*" what freemen can do in defence of their altars and firesides. Glory to the *militia*, that the "soldiers of *Wellington*," the boastful conquerors of the legions of *France*, have shrunk from the *liberty-directed* bullets of the high-souled sons of the west! Sons of freedom—saviors of *Orleans*—benefactors of your country and avengers of its wrongs, all hail! Hail glorious people—worthy, thrice worthy, to enjoy the blessings which heaven in bounteous profusion has heaped on your country! Never may its luxuriant soil be trodden unrevenged by insolent foreigners in arms!

The mail which is expected *this evening* will probably give the *finish* of the attack.

From Niles' Weekly Register, *Baltimore,*
Saturday, February 18, 1815.

GLORIOUS NEWS!

Orleans saved and peace concluded.

"The star spangled banner in triumph shall wave
O'er the land of the free and the home of the brave."

The matters detailed and recorded in the present number of the REGISTER, are of incalculable importance. The enemy has retired in disgrace from New Orleans, and peace was signed at *Ghent* on the 24th December, on honorable terms: At least, so we believe from the *dolefuls* of the British ministerialists. For particulars, see the several heads.

In our next paper, as we hope by that time to be a little more composed under those joyful tidings, we shall endeavor to arrange a great mass of interesting matter that lies over for insertion.

Who would not be an American? Long live the republic! All hail! last asylum of oppressed humanity! Peace is signed in the arms of victory!

The present number was held back on the hope of obtaining a copy of the TREATY.

THE CIVIL WAR

FOR SOME, THE RACIAL QUESTION WAS SIMPLE

IN WASHINGTON'S COLUMBIAN COLLEGE—later to be known as George Washington University—the racial question was a very clear-cut one indeed in the year 1847. It admitted of no debate, and, in whatever of its manifestations, offered no complexity to those confronted with it.

This is a letter from eighteen-year-old Thomas Pollard, senior at Columbian College, to his father, Colonel John Pollard, in eastern Virginia. Thomas Pollard died in 1852 after a brief teaching career, the last two years of it, 1848–50, at his alma mater.

The letter telling of the "great excitement" at the college, with the consequent prompt action by the faculty and others, is contained in the autobiography of one of Thomas Pollard's brothers, Henry Robinson Pollard, prominent Virginian lawyer. The latter was commonwealth attorney for King and Queen county for a dozen years, member of the Virginia House of Delegates, 1881–90, and for over two decades city attorney for Richmond.

From Memoirs and Sketches of The Life of Henry Robinson Pollard: An Autobiography.

There has been a great excitement in College for a few days, arising from an occurrence which you would little expect. As you are aware, there is a considerable number of students here from the North, and one of these gentlemen—Arnold by name (nearly related to old Benedict in the vileness of his purpose)—conceived a grand scheme for the relief of humanity. One of Capt. Haynes' servants having applied to him for his assistance to obtain his freedom, he seized with great delight upon the opportunity, and used his best exertions to acquire the end. He solicited several of his brother Yankees in the behalf of his wronged fellowman, and obtained $5 from one, which was afterwards withdrawn for fear of detection. But Arnold, still anxious to be the benefactor of the oppressed, persisted in his course and, either individually or by subscription raised for the servant $14.

But in a few days after he had given the money to the servant the whole affair was divulged. It, of course, soon reached the ears of the faculty and they immediately expelled him. The Southern students were very much excited and sent in to the faculty a protestation against further recitations until the matter was settled. The affair was found out on Monday morning, about 8 o'clock, and before 11 Arnold was ordered to leave. He went off amidst shouts of contempt. The individual who gave the $5 also left, and very judiciously too. President Bacon informed me that they intended to examine the case thoroughly and would not allow a man of that description to remain in College one day.

It seems that the law of the District[1] is such that, after having been here a certain time, a servant may sue for his freedom, and it was for this purpose that the money was needed. One of the negroes which the Capt. had charge of as guardian of Geo. Hoomes, having heard of the law, by some means, I know not what, raised the sum of $25, which he paid to the lawyer, and his suit was, in fact, instituted. He, of course, related his success to one of the Capt.'s and he tried the same project, but alas! both were discovered and are now on their way to the cotton fields of the South, and their abettors are fast travelling to the frozen North. I would not be at all surprised if others were implicated. They, however, will be dealt with promptly and rigidly. I am sorry that I have not time to give you a more intelligible description but you will doubtless learn from other sources with more accuracy.

Your affectionate son,
THO. POLLARD.

[1] District of Columbia.

RUNNING THE NORTHERN BLOCKADE—
DISASTER OR RICHES

RUNNING THE Northern blockade of Southern ports was an exciting and —when successful—highly profitable enterprise during the Civil War. The economically starved South wanted to sell its cotton, which brought high prices in England, and in return eagerly welcomed blankets, shoes, hardware, munitions—just about anything; soap and women's corsets are mentioned as bringing legendary returns.

The author of this description was Augustus Charles Hobart-Hampden (1822–86), a son of the sixth earl of Buckinghamshire, who had resigned a captaincy in the British navy to take a whirl, with some other former English naval officers, at blockade-running. This was in 1862–63. Later—he was never caught by the blockaders—he entered the Turkish service, was as usual daring and unorthodox, and rose to be admiral with the title of pasha, and then a marshal of the Turkish empire. He was restored to the British naval rolls as vice-admiral in 1885. Hobart-Hampden writes under the name of Hobart Pasha and has a "Captain Roberts"—himself—tell the blockade-breaking adventures.

This blockade-running constitutes a chapter in the Civil War that has not gathered the attention it warrants. Such history embraces the fabulous boom days in Nassau, headquarters for most of the runners, and the contrasting delineation of a port like Wilmington, North Carolina, at this end of the run; the solicitous cooperation between the runners and Southern soldiers and citizens, the dodges employed, and the tribulations and the triumphs—the North claimed seizure or destruction of about 1,500 ships—racked up by the blockaders.

From Sketches From My Life. *By the late Admiral Hobart Pasha.*

The vessel I had charge of—which I had brought out from England, was one of the finest double-screw steamers that had ever been built by D——n; of 400 tons burden, 250 horse-power, 180 feet long, and 22 feet beam—and was, so far as sea-going qualities, speed, etc, went, as handy a little craft as ever floated. Our crew consisted of a captain, three officers, three engineers, and twenty-eight men, including firemen, that is, ten seamen and eighteen firemen. They were all Englishmen, and as they received very high wages, we managed to have picked men. In fact, the men-of-war on the West India station found it a difficult matter to prevent their crews from deserting, so great was the temptation offered by the blockade-runners.

I will begin by explaining how we prepared the vessel for the work. This was done by reducing her spars to a light pair of lower masts, without any yards across them; the only break in their sharp outline being a small crow's nest on the foremast, to be used as a look-out place. The hull, which showed about eight feet above water, was painted a dull grey colour to render her as nearly as possible invisible in the night. The boats were lowered square with the gunnels. Coal was taken on board of a smokeless nature (anthracite). The funnel, being what is called "telescope," lowered close down to the deck. In order that no noise might be made, steam was blown off under water. In fact, every ruse was resorted to, to enable the vessel to evade the vigilance of the American cruisers, who were scattered about in great numbers all the way between Bermuda and Wilmington—the port at the time I write of most frequented by blockade-runners. While speaking of the precautions used I may mention that among the fowls taken on board as provisions, no cocks were allowed, for fear of their proclaiming the whereabouts of the blockade-runner. This may seem ridiculous, but it was very necessary.

The distance from Bermuda to Wilmington (the port we were bound to) is 720 miles. We started in the evening. For the first twenty-four hours we saw nothing to alarm us, but at daylight the second day there was a large American cruiser not half a mile from us, right ahead, who, before we could turn around, steamed straight at us, and commenced firing rapidly, but very much at random, the shot and shell all passing over or wide of us.

Fortunately, according to orders to have full steam on at daybreak, we were quite prepared for a run; and still more fortunately a heavy squall of wind and rain that came on helped us vastly, as we were dead to windward of the enemy; and having no top-weights we soon dropped him astern. He most foolishly kept yawing, to fire his bow-chasers, losing ground every time he did so. By eight o'clock we were out of range—unhit; and by noon out of sight of anything but smoke.

Luckily, the chase had not taken us much off our course, as the consumption of coal during a run of this sort, with boilers all but bursting from high pressure of steam, was a most serious consideration—there being no coal in the Confederate ports, where wood was only used, which would not suit our furnaces.

We were now evidently in very dangerous waters, steamers being reported from our mast-head every hour, and we had to keep moving about in all directions to avoid them; sometimes stopping to let one pass ahead of us, at another time turning completely round, and running back on our course. . . .

. . . During the day we got good observations with which our sounding agreed; and at sunset our position was sixty miles due east of the entrance to Wilmington river, off which place were cruising a strong squadron of blockading ships. The American blockading squadron, which had undertaken the almost impossible task of stopping all traffic along 3,000 miles of coast, consisted of nearly a hundred vessels of different sorts and sizes—*bona fide* men-of-war, captured blockade-runners, unemployed steam-packets, with many other vessels pressed into government service. Speed and sufficient strength to carry a long gun were the only requisites, the Confederate men-of-war being few and far between. These vessels were generally well commanded and officered, but badly manned. The inshore squadron off Wilmington consisted of about thirty vessels, and lay in the form of a crescent facing the entrance to Cape Clear river, the centre being just out of range of the heavy guns mounted on Fort Fisher, the horns, as it were, gradually approaching the shore on each side; the whole line or curve covered about ten miles.

I have mentioned that our position was well defined by observations and soundings, so we determined to run straight through the blockaders, and to take our chance. When it was quite dark we started steaming at full speed. It was extremely thick on the horizon, but clear overhead, with just enough wind and sea to prevent the little noise the engines and screws made being heard. Every light was out—even the men's pipes; the masts were lowered on to the deck; and if ever a vessel was invisible the D——n was that night.

As we got near, we could make out the outline of a vessel lying at anchor, head to wind, and conjectured that this must be the senior officer's vessel, which we were told generally lay about two miles and a half from the river's mouth, and which was obliged to show some sort of light to the cruisers that were constantly under weigh right and left of her.

Feeling pretty confident now of our position, we went on again at full speed, and made out clearly the line of blockaders lying to the right and left of the ship which showed the light; all excepting her being apparently under weigh. Seeing an opening between the vessel at anchor and the one on her left, we made a dash, and, thanks to our disguise and great speed, got through without being seen, and made the most of our way towards the land. As a strong current runs close inshore which is constantly changing its course, and there were no lights or landmarks to guide us, it was a matter of great difficulty to find the very narrow entrance to the river.

We were now nearly out of danger from cruisers, who seldom ventured very close inshore in the vicinity of the batteries; and our pilot, who had been thoroughout the voyage in bodily fear of an American prison, began to wake up, and, after looking well round, told us that he could make out, over the long line of surf, a heap of sand called "the mound," which was a mark for going into the river.

This good news emboldened us to show a small light from the inshore side of the vessel; it was promptly answered by two lights being placed a short distance apart on the beach, in such a position that, when the two were brought into line, or, as the sailors call it, into one, the vessel would be in the channel which led into the river. This being done without interruption from the cruisers, we steamed in and anchored safely under the batteries of Fort Fisher....

. . . The vessel's[1] cargo consisted of blankets, shoes, Manchester goods of all sorts, and some mysterious cases marked "hardware," about which no one asked any questions, but which the military authorities took possession of. This cargo was landed, and preparations made for taking on board THE paying article in this trade, namely, cotton.

I never bought it in any quantity, but I know that the price in the Southern States averaged from twopence to threepence a pound,[2] the price in Liverpool at that time being about a half-a-crown....

We left the quay at Wilmington cheered by the hurrahs of our brother blockade-runners, who were taking in and discharging their cargoes, and steamed a short distance down the river, when we were boarded to be *searched* and *smoked*. This latter extraordinary proceeding, called for perhaps by the existing state of affairs, took me altogether aback. That a smoking apparatus should be applied to a

[1] Hobart's blockade-runner.
[2] Threepence equaled about six cents and half a crown about 60 cents.

cargo of cotton seemed almost astounding. But so it was ordered, the object being to search for runaways, and, strange to say, its efficacy was apparent, when, after an hour or more's application of the process (which was by no means a gentle one), an unfortunate wretch, crushed almost to death by the closeness of his hiding-place, poked with a long stick till his ribs must have been like touchwood, and smoked the colour of a backwood Indian, was dragged by the heels into the daylight, ignominiously put into irons, and hurled into the guard-boat. This discovery nearly caused the detention of the vessel on suspicion of our being the accomplices of the runaway; but after some deliberation, we were allowed to go on.

Having steamed down the river a distance of about twenty miles, we anchored at two o'clock in the afternoon near its mouth. We were hidden by Fort Fisher from the blockading squadron lying off the bar, there to remain till some time after nightfall. . . .

Very faint lights, which could not be seen far at sea, were set on the beach in the same position as I have before described, having been thus placed for a vessel coming in; and bringing these astern in an exact line, that is the two into one, we knew that we were in the passage for going over the bar. The order was then given, "Full speed ahead," and we shot at a great speed out to sea.

Our troubles began almost immediately; for the cruisers had placed a rowing barge, which could not be seen by the forts, close to the entrance, to signalise the direction which any vessel that came out might take. This was done by rockets being thrown up by a designed plan from the barge. We had hardly cleared the bar when we saw this boat very near our bows, nicely placed to be run clean over, and as we were going about fourteen knots, her chance of escape would have been small had we been inclined to finish her. Changing the helm, which I did myself, a couple of spokes just took us clear. We passed so close that I could have dropped a biscuit into the boat with ease. I heard the crash of broken oars against our sides; not a word was spoken. . . .

. . . We steered a mile or two near the coast, always edging a little to the eastward, and then shaped our course straight out to sea. Several guns were fired in the pitch-darkness very near us. (I am not quite sure whether some of the blockaders did not occasionally pepper each other.) After an hour's fast steaming, we felt moderately safe, and by the morning had a good offing.

TILLIE PIERCE AT GETTYSBURG

TILLIE PIERCE ALLEMAN (1848–1914) was 15 years old when the tremendous experience of her life, the Battle of Gettysburg, upturned familiar scenes. Edges of that mighty conflict she passed through, fleeing artillery fire and helping care for wounded soldiers, while, outside the house, Confederate sharpshooters took fatal toll.

Gettysburg was her native town and all that normally beautiful and peaceful vicinage—suddenly to achieve fame by name of ridge and hill and stream and army regiment and division—was known and loved by her and her companions. It was from the Young Ladies Seminary that she was dismissed when the Confederates were seen entering the town; soon to be followed by the Union forces, and then the great three-day battle between the two.

Eight years later she was married in "the old College Church on Chambersburg Street" to Attorney Horace Alleman of Selinsgrove, Pa., who had served in the Union army. They lived in Selinsgrove where, according to one who remembers her, "she was active in church, civic and community affairs" and was known "as a woman of strong personality and cheerful disposition" who "enjoyed the company of her many friends."

From At Gettysburg, or What a Girl Saw and Heard of The Battle: A True Narrative. *By Mrs. Tillie (Pierce) Alleman.*

About three weeks before the battle,[1] rumors were again rife of the coming of the rebel horde into our own fair and prosperous State.

This caused the greatest alarm; and our hearts often throbbed with fear and trembling. To many of us, such a visit meant destruction of home, property and perhaps life.

We had often heard of their taking horses and cattle, carrying off property and destroying buildings.

[1] The battle of Gettysburg was fought July 1–3, 1863.

A week had hardly elapsed when another alarm beset us.

"The Rebels are coming! The Rebels are coming!" was passed from lip to lip, and all was again consternation.

We were having our regular literary exercises on Friday afternoon, at our Seminary, when the cry reached our ears. Rushing to the door, and standing on the front portico we beheld in the direction of the Theological Seminary, a dark, dense mass, moving toward town. Our teacher, Mrs. Eyster, at once said:

"Children, run home as quickly as you can."

It did not require repeating. I am satisfied some of the girls did not reach their homes before the Rebels were in the streets.

As for myself, I had scarcely reached the front door, when, on looking up the street, I saw some of the men on horseback. I scrambled in, slammed shut the door, and hastening to the sitting room, peeped out between the shutters.

What a horrible sight! There they were, human beings! clad almost in rags, covered with dust, riding wildly, pell-mell down the hill toward our home! shouting, yelling most unearthly, cursing, brandishing their revolvers, and firing right and left.

Soon the town was filled with infantry, and then the searching and ransacking began in earnest.

They wanted horses, clothing, anything and almost everything they could conveniently carry away.

Nor were they particular about asking. Whatever suited them they took. They did, however, make a formal demand of the town authorities, for a large supply of flour, meat, groceries, shoes, hats, and (doubtless, not least in their estimations), ten barrels of whiskey; or, in lieu of all this, five thousand dollars.

But our merchants and bankers had too often heard of their coming, and had already shipped their wealth to places of safety. Thus it was, that a few days after, the citizens of York were compelled to make up our proportion of the Rebel requisition.

That evening when these raiders were leaving, they ran all the cars that were about, out to the railroad bridge east of the town, set the bridge and cars on fire and destroyed the track. We were informed that they had gone to York. . . .

A little before noon on Tuesday, June 30th, a great number of Union cavalry began to arrive in the town. They passed northwardly along Washington Street, turned toward the west on reaching

The Battle of Gettysburg, sketched by Thomas Nast.

Chambersburg Street, and passed out in the direction of the Theological Seminary.

It was to me a novel and grand sight. I had never seen so many soldiers at one time. They were Union soldiers and that was enough for me, for I then knew we had protection, and I felt they were our dearest friends. I afterwards learned that these men were Buford's cavalry, numbering about six thousand men.

A crowd of "us girls" were standing on the corner of Washington and High Streets as these soldiers passed by. Desiring to encourage them, who, as we were told, would before long be in battle, my sister started to sing the old war song "Our Union Forever." As some of us did not know the whole of the piece we kept repeating the chorus.

Thus we sought to cheer our brave men; and we felt amply repaid when we saw that our efforts were appreciated. Their countenances brightened and we received their thanks and cheers.

After the battle some of these soldiers told us that the singing was very good, but that they would have liked to have heard more than the chorus.

The movements of this day in addition to what we beheld a few days previous, told us plainly that some great military event was coming pretty close to us. . . .

After I had eaten what that day[2] I called dinner, our neighbor, Mrs. Schriver, called at the house and said she would leave the town and go to her father's (Jacob Weikert), who lived on the Taney-town road at the eastern slope of the Round Top.

She requested that I be permitted to accompany her, and as it was regarded a safer place for me than to remain in town, my parents readily consented that I should go.

[2] July 1.

About one o'clock we started on foot; the battle still going on. We proceeded out Baltimore Street and entered the Evergreen Cemetery. This was our easiest rout, as it would bring us to the Taneytown road a little further on.

As we were passing along the Cemetery hill, our men were already planting cannon.

They told us to hurry as fast as possible; that we were in great danger of being shot by the Rebels, whom they expected would shell toward us at any moment. We fairly ran to get out of this new danger.

As I looked toward the Seminary Ridge I could see and hear the confusion of the battle.

We continued on our way, and had gotten to a little one and a half story house, standing on the west side of the road, when, on account of the muddy condition of the road we were compelled to stop. This place on the following day became General Meade's headquarters.

At last we reached Mr. Weikert's and were gladly welcomed to their home.

It was not long after our arrival, until Union artillery came hurrying by.

After the artillery had passed, infantry began coming. I soon saw that these men were very thirsty and would go to the spring which is on the north side of the house.

I was not long in learning what I could do. Obtaining a bucket, I hastened to the spring, and there, with others, carried water to the moving column until the spring was empty. We then went to the pump standing on the south side of the house, and supplied water from it. Thus we continued giving water to our tired soldiers until night came on, when we sought rest indoors.

The first wounded soldier whom I met had his thumb tied up. This I thought was dreadful, and told him so.

"Oh," said he, "this is nothing; you'll see worse than this before long."

"Oh! I hope not," I innocently replied.

Now the wounded began to come in greater numbers. Some limping, some with their heads and arms in bandages, some crawling, others carried on stretchers or brought in ambulances. Suffering, cast down and dejected, it was a truly pitiable gathering. Before night the barn was filled with the shattered and dying heroes of this day's struggle.

That evening Beckie Weikert, the daughter at home, and I went out to the barn to see what was transpiring there. Nothing before in my experience had ever paralleled the sight we then and there beheld. There were the groaning and crying, the struggling and dying, crowded side by side, while attendants sought to aid and relieve them as best they could.

We were so overcome by the sad and awful spectacle that we hastened back to the house weeping bitterly.

As we entered the basement or cellar-kitchen of the house, we found many nurses making beef tea for the wounded. . . .

I remember that at this time a chaplain who was present in the kitchen stepped up to me while I was attending to some duty and said:

"Little girl, do all you can for the poor soldiers and the Lord will reward you."

I looked up in his face and laughed, but at once felt ashamed of my conduct and begged his pardon. After telling him what Beckie and I had seen, how the nurses derided us for crying and that I now laughed when I should not, being unable to help myself, he remarked:

"Well it is much better for you and the soldiers to be in a cheerful mood."

During the early part of the forenoon[3] my attention was called to numerous rough boxes which had been placed along the road just outside the garden fence. Ominous and dismal as was the sight presented, it nevertheless did not prevent some of the soldiers from passing jocular expressions.

During the whole of this afternoon Mrs. Weikert and her daughters were busy baking bread for the soldiers. As soon as one ovenful was baked it was replenished with new, and the freshly baked loaves at once cut up and distributed. How eagerly and gratefully the tired-out men received this food!

It was shortly before noon that I observed soldiers lying on the ground just back of the house, dead. They had fallen just where they had been standing when shot. I was told that they had been picked off by Rebel sharpshooters, who were up in Big Round Top.

[3] Of July 2.

That night, in the house, I made myself useful in doing whatever I could to assist the surgeons and nurses. Cooking and making beef tea seemed to be going on all the time. It was an animated and busy scene. Some were cutting bread and spreading it, while I was kept busy carrying the pieces to the soldiers.

One soldier, sitting near the doorway that led into a little room in the southeast corner of the basement, beckoned me to him. He was holding a lighted candle in his hand, and was watching over a wounded soldier who was lying upon the floor. He asked me if I would get him a piece of bread, saying he was very hungry. I said certainly, ran away and soon returned. I gave him the bread and he seemed very thankful. He then asked me if I would hold the light and stay with the wounded man until he came back. I said I would gladly do so, and that I wanted to do something for the poor soldiers if I only knew what.

I then took the candle and sat down beside the wounded man. I talked to him and asked if he was injured badly. He answered:

"Yes, pretty badly."

I then asked him if he suffered much, to which he replied:

"Yes, I do now, but I hope in the morning I will be better."

I told him if there was anything I could do for him I would be so glad to do it, if he would only tell me what. The poor man looked so earnestly into my face, saying:

"Will you promise me to come back in the morning to see me."

I replied: "Yes, indeed." And he seemed so satisfied, and faintly smiled.

The sun was high in the heavens when I awoke the next day. . . .

I hastened down to the little basement room, and as I entered, the soldier lay there—dead. His faithful attendant was still at his side.

I had kept my promise, but he was not there to greet me.

As I stood there gazing in sadness at the prostrate form, the attendant looked up to me and asked: "Do you know who this is?" I replied: "No sir." He said: "This is the body of General Weed; a New York man."

As concerning many other incidents of the late war, so with the death of this brave general, I find an erroneous judgment has been formed; some claiming that he was instantly killed on Little Round Top, during the fight of the second day.

AS SHERMAN'S MARCH TO THE SEA
PASSED BURGE PLANTATION

MRS. THOMAS BURGE (1817–91) vividly portrays Sherman's ruthless March To The Sea (1864) as it reached and passed her plantation near Covington, Georgia. The writer, who depicts in her diary the frightening coming of the bluecoats and the pillaging, and who mourns the uprooting of the ties that bound around one hundred slaves to her cotton-raising lands, was a Maine native (Dolly Sumner Lunt) and a relative of the slavery foe, Senator Charles Sumner of Massachusetts.

When a young woman, she had moved to the South, where her married sister was already settled, to teach school in Covington. There she met her husband. He died less than three years before the War Between the States, leaving his widow—with their little daughter "Sadai"—to manage the plantation.

From A Woman's Wartime Journal. An Account of the Passage over a Georgia Plantation of Sherman's Army on the March to the Sea, as recorded in the Diary of Dolly Sumner Lunt (Mrs. Thomas Burge). *With Introduction and Notes by Julian Street.*

July 22, 1864.

(The day of the Battle of Atlanta)

We have heard the loud booming of cannon all day. . . . Suddenly I saw the servants running to the palings, and I walked to the door, when I saw such a stampede as I never witnessed before. The road was full of carriages, wagons, men on horseback, all riding at full speed. Judge Floyd stopped, saying: "Mrs. Burge, the Yankees are coming. They have got my family, and here is all I have upon earth. Hide your mules and carriages and whatever valuables you have."

Sadai (Mrs. Burge's nine-year-old daughter) said:

"Oh, Mama, what shall we do?"

"Never mind, Sadai," I said. "They won't hurt you, and you must help me hide my things."

I went to the smoke-house, divided out the meat to the servants, and bid them hide it. Julia (a slave) took a jar of lard and buried it. In the meantime Sadai was taking down and picking up our clothes, which she was giving to the servants to hide in their cabins; silk dresses, challis, muslins, and merinos, linens, and hosiery, all found their way into the chests of the women and under their beds; china and silver were buried underground, and Sadai bid Mary (a slave) hide a bit of soap under some bricks, that mama might have a little left. Then she came to me with a part of a loaf of bread, asking if she had not better put it in her pocket, that we might have something to eat that night. And, verily, we had cause to fear that we might be homeless, for on every side we could see smoke arising from burning buildings and bridges.

Sunday, July 24, 1864.

No church. Our preacher's horse stolen by the Yankees. This raid is headed by Guerrard and is for the purpose of destroying our railroads. They cruelly shot a George Daniel and a Mr. Jones of Covington, destroyed a great deal of private property, and took many citizens prisoners.

July 29, 1864.

Sleepless nights. The report is that the Yankees have left Covington for Macon, headed by Stoneman, to release prisoners held there. They robbed every house on the road of its provisions, sometimes taking every piece of meat, blankets and wearing apparel, silver and arms of every description. They would take silk dresses and put them under their saddles, and many other things for which they had no use. Is this the way to make us love them and their Union? Let the poor people answer whom they have deprived of every mouthful of meat and of their livestock to make any! Our mills, too, they have burned, destroying an immense amount of property.

August 2, 1864.

Just as I got out of bed this morning Aunt Julia (a slave) called me to look down the road and see the soldiers. I peeped through the blinds, and there they were, sure enough, the Yankees—the blue coats!

I was not dressed. The servant women came running in. "Mistress, they are coming! They are coming! They are riding into the lot! There are two coming up the steps!"

I bade Rachel (a slave) fasten my room door and go to the front door and ask them what they wanted. They did not wait for that, but came in and asked why my door was fastened. She told them that the white folks were not up. They said they wanted breakfast, and that quick, too.

"Thug" (short for "Sugar," the nickname of a little girl, Minnie Minerva Glass, now Mrs. Joe Carcy Murphy of Charlotte, North Carolina, who had come to pass the night with Sadai) and Sadai, as well as myself, were greatly alarmed. As soon as I could get on my clothing I hastened to the kitchen to hurry up breakfast. Six of them were there talking with my women. They asked about our soldiers and, passing themselves off as Wheeler's[1] men, said:

"Have you seen any of our men go by?"

"Several of Wheeler's men passed last evening. Who are you?" said I.

"We are a portion of Wheeler's men," said one.

"You look like Yankees," said I.

"Yes," said one, stepping up to me; "we are Yankees. Did you ever see one before?"

"Not for a long time," I replied, "and none such as you." (These men, Mrs. Burge says further, were raiders, Illinois and Kentucky men of German origin. They left after breakfast, taking three of her best mules, but doing no further injury.)

November 8, 1864.

I have never felt that slavery was altogether right, for it is abused by men, and I have often heard Mr. Burge say that if he could see that it was sinful for him to own slaves, if he felt that it was wrong, he would take them where he could free them. He

[1] Confederate Maj. Gen. Joseph Wheeler.

would not sin for his right hand. The purest and holiest men have owned them, and I can see nothing in the scriptures which forbids it. I have never bought or sold slaves and I have tried to make life easy and pleasant to those that have been bequeathed me by the dead. I have never ceased to work. Many a Northern housekeeper has a much easier time than a Southern matron with her hundred negroes.

November 12, 1864

Warped and put in dresses for the loom. Oh, this blockade gives us work to do for all hands!

November 18, 1864.

Slept very little last night. Went out doors several times and could see large fires like burning buildings. Am I not in the hands of a merciful God who has promised to take care of the widow and orphan? . . .

. . . We have done nothing all day—that is, my people have not. I made a pair of pants for Jack (a slave). Sent Nute (a slave) up to Mrs. Perry's on an errand. On his way back, he said, two Yankees met him and begged him to go with them. They asked if we had livestock, and came up the road as far as Mrs. Laura Perry's. I sat for an hour expecting them, but they must have gone back. Oh, how I trust I am safe! Mr. Ward is very much alarmed.

November 19, 1864.

I walked to the gate. There they came filing up.

I hastened back to my frightened servants and told them that they had better hide, and then went back to the gate to claim protection and a guard. But like demons they rush in! My yards are full. To my smoke-house, my dairy, pantry, kitchen, and cellar, like famished wolves they come, breaking locks and whatever is in their way. The thousand pounds of meat in my smoke-house is gone in a twinkling, my flour, my meat, my lard, butter, eggs, pickles of various kinds—both in vinegar and brine—wine, jars, and jugs are all gone. My eighteen fat turkeys, my hens, chickens, and fowls, my young pigs, are shot down in my yard and hunted as if they were rebels themselves. Utterly powerless I ran out and appealed to the guard.

"I cannot help you, Madam; it is orders."

As I stood there, from my lot I saw driven, first, old Dutch, my dear old buggy horse, who has carried my beloved husband so many miles, and who would so quietly wait at the block for him to mount and dismount, and who at last drew him to his grave; then came old Mary, my brood mare, who for years had been too old and stiff for work, with her three-year-old colt, my two-year-old mule, and her last little baby colt. There they go! There go my mules, my sheep, and, worse than all, my boys (slaves)!

Alas! little did I think while trying to save my house from plunder and fire that they were forcing my boys from home at the point of the bayonet. One, Newton, jumped into bed in his cabin, and declared himself sick. Another crawled under the floor,—a lame boy he was,—but they pulled him out, placed him on a horse, and drove him off. Mid, poor Mid! The last I saw of him, a man had him going around the garden, looking, as I thought, for my sheep, as he was my shepherd. Jack came crying to me, the big tears coursing down his cheeks, saying they were making him go. I said:

"Stay in my room."

But a man followed in, cursing him and threatening to shoot him if he did not go; so poor Jack had to yield. James Arnold, in trying to escape from a back window, was captured and marched off. Henry, too, was taken; I know not how or when, but probably when he and Bob went after the mules. I had not believed they would force from their homes the poor, doomed negroes, but such has been the fact here, cursing them and saying that "Jeff Davis wanted to put them in his army, but that they should not fight for him, but for the Union." No! Indeed no! They are not friends to the slave. We have never made the poor, cowardly negro fight, and it is strange, passing strange, that the all-powerful Yankee nation with the whole world to back them, their ports open, their armies filled with soldiers from all nations, should at last take the poor negro to help them out against this little Confederacy, which was to have been brought back into the Union in sixty days' time!

My poor boys! My poor boys! What unknown trials are before you! How you have clung to your mistress and assisted her in
every way you knew.

Never have I corrected them; a word was sufficient. Never
have they known want of any kind. Their parents are with me,
and how sadly they lament the loss of their boys. Their cabins are
rifled of every valuable, the soldiers swearing that their Sunday
clothes were the white people's, and that they never had money to
get such things as they had. Poor Frank's chest was broken open,
his money and tobacco taken. He has always been a money-making
and a saving boy; not infrequently has his crop brought him five
hundred dollars and more. All of his clothes and Rachel's clothes,
which dear Lou gave her before her death and which she had
packed away, were stolen from her. Ovens, skillets, coffee-mills, of
which we had three, coffee-pots—not one have I left. Sifters all gone!

As night drew its sable curtains around us, the heavens from
every point were lit up with flames from burning buildings. Dinner-
less and supperless as we were, it was nothing in comparison with
the fear of being driven out homeless to the dreary woods. Nothing to eat! I could give my guard no supper, so he left us. I appealed to another, asking him if he had wife, mother, or sister, and
how he should feel were they in my situation. A colonel from
Vermont left me two men, but they were Dutch, and I could not
understand one word they said.

My Heavenly Father alone saved me from the destructive fire.
My carriage-house had in it eight bales of cotton, with my carriage,
buggy, and harness. On top of the cotton were some carded cotton
rolls, a hundred pounds or more. These were thrown out of the
blanket in which they were and a large twist of the rolls taken and
set on fire, and thrown into the boat of my carriage, which was
close up to the cotton bales. Thanks to my God, the cotton only
burned over, and then went out. Shall I ever forget the deliver-
ance? . . .

November 20, 1864.

About ten o'clock they had all passed save one, who came in
and wanted coffee made, which was done, and he, too, went on. A
few minutes elapsed, and two couriers riding rapidly passed back.

Then, presently more soldiers came by, and this ended the passing of Sherman's army by my place, leaving me poorer by thirty thousand dollars than I was yesterday morning. And a much stronger Rebel!

My boys have not come home. I fear they cannot get away from the soldiers. Two of my cows came up this morning, but were driven off again by the Yankees.

I feel so thankful that I have not been burned out that I have tried to spend the remainder of the day as the Sabbath ought to be spent. Ate dinner out of the oven in Julia's (the cook's) house, some stew, no bread. She is boiling some corn. My poor servants feel so badly at losing what they have worked for; meat, the hog meat that they love better than anything else, is all gone.

December 25, 1864.

Sadai jumped out of bed very early this morning to feel in her stocking. She could not believe but that there would be something in it. Finding nothing, she crept back into bed, pulled the cover over her face, and I soon heard her sobbing. The little negroes all came in: "Christmas gift, mist'ess! Christmas gift, mist'ess!"

I pulled the cover over my face and was soon mingling my tears with Sadai's.

May 29, 1865.

Dr. Williams, from Social Circle, came this morning to trade me a horse. He tells me the people below are freeing their servants and allowing those to stay with them that will go on with their work and obey as usual. What I shall do with mine is a question that troubles me day and night. It is my last thought at night and the first in the morning. I told them several days ago they were free to do as they liked. But it is my duty to make some provision for them. I thank God that they are freed, yet what can I do with them? They are old and young, not profitable to hire. What provision can I make?

THE NIGHT OF FIRE IN COLUMBIA, S.C.

THE NIGHT of fire-lit horror in Columbia, South Carolina, following its capture by the Union forces, is painted here by the Reverend A. Toomer Porter. It was near the end of the war—February 17, 1865—and the capital of the state was undefended against the army of General Sherman.

The Reverend Dr. Porter (1828–1902) was of Charleston, South Carolina, a chaplain with Confederate troops during the war. He was a competent person, whose clerical calling did not weaken or too closely confine his forceful character and diverse abilities. For forty-four years, 1854–98, he was rector of the Church of the Holy Communion, Charleston, and in connection with the church founded what later became known as the Porter Military Academy. In this and other directions, he did much for education in his region.

Further recollections of the night of the fire were gathered by the northern writer, John Townsend Trowbridge, when he visited Columbia a year after the disaster.

From Led On! Step by Step. Scenes from Clerical, Military, Educational and Plantation Life in the South, 1828–1898. *An Autobiography by* A. Toomer Porter, D. D.

I ran to the Main Street, and met the advancing column of the incoming enemy, soon after they entered the town. As they were marching down the street, many stragglers fell out of the ranks; but I moved on among them unmolested, for I had taken the precaution to put on my clerical clothes. Very soon I saw with great apprehension many persons, white and colored, rushing out of stores and houses with pitchers and buckets. I heard this was done to propitiate the thirsty soldiers. It was soon evident what was in those vessels, for many of the soldiers became intoxicated, and to this cause we owed some of the horrors that followed.

As soon as the column halted and stacked arms, the weary and drunken men threw themselves on the cotton bales in the middle of the street. Thinking the officer in command would make his head-quarters at the State House, which stood at the head of Main Street, I went there, and found a perfect orgie in progress. Many trophies and mementoes of a not inglorious past, especially of the War of 1812, the Florida War, and the Mexican War, battle-flags and swords, etc., were in the possession of drunken soldiers, and were being pulled to pieces and tossed about. Some of the men were wrestling and boxing. Altogether, the scene was so intensely painful and mortifying, that I quickly returned.

Going back down Main Street, I found Colonel Stone, the officer in command, and told him the city was full of unprotected women and children, and appealed to him as a man and a soldier to give me some guards for them, calling his attention to the drunken state of his men. He courteously directed me to go to the Market House, farther down the street, where I could find his Provost Marshal. He at the same time wrote on one of the notes orders for as many guards as I needed.

On my way to the Market House I saw the first bale of cotton take fire. The soldiers who were sitting and lying on the cotton had begun to light their pipes, and a spark or a lighted match must have fallen on the loose cotton, which of course took fire. I was within twenty feet of the first cotton fired that day. The flames soon spread, and the men, cursing those who had deprived them of their resting-place, quickly got away from the burning piles.

I saw General Sherman and his staff ride down Main Street, at about 9 o'clock A.M., and when he came in, the burning cotton was still smouldering. At that time he was ignorant of the cause of the fire, and naturally supposed it had been kindled by the retreating Confederates. I met him that afternoon at the house of Mr. Harris Simons.

On leaving, I walked some distance with the General, and had some conversation regarding the preservation of the library of the College. He remarked that he would sooner send us a library, than destroy the one we had; adding, that if better use had been made of it, this state of things would not exist, and that I must go and tell the ladies they were as safe as if he were a hundred miles away.

A Captain of the Federal army had billeted himself on us, and was welcomed by us, as we thought he could protect the house.

*Ruins of Columbia from the front of the Capitol, looking
north.*

This officer went with me to the roof of the house, and we there saw
that the whole of Columbia was surrounded with flames. I pointed
this out to the Captain, and said I believed they were going to burn
Columbia.

"No," he said; "those are camp-fires."

I told him that I had been four years in camp, and thought I
knew what a camp-fire was. Then I pointed out several residences
on fire, the owners of which I knew, namely, Mr. Trenholm, General
Hampton, Colonel Wallace, and a number of others. The environs
of the town were ablaze. Then a fire broke out in Main Street, near
Hunt's Hotel, caused by an overturned lamp in a saloon, which
ignited the liquor, and as the flames spread, two or three small hand-
engines were brought out which I saw Federal soldiers work on. Suddenly three fire-balloons went up, and in ten minutes eight fires
broke out simultaneously across the northern street of the city, about

equal distance from each other, and stretched almost entirely across the town.

At once the men who had been on the engines a moment before turned in and broke them to pieces. I saw this from the roof of the house.

"See that?" I said to the Captain.

He gave one long look, then darted down the skylight, and we never saw him again.

A gale of wind was blowing from the north that night, and that soon caused the fire to burn freely, so that in a short time the city was wrapped in a lurid sheet of flames.

Going into the street I there beheld a scene which, while memory lasts, I can never forget. Streams of pale women, leading their terrified children, with here and there an infant in arms, went by, they knew not whither, amid the fierce flames. They hurried on, leaving behind them forever their burning homes, and all they contained. To their everlasting honor be it said, no cry escaped their lips, no tears rolled down their cheeks. Fearless and undaunted, they moved amid the surrounding horrors, silent, self-contained, enduring. In silence, the pale procession passed on. When the history of heroic women is written, let not those Carolina women be forgotten.

The streets were filled with soldiers mounted and on foot, in every stage of drunkenness. The whole of General Howard's Fifteenth Corps, we learned, had been turned loose upon us. Shouts of derision and blasphemy filled the air. Cries of "There are the aristocrats!" "Look at the chivalry!" were yelled into the ears of these defenseless women. Men seemed to have lost their manhood, and the mere beast was in the ascendant. Be it said, however, that although these poor women were in their power, there is no recorded instance of a white woman having been assaulted or outraged. So much cannot be said about the colored women, who were not so well treated. . . .

General Sherman[1] came by. The burning city made it bright as day; the General recognized me, and I said in reply to his remark, "This is terrible," "Yes, when you remember that women and children are your victims."

I was desperate and had lost all fear of him.

"Your Governor is responsible for this," he said.

"How so?" I asked.

He said: "Whoever heard of evacuating a place and leaving it full of liquor? My men are drunk, and this is the cause of all. Why did not your Governor destroy all this liquor before he left? There was a very great quantity of whiskey in the town when we arrived."

"The drunken men have done much," I replied; "but I have seen sober men fire house after house."

Just then an officer rode up, and saluted the General, who recognized him and said, "Captain Andrews, did I not order you that this should stop?"

"Yes, General, but the First Division are as drunk as the first regiment that came in yesterday morning."

"Then, sir, go, and bring the Second Division and have this stopped. I hold you personally responsible for the immediate cessation of this riot."

[1] This was about 3:30 A.M. the following morning.

Captain Andrews rode off. The Second Division from Stark Hill, General Woods commanding, was brought in; the drunken mob was swept by them out of the city, and in less than half an hour, not another house was burned. The discipline of that army was superb, and we all felt that fire and disorder could have been prevented or sooner arrested, for thirteen hundred houses were burned that night, and seven thousand women and children driven into the streets amidst the scenes which, as an eye-witness, I have described.

A NORTHERNER VISITS THE RUINS

JOHN TOWNSEND TROWBRIDGE (1827–1916) was a popular and prolific writer of stories for boys, which appeared chiefly in Boston publications, as well as a novelist and poet. Before and during the Civil War he produced some anti-slavery and pro-Union novels and articles. In the fall of 1865 he started on a tour to gather material for his book: *The South: Its Battle-Fields, Desolated States and Ruined Cities, Its People and Prospects*. He arrived in Columbia during the first weeks of 1866.

From My Own Story: With Recollections of Noted Persons. *By John Townsend Trowbridge.*

What the rebel invaders of Pennsylvania did in a small way at Chambersburg, our army repeated on a scale of appalling magnitude at Columbia.

Through Governor Orr, to whom I had letters, I made acquaintance with Mayor Gibbes and other citizens; and to them I was indebted for many reminiscences and anecdotes. On the night of the fire, a thousand men could be seen, in the yards and gardens of the city, by the light of the flames, probing the earth with their bayonets for buried plunder. The dismay and terror of the inhabitants can hardly be conceived. Trunks and bundles were snatched from the hands of hurrying fugitives, broken open, rifled, and then hurled into the flames. Ornaments were plucked from the necks and arms of ladies and caskets from their hands.

An old gentleman who had purchased two watches for his grandchildren had one snatched from him by a soldier. In his rage and grief he exclaimed, "You may as well take the other!" and his suggestion was cheerfully complied with.

Another sufferer said, "That watch will be good for nothing without the key. Won't you stop and take it?" "Thank you," said the soldier; and he went off proudly winding his new chronometer.

The soldiers were full of humorous remarks about the ruined city. "What curious people you are!" said one. "You run up your chimneys before you build your houses."

One man's treasure, buried by his garden fence, escaped the soldiers' divining rods, but was afterwards discovered by a hitched horse pawing the earth over it. Some treasures were hidden in cemeteries, but they did not always escape the search of the soldiers, who showed a strong mistrust of new-made graves.

RETREAT FROM RICHMOND— AND APPOMATTOX

THE RETREAT and surrender of General Robert E. Lee's forces have usually been presented from a Northern point of view. Here is the scene from the witness of one of the losers, an officer of the 7th South Carolina Cavalry. In steadfast spirit and with quiet eloquence, he makes felt this closing drama of the War between the States.

Edward Mortimer Boykin (1820–91), who published his war reminiscences anonymously, was a doctor of Camden, South Carolina. He married Mary Chesnut Lang in 1841. By the end of the war, in which he lost a son and was himself wounded, Boykin had been promoted to lieutenant colonel. At home again, he resumed the practice of medicine. He always limped from his wound but lived to celebrate his golden wedding anniversary.

One may catch glimpses of this capable soldiering doctor in the pages of Mary Boykin Chesnut's well-known book, A *Diary From Dixie*. Mrs. Chesnut and Dr. Boykin were cousins and the Chesnut plantation, Mulberry, was not far from the Boykin plantation. In 1862, Mrs. Chesnut noted in her diary that she had heard it said of the doctor that "in whatever company you may meet him he is the pleasantest man there." In 1864, she saw Boykin, promoted to major, stout and jolly, as "the very picture of a debonaire devil-may-care cavalier," and in May 1865, after the southern defeat, she wrote that "E. M. Boykin is awfully sanguine. His main idea is joy that he has no Negroes to support, and can hire only those he really wants."

From The Falling Flag. Evacuation of Richmond, Retreat and Surrender at Appomattox. *By An Officer of The Rear Guard.*

We passed into the "Rockets," the southern suburb of Richmond, at an easy marching gait, and there learned that the bridge had taken fire from some of the buildings, which by this time we could see were on fire in the city. Fearing our retreat would be cut off at that point, which would throw us from our position as rear guard, we pushed on rapidly, the column moving at a trot through the "Rockets."

The peculiar population of that suburb were gathered on the sidewalk; bold, dirty looking women, who had evidently not been improved by four years' military association, dirtier (if possible) looking children, and here and there skulking, scoundrelly looking men, who in the general ruin were sneaking from the holes they had been hiding in—not, though, in the numbers that might have been expected, for the great crowd, as we soon saw, were hard at it, pillaging the burning city.

Bare-headed women, their arms filled with every description of goods, plundered from warehouses and shops, their hair hanging about their ears, were rushing one way to deposit their plunder and return for more, while a current of the empty-handed surged in a contrary direction towards the scene.

*The grim ruins of the Gallego flour mills, on Richmond's
waterfront.*

The roaring and crackling of the burning houses, the trampling
and snorting of our horses over the paved streets as we swept along,
wild sounds of every description, while the rising sun came dimly
through the cloud of smoke that hung like a pall around him, made
up a scene that beggars description, and which I hope never to see
again—the saddest of many of the sad sights of war—a city undergoing pillage at the hands of its own mob, while the standards of an
empire were being taken from its capitol, and the tramp of a
victorious enemy could be heard at its gates.

Richmond had collected within its walls the refuse of the war
—thieves and deserters, male and female, the vilest of the vile were
there, but strict military discipline had kept it down. Now, in one
moment, it was all removed—all restraint was taken off—and you
may imagine the consequences. There were said to be 5,000 deserters in the city, and you could see the grey jackets here and there
sprinkled in the mob that was roaring down the street. When we

reached somewhere between Twentieth and Twenty-fifth streets—
I will not be certain—the flames swept across Main street so we
could not pass. The column turned to the right, and so got into
the street above it. On this (Franklin street) are many private
residences; at the windows we could see the sad and tearful faces
of the kind Virginia women, who had never failed the soldier in
four long years of war and trouble, ready to the last to give him
devoted attendance in his wounds and sickness, and to share with
his necessities the last morsel.

At last we were on the main bridge, along which were scattered
faggots to facilitate the burning. Lieut. Cantey, Sergt. Lee and
twenty men from the Seventh were left, under the supervision of
Colonel Haskell, to burn the bridge, while the rest went slowly up
the hill on which Manchester is built, and waited for them. Just
as the canal bridge on which we had crossed took fire, about forty of
Kautz' cavalry galloped easily up Main street, fired a long shot with
their carbines on the party at the bridge, but went on up the street
instead of coming down to the river. They were too late to secure the
bridge, if that had been their object, which they seemed to be aware
of, as they made no attempt to do so. Their coming was of service
to the city. General Ord, as we afterwards understood, acted with
promptness and kindness, put down the mob, and put out the fire,
and protected the people of Richmond from the mob and his own
soldiers, in their persons and property.

"Mount the brigade and move up at once!" The enemy had
gotten in force between us and Burkville, and his cavalry had struck
our wagon and ordnance train some three or four miles from where
we were. So there was mounting in hot haste, and off we went at a
gallop.

We soon reached the point they had first attacked and set fire
to the wagons—the canvas covers taking fire very easily. Their plan
of operation seemed to be to strike the train, which was several
miles long at a given point, fire as many wagons as their number
admitted of doing at once, then making a circuit and striking it
again, leaving an intermediate point untouched.

We did not suppose the troops actually engaged in the firing
exceeded three or four hundred well mounted men, but had a large

body of cavalry moving parallel with them in easy supporting distance. This was a very effectual mode of throwing the march of the wagon train into confusion, independent of the absolute destruction they caused.

We moved on slowly after them—the sun being nearly down—to "Amelia Springs," some two miles off, crossed the creek, and, though we had commenced the fight in the morning, were politely requested (everybody knows what a military request is) by General Lee to move down the road until we could see the Yankee pickets, put the brigade into camp, post pickets, and make the best of it—all of which we did.

All around us through the stillness floated the music of the Yankee bands, mocking with their beautiful music our desperate condition; yet our men around their fires were enjoying it as much, and, seemingly, with as light hearts as the owners of it. Occasionally, as a bugle call would ring out, which always sounds to a trooper as a challenge to arms, a different expression would show itself, and a harder look take the place of the softer one induced by "Home, Sweet Home," or "Annie Laurie."

At about ten o'clock a quiet order mounted us, almost before, as the little boys say, we got the "sleep out of our eyes." We were in column on the road, and non-commissioned officers under the direction of the adjutant riding down it, each with a handkerchief full of cartridges, supplying the men with that very necessary "article of war." And then commenced that most weary night march, that will always be remembered by the tired men who rode it, that ended only (without a halt, except a marching one,) at Appomattox Courthouse.

The line of retreat had been changed, and by a forced night march on another road a push was being made for the mountains at Lynchburg. Had we gotten there (and Appomattox Court-house was within twenty miles of Lynchburg) with the men and material General Lee still had with him, Lee's last struggle among the mountains of his native State would have made a picture to swell the soldier's heart with pride to look upon. The end we know would have been the same.

Not long after resuming our march we posted pickets at some cross roads, under the immediate direction of General R. E. Lee

General Lee, on his horse, Traveler.

himself. We moved steadily on to-day without molestation of any kind, the wagons moving in double lines, the road being wide enough to admit it. About twelve o'clock or a little later we had halted to water our horses at a stream that crossed the road.

I had dismounted and was leaning across my horse, when I saw, as I thought, Captain Allen, of the Twenty-fourth Virginia, of our brigade, having watered his horse where the stream crossed the road. The captain was a fine specimen of a Virginia soldier and gentleman, some sixty years of age, of fine presence, who was always said to resemble General Lee, wearing his grey beard trimmed after the fashion of that of our great leader, and in the saddle having about the same height, though dismounted, the captain, I should say, was the taller. However, I watched the old captain, as I thought, riding up the hill toward me, on a very fine grey horse, and was thinking what a type of the veteran soldier he looked, as indeed I had often thought before, until he got within a few feet of me, when I changed my intended rather familiar, but still most respectful salute, meant for the captain, for the reverence with which the soldier salutes the standard of his legion—which represents to him all that he has left to love and honor—as I discovered that it was General R. E. Lee himself, riding alone—not even an orderly in attendance. He turned our salute, his eye taking it all in, with a calm smile, that assured us our confidence was not misplaced.

April 9th.—The sun rose clear on this the last day, practically, of the Southern Confederacy. It was cool and fresh in the early morning so near the mountains, though the spring must have been a forward one, as the oak trees were covered with their long yellow tassels.

Firing was going on, artillery and small arms, beyond the town, and there was General R. E. Lee himself, with Longstreet, Gordon, and the rest of his paladins.

When we rode into the open field we could see the enemy crowding along the edge of the woods—cavalry apparently extending their line around us. We kept on advancing towards them to get a nearer view of things, and were midway on the Richmond side between the town and a large white house with a handsome grove around it. In the yard could be seen a body of cavalry, in number about our own; we saw no other troops near. Two or three hundred yards to the right of the house an officer, apparently of rank, with a few men—his staff, probably—riding well forward, halted, looking toward the town with his glass. Just as he rode out General Gary had given the order to charge the party in the yard. Some one remarked that it looked like a flag of truce. "Charge!" swore Gary in his roughest tones, and on we went. The party in the yard were taken by surprise; they had not expected us to charge them, as they were aware that a parley was going on (of which, of course, we knew nothing), and that there was a suspension of hostilities.

We drove them through the yard, taking one or two prisoners

—one little fellow, who took it very good-humoredly; he had his head tied up, having got it broken somewhere on the road, and was riding a mule. We followed up their retreat through the yard, down a road, through the open woods beyond, and were having it, as we thought, all our own way—when, stretched along behind the brown oaks, and moving with a close and steady tramp, was a long line of cavalry, some thousands strong—Custer's division—our friends of last night. This altered the complexion of things entirely; the order was instantly given to move by the left flank—which, without throwing our back to them, changed the forward into a retrograde movement.

The enemy kept his line unbroken, pressing slowly forward, firing no volley, but dropping shots from a line of scattered skirmishers in front was all we got. They, of course, knew the condition of things, and seemed to think we did not. We fell back toward a battery of ours that was behind us, supported, I think, by a brigade of North Carolina infantry. We moved slowly, and the enemy's skirmishers got close enough for a dash to be made by our acting regimental adjutant—in place of Lieutenant Capers, killed the night before—Lieutenant Haile, who took a prisoner, but just as it was done one of our couriers—Tribble, Seventh regiment—mounted on a fine black horse, bareheaded, dashed between the two lines with a handkerchief tied upon a switch, sent by General Gordon, announcing the "suspension of hostilities."

The articles of capitulation were signed next morning under the famous "apple tree," I suppose; what we saw of it was this: General Lee was seen, dressed in full Confederate uniform, with his sword on, riding his fine grey charger, and accompanied by General Gordon, coming from the village, and riding immediately in front of where we were lying. He had not been particularly noticed as he had gone toward the town, for, though with the regiment, I have no recollection of his doing so. As soon as he was seen it acted like an electric flash upon our men; they sprang to their feet, and, running to the roadside, commenced a wild cheering that roused our troops. As far as we could see they came running down the hillsides, and joining in, along the ground, and through the woods, and up into the sky, there went a tribute that has seldom been paid to mortal man. "Faithful, though all was lost!"

PRISONER JEFFERSON DAVIS TALKS WITH HIS DOCTOR

THEY CAPTURED President Jefferson Davis of the Confederate States of America in Georgia on May 10, 1865, and confined him in Fortress Monroe, Virginia. Under the emotional and vindictive climate of the time the details of his imprisonment were cruelly severe.

The two main accusations against him were that he was involved in the assassination of President Lincoln and that he was responsible for inhuman treatment of Union war prisoners. The case could not stand up in court and he was never brought to trial, languishing in prison until at long last he was freed on bail May 14, 1867, Editor Horace Greeley of the New York *Tribune* and Gerrit Smith, philanthropic abolitionist, being among the signers of his bond.

Brevet Lieutenant Colonel John Joseph Craven (1822–93) was the doctor assigned to Jefferson Davis (1808–89) during the first eight months of his incarceration. Craven, a Union surgeon and strong anti-slavery man, had served as medical director of the Department of the South and then of the 10th Corps, which included Fortress Monroe. He constantly visited his prisoner, came to sympathize with him and converse with him, and continually sought alleviation of the harsh terms of his confinement. It was Craven's assertion at that time that the most bloodthirsty and revengeful are noncombatants.

This account of Lieutenant Colonel Craven's talks with Jefferson Davis published in 1866, constituted, claimed the author, "absolutely the first statement in his favor—if so it can be regarded—which the Northern press has yet given to the world."

Mrs. Davis in her book, *Jefferson Davis, A Memoir*, refers to Craven as "the good doctor," and Davis himself in a letter to his wife, during his confinement, wrote: "I feel deeply indebted to Dr. Craven and the ladies of his family for a benevolence which had much to suppress, and nothing to excite it, and but for which my captivity would soon have ended in death."

Craven drew official critical attention for ordering an overcoat and heavy underwear for his prisoner and was mustered out of the service in January 1866. He returned to Newark, New Jersey, where he was postmaster for four years, then took up the practice of medicine till he moved to Patchogue, Long Island in 1883. There he held various civic offices till his death.

From The Prison Life of Jefferson Davis,
embracing Details and Incidents of his Captivity, particulars Concerning his Health
and Habits, together with many Conversa-
tions on topics of great Public Interest. *By*
Bvt. Lieut. Col. John J. Craven, M.D.

On the morning of May 24th, I was sent for about half-past
8 A.M., by Major-General Miles;[1] was told that State-prisoner Davis
complained of being ill, and that I had been assigned as his medical
attendant.

Calling upon the prisoner—the first time I had ever seen him
closely—he presented a very miserable and afflicting aspect. Stretched
upon his pallet and very much emaciated, Mr. Davis appeared a
mere fascine of raw and tremulous nerves—his eyes restless and
fevered, his head continually shifting from side to side for a cool
spot on the pillow, and his case clearly one in which intense cerebral
excitement was the first thing needing attention. He was extremely
despondent, his pulse full and at ninety, tongue thickly coated,
extremities cold, and his head troubled with a long-established
neuralgic disorder. Complained of his thin camp mattress and
pillow stuffed with hair, adding, that he was so emaciated that his
skin chafed easily against the slats; and, as these complaints were
well founded, I ordered an additional hospital mattress and softer
pillow, for which he thanked me courteously.

Mr. Davis turned to the officer of the day, and demanded
whether he had been shackled by special order of the Secretary of
War, or whether General Miles had considered this violent course
essential to his safe-keeping? The Captain replied that he knew
nothing of the matter; and so our first interview ended.

On quitting Mr. Davis, at once wrote to Major Church, Assistant Adjutant-General, advising that the prisoner be allowed
tobacco—to the want of which, after a lifetime of use, he had referred as one of the probable partial causes of his illness—though not
complainingly, nor with any request that it be given. This recom-
mendation was approved in the course of the day; and on calling
in the evening brought tobacco with me, and Mr. Davis filled his

[1] Major General Nelson A. Miles, commanding at Fortress Monroe.

Jefferson Davis bidding farewell to his escort two days before his capture.

pipe, which was the sole article he had carried with him from the *Clyde*,[2] except the clothes he then wore.

"This is a noble medicine," he said, with something as near a smile as was possible for his haggard and shrunken features. "I hardly expected it; did not ask for it, though the deprivation has been severe. During my confinement here I shall ask for nothing."

He was now much calmer, feverish symptoms steadily decreasing, pulse already down to seventy-five, his brain less excitable, and his mind becoming more resigned to his condition. Complained that the foot-falls of the two sentries within his chamber made it difficult for him to collect his thoughts; but added cheerfully that, with this —touching his pipe—he hoped to become tranquil.

This pipe, by the way, was a large and handsome one, made of meerschaum, with an amber mouth-piece, showing by its color that it had seen "active service" for some time—as indeed was the

[2] The ship that brought the captured Jefferson Davis to Fortress Monroe, May 19.

case, having been his companion during the stormiest years of his late titular Presidency. It is now in the Writer's possession, having been given to him by Mr. Davis, and its acceptance insisted upon as the only thing he had left to offer.

Morning of 25th May. My patient much easier and better. Had slept a little, and thanked me for the additional mattress.

Happening to notice that his coffee stood cold and apparently untasted beside his bed in its tin cup, I remarked that here was a contradiction of the assertion implied in the old army question, "Who ever saw cold coffee in a tin cup?" referring to the eagerness with which soldiers of all classes, when campaigning, seek for and use this beverage.

"I cannot drink it," he remarked, "though fond of coffee all my life. It is the poorest article of the sort I have ever tasted; and if your government pays for such stuff as coffee, the purchasing quartermaster must be getting rich. It surprises me, too, for I thought your soldiers must have the best—many of my Generals complaining of the difficulties they encountered in seeking to prevent our people from making volunteer truces with your soldiers whenever the lines ran near each other, for the purpose of exchanging the tobacco we had in abundance against your coffee and sugar."

Replied that the same difficulty had been felt on our side, endangering discipline and calling for severe measures of repression. The temptation to obtain tobacco was uncontrollable. One of our lads would pop his head up from his riflepit and cry: "Hey, Johnny, any tobacco over your way?" to which the reply would instantly come, "Yes, Yank, rafts of it. How is it with you on the coffee question?" A satisfactory reply being given, the whisper would run along each line, "Cease firing, truce for coffee and tobacco"; and in another moment scores of the combatants, on either side, would be scrambling over their respective earthworks, and meeting on the debatable land between, for commerical dicker and barter in true Yankee style.

This picture seemed to amuse the patient. His spirits were evidently improving. Told him to spend as little time in bed as he could; that exercise was the best medicine for dyspeptic patients. To this he answered by uncovering the blankets from his feet and showing me his shackled ankles.[3]

[3] He had been shackled the 23rd; the shackles were removed the 28th.

"It is impossible for me, Doctor; I cannot even stand erect. These shackles are very heavy; I know not, with the chain, how many pounds. If I try to move they trip me, and have already abraded broad patches of skin from the parts they touch. Can you devise no means to pad or cushion them, so that when I try to drag them along they may not chafe me so intolerably? My limbs have so little flesh on them, and that so weak, as to be easily lacerated."

At sight of this I turned away, promising to see what could be done, as exercise was the chief medical necessity in his case; and at this moment the first thrill of sympathy for my patient was experienced.

That afternoon, at an interview sought with Major-General Miles, my opinion was given that the physical condition of State-prisoner Davis required the removal of his shackles, until such time as his health should be established on some firmer basis. Exercise he absolutely needed, and also some alleviation of his abnormal nervous excitement.

HORACE GREELEY EXPLAINS WHY HE SIGNED DAVIS' BOND

EDITOR HORACE GREELEY of the New York *Tribune* followed his own earnest thought. His record during the Civil War period can be condensed thus: A strong free-soiler, he supported the war while grieving at its bloodshed; in 1863 he proposed foreign mediation, and in 1864, with Lincoln's unofficial assent, was delegate to unsuccessful peace negotiations with Confederate emissaries in Canada, after which Greeley urged a year's armistice; at the war's end he favored the 14th and 15th amendments and proposed a general amnesty.

As former President Jefferson Davis was held prisoner without indictment and without formal charge, Greeley pointed out the unconstitutional character of the performance and then was one of those who signed Davis' bond. This action cost Greeley northern popularity and money, the latter in loss of subscriptions to his book about the war and to his newspapers, especially the weekly *Tribune*.

From Recollections of a Busy Life. *By*
Horace Greeley.

Mr. Andrew Johnson had seen fit to change his views and his
friends since his unexpected accession to the Presidency, and had,
from an intemperate denouncer of the beaten Rebels as deserving
severe punishment, become their protector and patron. Jefferson
Davis, in Fortress Monroe, under his proclamation aforesaid, was
an ugly elephant on Johnson's hands; and thousands were anxious
that he should remain there. Their view of the matter did not im-
press me as statesmanlike, nor even sagacious.

The Federal Constitution expressly provides[1] that,

> In all criminal prosecutions, the accused shall enjoy the right
> to a speedy and public trial, by an impartial jury of the State
> and district wherein the crime shall have been committeed,
> etc. . . .

Mr. George Shea, the attorney of record for the defence in the
case of The United States *versus* Jefferson Davis, indicted for treason, is the son of an old friend, and I have known and liked him
from infancy. After it had become evident that his client had no
immediate prospect of trial, if any prospect at all, Mr. Shea became
anxious that said client be liberated on bail. Consulting me as to the
feasibility of procuring some names to be proffered as bondsmen of
persons who had conspicuously opposed the Rebellion and all the
grave errors which incited it, I suggested two eminent Unionists,
who, I presumed, would cheerfully consent to stand as security that
the accused would not run away to avoid the trial he had long but
unsuccessfully invoked. I added, after reflection, "If *my* name should
be found necessary, you may use that." He thanked me, and said
he should proffer it only in case the others abundantly at his command would not answer without it. Months passed before I was
apprised, by a telegram from Washington, that my name *was*
needed; when I went down and proffered it. And when, at length,
the prisoner was brought before the United States District Court at
Richmond,[2] I was there, by invitation, and signed the bond in due
form.

[1] "Amendments, Art. VI."
[2] May 13, 1867.

I suppose this would have excited some hubbub at any rate; but the actual tumult was gravely aggravated by gross misstatements. It was widely asserted that the object of giving bail was to screen the accused from trial,—in other words, to enable him to run away,—when nothing like this was ever imagined by those concerned. The prisoner, through his counsel, had assiduously sought a trial, while the prosecution was not ready, because (as Judge Underwood was obliged to testify before a Committee of Congress) no conviction was possible, except by packing a jury. The words "straw bail" were used in this connection; when one of the sureties is worth several millions of dollars, and the poorest of them is abundantly good for the sum of $5,000, in which he is "held and firmly bound" to produce the body of Jefferson Davis whenever the plaintiff shall be ready to try him. If he only *would* run away, I know that very many people would be much obliged to him; but he won't.

It was telegraphed all over the North that I had a very affectionate meeting and greeting with the prisoner when he had been bailed; when in fact I had never before spoken nor written to him any message whatever, and did not know him, even by sight, when he entered the court-room. After the bond was signed, one of his counsel asked me if I had any objection to being introduced to Mr. Davis, and I replied that I had none; whereupon we were introduced, and simply greeted each other. I made, at the request of a friend, a brief call on his wife that evening, as they were leaving for Canada; and there our intercourse ended, probably forever.

When the impeachment of President Johnson was fully resolved on, and there was for some weeks a fair prospect that Mr. Wade[3] would soon be President, with a Cabinet of like Radical faith, I suggested to some of the prospective President's next friends that I had Jefferson Davis still on my hands, and that, if he were considered a handy thing to have in the house, I might turn him over to the new Administration for trial at an hour's notice, the suggestion evoked no enthusiasm and I was not encouraged to press it.

The sale of my history[4] was very large and steady down to the date of the clamor raised touching the bailing of Jefferson Davis,

---

[3] Benjamin F. Wade of Ohio, president pro-tem of the Senate, in line for presidency if Johnson found guilty.

[4] *The American Conflict.*

when it almost ceased for a season; thousands who had subscribed for it refusing to take their copies, to the sore disappointment and loss of the agents, who had supplied themselves with fifty to a hundred copies each, in accordance with their orders; and who thus found themselves suddenly, and most unexpectedly involved in serious embarrassments. I grieved that they were thus afflicted for what, at the worst, was no fault of theirs; while their loss by every copy thus refused was twenty times my own. I trust, however, that their undeserved embarrassments were, for the most part, temporary,— that a juster sense of what was due to them ultimately prevailed,— that all of them who did not mistake the character of a fitful gust of popular passion, and thereupon sacrifice their hard earnings, have since been relieved from their embarrassments; and that the injury and injustice they suffered without deserving have long since been fully repaired. At all events, the public has learned that I act upon my convictions without fear of personal consequences; hence, any future paroxysm of popular rage against me is likely to be less violent, in view of the fact that this one proved so plainly ineffectual.

FOOD,
FASHION AND MANNERS

MASSACHUSETTS FAMILY LIFE—UNGLOSSED

AN ILLUMINATING glimpse of daily life with a Pepperell, Massachusetts, family in 1777, furnished through the unflattering eyes of a captured British army officer, is printed below. Ensign Thomas Hughes, son of a British major and one of four brothers all of whom entered the army, was eighteen years old when he penned this. He was a prisoner on parole, having been captured by the Americans at Ticonderoga earlier in the year, and was boarding with this Pepperell family.

Young Hughes was our prisoner in various cities and towns, mostly in Massachusetts and Pennsylvania, until four months before Yorktown (1781). He and his comrades had a reasonably livable time in those days when parole was accepted and exercised at face value. His narrative clashes with the admiring memoirs of our French allies. Hughes soundly disliked Americans and democracy. He died in Canada, 1790.

From A Journal by Thos: Hughes 1778–1789, for his Amusement and Designed only for his Perusal by the time he attains the Age of 50 if he lives so long.

Oct: 20th. All landed at Charlestown, where both officers and servants were immediately put into one horse chairs—and off we went for Pepperell under the care of a conductor. Lay this night at Concord—22 miles.

Oct: 21st. Arrived at Pepperell, and were delivered over to the Committee of the town, who distributed us about the neighbourhood for this night.

Oct: 22nd. Procur'd quarters in a house, in which I have agreed to pay two silver dollars pr week for board &c &c. The family are very civil—it consists of Father (who is almost deaf), Mother (a talkative old woman), and two daughters, who are of the order of old maids, confounded ugly, with beards an inch long.

Oct: 25th. This town is quite a new settlement and so little clear'd that in some places the houses are a mile distant. We are almost as much out of the world here, as if we were in the deserts of Arabia, and the inhabitants as ignorant as the Hottentots. I have been asked how often I have visited Jerusalem and if I did not live close by it, though I told them I lived in England; and then they ask'd, if England was not a fine town. What a life am I to lead? I am sick of their absurdities.

Oct: 26th. I find that the people here have not the least idea of a gentleman. Our servants are treated just like ourselves, and they are surpris'd to find our men won't eat at the same table with us, to which they are always invited. Two of our gentlemen agreeing with some inhabitant about boarding, the only thing the people objected to, was the article of washing. Oh! if that is the only obstacle (says a Committee man, who went with them) it is easily remov'd; send them a tub, and give them a little soap, and they can wash their own clothes.

November 1st. This life being such a one as perhaps I may never see again, I cannot refrain describing it. We have but one room to eat and sit in, which is in common with all the family, master, mistress, and servant, and what to call it, I know not, as it serves for parlour, kitchen and workroom. About 9 o'clock, Lt Brown (who lives with me) and myself breakfast, but they all wonder how we can sleep so long. Our breakfast is bread and milk, or boil'd Indian corn with butter and treacle spread over it. This is pretty substantial, and after it we generally walk into the woods, to gather chestnuts, or throw stones at squirrels. About 12 o'clock the whole family collects for dinner, which soon after smokes upon the board; and whilst it is cooling, Father shuts his eyes, mutters an unintelligible monstrous long grace and down we all sit with no other distinction, but Brown and me getting pewter plates— whereas the others have wooden platters. Our food is fat salt pork, and sauce (the name they give to roots and greens). We never get fresh meat, but when a fox, or hawk, seizes an unfortunate fowl, but being discover'd by the noise we made, is frighten'd, and lets fall the prey, generally with the loss of a leg or wing. The fowl on this disaster is immediately pickt and put into the pot. The dinners are upon that free and easy mode, that neither gentleman or lady use any ceremony—all hands in the dish at once—which gives many pretty opportunities for laughter, as two or three of us often catch hold of the same piece. This meal over, another grace is said, and we all disperse to our different employments, theirs working and ours the best we can find. At night fall a large fire is made on the hearth, and the kitchen (or whatever it is) receives the whole family, which would present an high scene to an unconcern'd spectator—Mother, Brown and me round the fire, she knitting and asking us silly questions; our servant at the opposite corner of the chimney from us; at our back two or three women spinning with large noisy wheels, and in the middle of the room sits Father, and one or two apprentice boys shelling Indian corn. We have no candles, but the room is lighted by splinters of pine wood flung into the fire. About 8 o'clock, we get bread and milk for supper; a little after Father begins to yawn—upon which we stand up. He says prayers, and we depart to our beds. Our apartment, or rather the place we lay in, extends over the whole house, and is what is commonly call'd the garret. We have three beds in it—one of which contains Brown and me, in the second sleep our two young ladies, and close at their feet, in the third, rest the servant and apprentice. Our room is not the worse for being a repository of fruit, and nuts, as we generally make an attack on the apples before we get up of a morn. If this is the kind of life the poets say so much of, and call Rural Happiness, I wish to my soul that they were here, and I in London.

Nov: 20th. There is something in the characters of these New Englanders that I cannot illustrate. They are certainly all very religious, and very industrious—and yet the men are not over nice in point of honesty, and the loss of virtue amongst the women does

*The Surrender of General Burgoyne. From the painting
by John Trumbull in the United States Capitol.*

not sully their reputation. I believe they think different from the
rest of the world.

Nov: 29th. Not having seen each other for some time, we met
to day by appointment, and dined together at a public house. We
were all very merry, but in the end one or two getting mellow and
kicking up a dust, they were sent to prison, for talking disrespect-
fully of the Congress, by one Scott, an Irishman and a captain in the
rebel service who was (by his own confession) oblig'd to leave his
country for none of his good deeds.

December 9th. An order from the Council of Boston, to take
us all to gaol for exceeding our limits by dining at the public
house; which it seems we had (by almost 150 yards). The Sheriff
took us into custody and, as he had two prisons under his jurisdic-
tion, was so polite as to offer us the choice of Concord or Cam-

bridge. We chose the latter as Genl Burgoyne's army[1] are quarter'd there. We lay this even at Lexington.

Dec: 10th. Our sheriff was so far from taking any care for preventing an escape that he left us entirely to ourselves, and upon our arrival we were 3 hours in the town of Cambridge before we could find him; but at last meeting him in the street, we stopt him. Well, says he, I am a little busy, but I will settle you first. The prison being near he deliver'd us to the jailor—with an injunction to use us well.

FIRST AMERICAN GEOGRAPHER DESCRIBES NEW YORK

JEDIDIAH MORSE (1761–1826), who was the father of Samuel F. B. Morse, inventor of the telegraph, has also been called the father of American geography. At the age of twenty-three he published *Geography Made Easy*, which flourished through twenty-five editions. The *American Universal Geography*, published both in this country and Europe, came five years later and the *American Gazeteer* in 1797. All were popular and eminently readable and informative, and more accurate concerning the U.S. than those English geographies Morse disliked.

This geographer was for most of his adult life—for thirty years— a Congregational minister in Charlestown, Massachusetts. In 1819 he complied with a government request for a report on our Indian nations. He helped found the New England Tract Society and the American Bible Society. Edinburgh University gave him the degree of Doctor of Sacred Theology.

One of his sons, Sidney E. Morse, described him: "The tall slender form and the well-shaped head, a little bald, but covered thinly with fine silken powdered hair falling gracefully into curls, gave him, when only middle-aged, a venerable aspect, while the benignant expression of his whole countenance and especially of his bright speaking eye, won for him at first sight respect and love."

[1] Burgoyne had surrendered at Saratoga in October; his army was being held at Cambridge.

Here Mr. Morse pictures the New York of over a century and a half ago.

From Geography Made Easy: being An Abridgement of the American Universal Geography. *By Jedidiah Morse.*

There are three incorporated cities in this state; New-York, Albany, and Hudson. New-York is the capital of the state, and stands in the southwest point of Manhattan, commonly called York-Island, at the confluence of the Hudson and East rivers. The principal part of the city lies on the east side of the Island, although the buildings extend from one river to the other. The length of the city on East river is about two miles; but falls much short of that distance on the banks of the Hudson. Its breadth, on an average, is nearly three-fourths of a mile; and its circumference may be four miles.

The houses are generally built of brick, and the roofs tiled. There are remaining a few houses, built after the old Dutch manner.

The most magnificent edifice in this city is Federal Hall, situated at the head of Broad street, where its front appears to great advantage.

The other publick buildings in the city, are 3 houses for publick worship for the Dutch Reformed church—five presbyterian churches—four Episcopal churches—two for German Lutherans and Calvinists—two Friends meeting houses—two for Baptists—two for Methodists—one for Moravians—one Roman Catholick church—and one French Protestant church out of repair, and a Jews' synagogue. Besides these, there is the Governour's house, a splendid building— the college, gaol, a new and spacious prison, and several other buildings of less note. The city is accomodated with four markets in different parts, which are furnished with a great plenty and variety of provisions, in neat and excellent order.

This city is esteemed the most eligible situation for commerce in the United States. It almost necessarily commands the trade of one half of New-Jersey, most of that of Connecticut, part of that of Massachusetts and New-Hampshire, and almost the whole of

New York City in 1800, viewed from the Hobuck (Hoboken),
New Jersey, ferry landing.

that of Vermont, besides the whole fertile interiour country, which
is penetrated by one of the largest rivers in the United States.

A want of good water has been a great inconvenience to the
citizens; there being few wells in the city. Most of the people were
supplied every day with fresh water conveyed to their doors in
casks, from a pump near the head of Queen street, which receives
it from a spring almost a mile from the center of the city. This
well is about 20 feet deep, and 4 feet diameter. The average quantity drawn daily from this remarkable well, was 110 hogsheads, of
130 gallons each. In some hot summer days, 216 hogsheads have
been drawn from it; and what is very singular, there is never more
or less than about three feet of water in the well. The water was
sold commonly at three pence a hogshead, at the pump. The Manhattan company was incorporated in 1798, for the purpose of con-
veying good water into the city, and their works are now nearly or
quite completed.

In point of sociability and hospitality, New-York is hardly exceeded by any town in the United States.

On a general view of this city, as described thirty years ago, and in its present state, the comparison is flattering to the present age; particularly the improvements in taste, elegance of manners, and that easy unaffected civility and politeness which form the happiness of social intercourse.

HOW THEY DRESSED TO VISIT DOLLY MADISON

DOLLY MADISON is as famed as her husband-president in current memory. The glint and vivaciousness of her personality shone in and out of the White House. These somewhat breathless fashion notes of Washington society in the winter of 1815–16, by a Massachusetts cabinet wife, are the more worthwhile because unpolished.

Mary Boardman Crowninshield (1778–1840) was the wife of Benjamin W. Crowninshield, Secretary of the Navy from December 1814 to October 1818, when he resigned; later he was in the House, 1823–31. The Crowninshields—they were both from Salem—were married in 1804 and had six children when Mrs. Crowninshield decided to accompany her husband to Washington for the 1815–16 winter. The two eldest daughters, Elizabeth and Mary, went with them. Mrs. Crowninshield liked the family together. A century later (1913) one of her relatives wrote that "she was continually upbraiding her husband for living in Washington and leaving her and her children alone in Salem."

From Letters of Mary Boardman Crowninshield, 1815–1816. *Edited by Francis Boardman Crowninshield.*

Thursday Morning, December 7th, 1815.

Dear Mother:—

Ball to-night. Last eve I went to the drawing-room.[1] We were

[1] Mrs. Madison gave frequent drawing-rooms or receptions. President and Mrs. Madison were living at the corner of Pennsylvania Avenue and 19th Street, the White House being still unoccupied after its burning by the British the previous year.

Mary Boardman Crowninshield in
1816. From a painting by John Vanderlyn.

not crowded, but one room well filled;—all much dressed, but their new dresses saved for this eve. Mrs. Madison's is a sky-blue striped velvet,—a frock,—fine elegant lace round the neck and lace handkerchief inside and a lace ruff, white lace turban starred in gold, and white feather. Clothes so long that stockings or shoes are not seen, but white shoes are generally worn. Mrs. Dallas[2] a dark green velvet trimmed with a lace footing half a quarter wide. It was beautiful lace, but did not look well on so dark a color—a green and white turban helmet front and green feathers waving over. Several black velvets, crepes, brocades, satins;—any one who has tolerable hair does not care to cover it up,—the object is to look as young as you can. The folks here in the house say I must dress my hair,

2 Wife of Alexander James Dallas, secretary of treasury.

This gown, once worn by Dolly Madison, might well be the yellow satin admired by Mrs. Crowninshield at the President's levee.

not cover it up, so last eve it was combed up as high on the top as I could get it, braided, and a bunch of flowers pinned in with one of my best ornaments—the green and gold one. In the evening Mrs. Madison said, "Oh, Mrs. C., your butterfly is too much hidden." I asked what she meant. She replied, "that elegant ornament in your hair—it is superb indeed." I imagine she took a liking to it, for she had little neat ornaments—emeralds set in gold. I had on my plain muslin trimmed with lace over white satin. The newest fashion to make a gown is like my English ones that go down in a peak before and behind. I have just brought in a pretty white silk one that is made in that way, but I have no pretty trimming for it, so think of preparing my gold muslin for this eve; as I got in Philadelphia a beautiful gold trimming for that and we do not have many balls here—perhaps not one again till Washington's birth-night. I am so sorry I did not take on my feathers, for I have to give nine dollars for two to wear this eve. You cannot get the most ordinary headdress for less than eight, up to fifteen dollars, and you must have a new one almost every time you go into company, so I save much expense by not wearing turbans.

Washington, January 2, 1816.

Yesterday I was at the President's levee. Mary went with us, but Elizabeth would not go. Such a crowd I never was in. It took us ten minutes to push and shove ourselves through the dining room; at the upper part of it stood the President and his lady, all standing—and a continual moving in and out. Two other small parlours open and all full—likewise the entry. In every room was a table with wine, punch, and cakes, and the servants squeezing through with waiters for those who could not get to the table. Some of the ladies were dressed very elegantly, beautiful bonnets and pelisses, shawls, etc. Mrs. Madison was dressed in a yellow satin embroidered all over with sprigs of butterflies, not two alike in the dress; a narrow border in all colors; made high in the neck; a little cape, long sleeves, and a white bonnet with feathers. Mrs. Baldwin, a sister of Mrs. Barlow,[3] was dressed first in a pretty white gown, high and much ruffled, the ruffles worked, which is

---

[3] Widow of Joel Barlow, writer and cosmopolitan.

thought handsomer than lace, and over it a scarlet merino dress made short above the ruffles of her gown, crossed before and behind about the waist, and short sleeves; it looked very tasty, trimmed with merino trimming with fringe; a black velvet hat turned up in front, with a large bunch of black feathers. Mrs. Clay,[4] a white merino dress with a deep border and a shawl to match. Mrs. Brown,[5] an orange dress of the same kind. Mrs. Decatur,[6] a blue lustre trimmed with satin ribbon high like a pelisse, a white hat turned up in front. Mrs. Dallas, a light pelisse trimmed round with velvet the same color. Her daughter, who had just arrived from Philadelphia, a brown merino pelisse trimmed with a rich trimming all colors. Mathilda, a very young girl, a scarlet merino, a blue hat with a large blue and white feather. In short, the greatest variety of dresses, for all the ladies in the city were there;—began to go at one o'clock. At three it was all over and done. I was disappointed in my pelisse. First it was made too short—it was then pieced down and the border quilted; it really looked handsomer, but she charged me ten dollars more than she engaged to make it for, so I sent it back. I ought to go out to-day and get another, or I shall not have one till spring.

Friday
Washington, 16th *February,* 1816

I was at the drawing room on Wednesday—expected to be the only one, as there were so many the last Levee, and there was another party on the same eve. Soon after I got in Mrs. Madison said how much we think alike—both with a little blue and flowers. I had on my blue velvet, and flowers on my head. Mrs. Madison a muslin dotted in silver over blue—a beautiful blue turban and feathers. I have never seen her look so well. There was a lady there I had never seen—monstrous large, dressed in a plain muslin, not even a piece of lace about the neck—just like a little girl's frock. Neck bare, a pink turban with a black feather. All the gentlemen

---

[4] Wife of Henry Clay.
[5] Wife of General Jacob Brown, later commander of the United States Army.
[6] Wife of Commodore Stephen Decatur.

thought her very handsome, but Miss Randolph is the most admired,—not pretty but very accomplished. Her grandfather, Mr.
Jefferson,[7] has taken much pains in educating her. I can never get
a chance to speak to her, she is so surrounded by gentlemen—for
here there are half a dozen gentlemen to one young lady.

Saturday
Washington, February 24, 1816.

You can have no idea of the great crowd at the ball. The
hall was as full as it could possibly be. They danced cotillions,
but you could only see the heads. We stood up on the benches. I
was afraid to move about much lest I should lose the girls. Mrs.
Chappell took care of Mary. Finally the heat was so great, I moved
on for the bottom of the hall, but was half an hour getting there.
After taking some refreshment, one of the managers said there was
a parlor opened below for the ladies who wished to go, so I took
the girls down. It was more pleasant there. From this room we
went to the supper table. The managers appoint gentlemen to
wait on the ladies, and take their seats according to their rank. Mrs.
Madison headed the table, Mrs. Brown on her right, Mrs. Dallas
on the left, then came my turn. Gen. Brown was my gallant. My
dress got entangled in his spurs and I fell over his sword going
upstairs, but arrived safe at the table, which was very large, but
not one quarter could come to table; indeed, half of the company
did not get anything. The girls fared very well. Don't, dear, tell
everybody what I write—it might be thought vanity for me to tell
who waited on me or where my seat was at table, so don't say I
wrote it. Mrs. Madison, dressed in black velvet trimmed with gold
[and] a worked lace turban in gold, looked brilliant,—a lace and
gold kind of a something over her shoulders. The greatest variety
of dresses as to colors and materials, but nothing entirely new. We
came home some of the first. I bought the girls new white kid
shoes. Gave five dollars for both, and new gloves, but such sights
when they got home,—so dirty, and yet they did not dance.

[7] Former President Thomas Jefferson.

HOW TO MAKE A GOOD QUILL PEN

DURING AMERICA's early years the quill pen was a necessity of existence. The manufacture of steel pens in this country did not begin until about 1860, although some were being made in England by 1820. Nathaniel P. Willis, the essayist and editor, is said to have brought some of the English pens to Washington in the 1830s. "Before this," wrote Ben: Perley Poore, Capitol official and newspaperman, "goose-quill pens had been exclusively used, and there was in each House of Congress and in each Department a penmaker, who knew what degree of flexibility and breadth of point each writer desired. Every gentleman had to carry a penknife, and to have in his desk a hone to sharpen it on, giving the finishing touches on one of his boots."

From The Private Instructor and Young Gentleman's Pocket Companion. *By John Blake.*[1]

On the choice of pen-knives and quills, for making pens, &c.
The young penman should be very careful to provide himself with a good pen-knife. The blade should be strong, and not over too large; for the middle sized blades will take off the nib the clearer. The edge should be straight and not too keen. The round pointed blades hinder the nibbing of the pen square; and if too keen, when nibbing a strong pen, the edge will be apt to turn.

Next to a good pen-knife, the young penman should furnish himself with good pens, good free ink, and also good paper, when arrived to commendable performances; likewise a flat ruler for sureness, and a round one for dispatch, with a leaden plummet or pencil to rule lines with; also, sand-paper and gum elastic, or Indian rubber; the one to scratch out a letter or word, when occasion should require it, and the other to rub out the lead lines, after using a black lead pencil.

[1] Published in 1815.

As to the choice of quills, of which there are great varieties, those called seconds are the best, as being hard, long, and round in the barrel. Natural quills are made of greater service by dutching or clarifying them. The first is effected by running them into a clear fire, and afterwards rubbing or scraping off the superfluous scurf while warm; the other by boiling them in water, and then clearing them over a charcoal fire, or dipping them into dry hot sand, and rubbing them well with a clean woollen cloth, while warm, until clear. The last is much the best way, and it leaves the quill much the clearer.

The best way of making a pen.

The making of a pen is gained sooner by experience and observation from others that can make one well, than by any verbal or written directions. But nevertheless, in order to make a good pen, care must be taken that the slit be-not forced so hard as to gape or open; neither should the nib be bent inwards; both these deficiencies tending to the same bad end. The first causes the pen to cast ink; the last, after a very little using, occasions a double stroke; and when the nib is recovered from that forced strain, the slit opens, not much unlike that which was forced too much. The slit should be always easy and clear. Make each cheek or side of the slit as equal as possible. Nib it even or square; the common practice of making that part next the hand both narrower and shorter than the other, being a great error; for should the nib in that part be the narrowest, it must, of course, be the weakest; and if it be the shortest, the other part of the nib must touch the paper before it, and then one may as well have no slit at all.— Make the slit long or short, according to the usual pressure of the hand in writing, and to the strength of the quill.

AMERICAN FARM HANDS BEAT THE ENGLISH ONES

THE WRITINGS of William Cobbett, like those of Daniel Defoe, exhibit an extraordinary native lucidity and force. The contentious Cobbett (1762–1835) arrived in Philadelphia 1792, published Porcupine's (daily)

Gazette 1797–99, was a bitter Federalist, got fined for libel; returned to England in 1800, and was welcomed by leaders of the Tory Government. There, with minor interruptions, he published Cobbett's *Weekly Political Register* from 1802 to his death.

In 1804 he turned anti-Tory and became a champion of the common people and of parliamentary reform. He revisited America, 1817–19, spending most of the time on his Long Island farm, when he wrote the observations that follow. He was elected to Parliament soon before he died; was instrumental in producing a thirty-six-volume parliamentary history, also a history of state trials. His books, diverse and many, all compel the reader's interest.

Essayist William Hazlitt describes Cobbett: "His figure is tall and portly; he has a good sensible face, rather full, with little grey eyes, a hard, square forehead, a ruddy complexion, with hair grey or powdered." He seemed "a very pleasant man."

From A Year's Residence In America. *By William Cobbett.*

It is, too, of importance to know, *what sort* of labourers these Americans are; for, though a labourer is a labourer, still there is some difference in them; and, these Americans are *the best that I ever saw.* They mow *four acres* of *oats, wheat, rye,* or *barley* in a day, and, with a cradle, lay it so smooth in the swarths, that it is tied up in sheaves with the greatest neatness and ease. They mow *two acres and a half of grass* in a day, and they do the work well. And the crops, upon an average, are all, except the wheat, *as heavy* as in England. The English farmer will want nothing more than these facts to convince him, that the labour, after all, is not so *very dear.*

The causes of these performances, so far beyond those in England, is first, the men are *tall* and well built; they are *bony* rather than *fleshy;* and they *live,* as to food, as well as man can live. And, secondly, they have been *educated* to do much in a day. The farmer here generally is at the *head* of his "boys," as they, in the kind language of the country, are called. Here is the best of examples. My old and beloved friend, Mr. JAMES PAUL, used, at the age of nearly *sixty* to go at *the head of his mowers,* though his fine farm was his own, and though he might, in other respects, be called a rich man; and, I have heard, that Mr. ELIAS HICKS, the famous Quaker Preacher, who lives about nine miles from this spot, has this year, at *seventy* years of age, cradled down four acres of rye in a day. I wish some of the *preachers* of other descriptions, especially our fat parsons in England, would think a little of this, and would betake themselves to "work with their hands" the things which be good, that they may have to give to "him who needeth," and not go on any longer gormandizing and swilling upon the labour of those who need.

Besides the great quantity of work performed by the American labourer, his *skill*, the *versatility* of his talent, is a great thing. Every man can use an *ax*, a *saw*, and a *hammer*. Scarcely one who cannot do any job at rough carpentering, and mend a plough or a waggon. Very few indeed, who cannot kill and dress pigs and sheep, and many of them Oxen and Calves. Every farmer is a *neat* butcher; a butcher for *market*; and, of course, "the boys" must learn. This is a great convenience. It makes you so independent as to a main part of the means of housekeeping. All are *ploughmen*. In short, a good labourer here, can do *any thing* that is to be done upon a farm.

The operations necessary in miniature cultivation they are very awkward at. The *gardens are ploughed* in general. An American labourer uses a *spade* in a very awkward manner. *They poke the earth about* as if they had no eyes; and toil and muck themselves half to death to dig as much ground in a day as a Surrey man would dig in about an hour of hard work. *Banking, hedging,* they know nothing about. They have no idea of the use of a *bill-hook*, which is so adroitly used in the coppices of Hampshire and Sussex. An *ax* is their tool, and with that tool, at *cutting down* trees or *cutting them up*, they will do *ten times* as much in a day as any other men that I ever saw. Set one of these men on upon a wood of timber trees, and his slaughter will astonish you.

WHAT NEW ENGLAND ATE AND DRANK IN 1832

OVER A century ago, school children, and many older people as well, had life made easier and the world more intelligible by Samuel Griswold

Goodrich (1793–1860). This New England editor, publisher and author brought to his literary age the unusual gift of commonsense clarity. His geographies, for example, followed the pleasantly informative footsteps of Geographer Jedidiah Morse and improved upon the latter in liveliness and a working breadth of knowledge.

His industry was ceaseless and his output amazing. He was editor and chief author of about 170 volumes, 116 of them under his famous pseudonym of Peter Parley, a name frequently pirated. Many were the fields of Goodrich's learning and instruction; the range of his books encompassed most subjects of education and thought. Of the 170 books, Goodrich was probably sole author of a majority. Four years before his death he wrote that 7,000,000 copies of his works had been sold and that "about three hundred thousand volumes are now sold annually."

From A System of Universal Geography, Popular and Scientific . . . Embracing Numerous Sketches from Recent Travels. *By* S. G. Goodrich.[1]

Food and Drink. The food may be well called substantial, and the variety and quantity are enough to denote a land of plentiful supply. An English traveller in New England remarks that Henry IV who wished that each of his subjects might be so rich as to have a chicken for his Sunday dinner, could here have had his generous desire more than gratified. The breakfast, which in the country, is held at an early hour, and often by sunrise, is no evanescent thing. In a farmer's family, it consists of little less than ham, beef, sausages, pork, bread, butter, boiled potatoes, pies, coffee, and cider. The use of coffee in the morning, and of tea at night, is almost universal. At hotels and boarding houses, the standing breakfast is of beef, mutton, ham, broiled chickens, sausages, tripe, various kinds of fish, tongue, bread, butter, coffee, and cider. Few people are so poor as not to have animal food, at least twice a day; on Saturday, it is usual to have for dinner, salted cod fish.

Cider which is drunk so early in the day is used in every house; in common seasons, it is worth about a dollar the barrel. In the country, it is hardly considered reputable among farmers to omit to offer cider to any casual visitor, or traveller; it is usually

[1] Published in 1832.

Fun and feasting at a Fourth of July picnic.

drawn in a mug or bowl. It is slightly an intoxicating liquor; but is seldom taken in a quantity that intoxicates.

The most usual bread in cities is made of wheat flour; in the country the common bread is made of a mixture of rye and indian corn. The meal of the latter is also boiled in water to the consistency of a thick paste, called "mush" or "hasty-pudding," which is eaten in milk, or with butter and molasses; and when cold cut into slices, and fried in butter or lard. This is the subject of a poem, which, if not the best, is at least one of the most popular in New England. Perhaps however the true national dish for which the absentee has the greatest longing, is the white bean, which is baked with salt pork, and saturated with the fat. No feast in the country is perfect or indeed excusable without it. The common dinner hour in the country is at noon, and in cities from one to two o'clock. The dinners are despatched in such haste that the table is often cleared in half an hour.

The artificial or intoxicating drinks the most general after cider, are beer, and the various kinds of spirits. The use of beer however has much diminished the consumption of spirits; and the light French wines which are growing into use, are excellent sub-stitutes for the deleterious mixtures of brandy and other ingredients, that were sold as the wines of Portugal or Madeira.

To render light and pure wines cheap and common, until our own vineyards supply us, would be of national advantage. Intemperance is not the vice of countries where wines are abundant. In France and Italy it is a rare sight to behold an intoxicated man. In New England, the West India rums, and brandy, gin, and whiskey are much consumed; they are found at every inn, and in too many other places. But the most deleterious spirit is the New England rum, which is distilled from molasses, and sold so cheap that the wages of a day's labor, will purchase three gallons of it.

Intemperance has been the great domestic curse of New England, compared with which the sweeping of a plague would have been a visit of mercy. Three fourths of the poverty and crime that lead to the alms-house and the prison, spring from this fruitful source. There is hardly a village in New England, where the traveller will not see more than one miserable object and often the wreck of a noble man, degraded below the rank of brutes, by habitual intoxication.

The tide of ruin, however, is fast receding. Numerous associations called temperance societies, have done much to check the evil. The members of these agree to taste no spirits themselves, to supply none to their laborers, and often, to hold no traffic with those who do. In Massachusetts there are upwards of 200 of these associations, and in the United States there have been returns from 2,200, which is perhaps about half the number of the whole. These have all been established of late years. According to the report of the American temperance society, not less than 3000 persons have been rescued from intemperance, that hard road to leave, by the influence of these societies, and there can be no record of the far greater number saved from falling. More than 1000 distilleries have been stopped; and more than half that were in operation in New York, a year ago, are disused, and three thousand venders of spirits have openly renounced the traffic. The diminution of foreign liquors passing through the New York customhouse, for the last three years, is more than 53 per cent. An instance of the reduction may be seen in Belchertown, Massachusetts, where all the taxes of the place amounted to $3430. A society was formed, and the result was, that while in 1824, 8055 gallons of spirits were consumed, at the cost of $4883, in 1828, but 1090 gallons were sold, at $1440. The saving thus made, was $13 more than all the taxes of the town.

THIS WAS JUST A SMALL DINNER

TABLES GROANED in the days of Andrew Jackson. This selection concerns the menu for a small dinner, for a dozen persons all told, that Margaret Bayard Smith gave for Harriet Martineau in 1835. Mrs. Smith has already described for us Admiral Cockburn's activities during the occupation of Washington. Miss Martineau commented, some pages back, on the American's use of tobacco.

From The First Forty Years of Washington Society. *Portrayed by the Family Letters of Mrs. Samuel Harrison Smith (Margaret Bayard). From the Collection of her Grandson, J. Henley Smith. Edited by Gaillard Hunt.*

TO MRS. KIRKPATRICK

Washington, Febr. 4th 1835.

Friday 5th. And now for Miss Martineau, since you desire to hear a little more about her, particularly of the day she passed here. But I really must give you a previous scene which amused me extremely and will not be without some diversion for you. The day previous to our little dinner party, I sent for Henry Orr, whom I had always employed when I had company and who is the most experienced and fashionable waiter in the city. He is almost white, his manners gentle, serious and respectful, to an uncommon degree and his whole appearance quite gentlemanly. "Henry," said I, when he came, "I am going to have a small dinner party, but though small, I wish it to be peculiarly nice, every thing of the best and most fashionable. I wish you to attend, and as it is many years since I have dined in company, you must tell me what dishes will be best." "Boulli,[1] I suppose, is not out of fashion?" "No, indeed, Ma'am! A Boulli at the foot of the table is indispensable, no dinner without it." "And at the head?" "After the soup, Ma'am, fish, boil'd fish, and after the Fish, canvas-backs, the Boulli to be removed, and Pheasants." "Stop, stop Henry," cried I, "not so many removes if you please!" "Why, ma'am, you said your company was to be a dozen and I am only telling you what is absolutely necessary. Yesterday at Mr. Woodbury's[2] there was only 18 in company and there were 30 dishes of meat." "But Henry I am not a Secretary's lady. I want a small, genteel dinner." "Indeed, ma'am, that is all I am telling you, for side dishes you will have a very small ham, a small Turkey, on each side of them partridges, mutton chops, or sweetbreads, a macaroni pie, an oyster pie"—"That will do, that will do, Henry. Now for vegetables." "Well, ma'am, stew'd celery, spinage, salsify, cauliflower." "Indeed, Henry, you must substitute potatoes, beets, etc." "Why ma'am, they will not be genteel, but to be sure if you say so, it must be so. Mrs. Forsyth[3] the other day, *would* have a plum-pudding, she will keep to old fashions." "What, Henry, plum-pudding out of fashion?" "La, yes, Ma'am, all kinds of puddings and pies." "Why, what then must I have at the head and foot of the table?" "Forms of ice cream at the head, and a pyramid of anything, grapes, oranges, or anything handsome at the foot." "And the other dishes?" "Jellies, custards, blanc-mange, cakes, sweet-meats, and sugar-plums." "No nuts, raisons, figs, etc., etc.?" "Oh, no, no, ma'am, they are quite vulgar." "Well, well, Henry. My dessert is, I find, all right, and your dinner I suppose with the exception of one or two things. You may order

[1] Boulli was boiled or stewed meat.
[2] Levi Woodbury of New Hampshire was Secretary of the Treasury.
[3] Probably the wife of John Forsyth of Georgia, Secretary of State.

me the pies, partridges, and pheasants from the French cook, and Priscilla can do the rest." "Indeed, Ma'am, you had best"—"No more, Henry," interrupted I. "I am not Mrs. Woodbury." But I carried my point in only having 8 dishes of meat, tho' I could not convince Henry, it was more genteel than a grander dinner.

WHEN OUR MODESTY RAN WILD

OVERDONE DELICACY and modesty was an American trait that marshaled remarks from more than one commentator in the first half of the nineteenth century. Like all human reactions, this one had traveled past center.

Captain Frederick Marryat (1792–1848) was in the British navy until 1830, when he resigned to fix his attention on writing. In the latter part of the War of 1812, the ship Marryat was on cruised off our coast and, it is stated, helped in capturing several "merchant ships and privateers." It was in 1837–38 that Marryat journeyed in the United States and Canada and brought out two books on his impressions. These, allowing for prejudice, throw some lively light upon our people and their ways. This former navy man wrote a number of popular novels— *Mr. Midshipman Easy*, for instance—and then, toward the end of his life, continued with books for younger readers.

From A Diary In America, with Remarks On Its Institutions. *By Capt. Marryat, C. B.*

They[1] object to everything nude in statuary. When I was at the house of Governor Everett, at Boston, I observed a fine cast of the Apollo Belvidere; but in compliance with general opinion, it was hung with drapery, although Governor Everett himself is a gentleman of refined mind and high classical attainments, and

[1] The Americans, in 1837.

What well-dressed city folk were wearing during Captain Marryat's visit to the U. S. This Currier print displays fall and winter fashions for 1837 and 1838.

quite above such ridiculous sensitiveness. In language it is the same thing. There are certain words which are never used in America, but an absurd substitute is employed. I cannot particularize them after this preface, lest I should be accused of indelicacy myself. I may, however, state one little circumstance which will fully prove the correctness of what I say.

When at Niagara Falls I was escorting a young lady with whom I was on friendly terms. She had been standing on a piece of rock, the better to view the scene, when she slipped down, and was evidently hurt by the fall: she had, in fact, grazed her shin. As she limped a little in walking home, I said, "Did you hurt your leg much?" She turned from me, evidently much shocked, or much offended,—and not being aware that I had committed any very heinous offence, I begged to know what was the reason of her dis-

A BEAUTIFUL PAIR.

*Some very slight waning of that sense of modesty which put pantaloons
on piano legs in 1837, to the amazement of Captain Marryat,
can be observed in this Currier and Ives print made 45 years later.
But the bikini bathing suit remained almost a century
away.*

pleasure. After some hesitation, she said that as she knew me well,
she would tell me that the word *leg* was never mentioned before
ladies. I apologized for my want of refinement, which was attributa-
ble to having been accustomed only to *English* society; and added,
that as such articles must occasionally be referred to, even in the
most polite circles in America, perhaps she would inform me by
what name I might mention them without shocking the company.
Her reply was, that the word *limb* was used; "nay," continued she,
"I am not so particular as some people are, for I know those who
always say limb of a table, or limb of a piano-forte."

There the conversation dropped; but a few months afterwards
I was obliged to acknowledge that the young lady was correct when
she asserted that some people were more particular than even she
was.

I was requested by a lady to escort her to a seminary for young ladies, and on being ushered into the reception-room, conceive my astonishment at beholding a square piano-forte with four *limbs*. However, that the ladies who visited their daughters might feel in its full force the extreme delicacy of the mistress of the establishment, and her care to preserve in their utmost purity the ideas of the young ladies under her charge, she had dressed all these four limbs in modest little trousers, with frills at the bottom of them!

NATHANIEL HAWTHORNE'S NOTES ON RURAL FESTIVITIES

THIS IS not a story of war and crises but a rural spectacle in western Massachusetts, meet for pleasant and unhurried contemplation.

Nathaniel Hawthorne (1804–64), in some of his earlier years, was accustomed to take a summer walking trip through various parts of New England. In August 1838, he was in Williamstown, Massachusetts, at commencement time. The previous year his first book had been published, *Twice Told Tales*, and the public response had been languid. Fame had not reached him. *Mosses From An Old Manse*, *The Scarlet Letter*, *The Snow Image* and all the rest were still to come.

His *American Note Books*, well worth scanning, came from the journals in which he recorded daily happenings, at home and on his journeys, as well as reflections and ideas for articles and books.

From Passages from the American Note-Books. *By Nathaniel Hawthorne.*

Wednesday, August 15th.—I went to Commencement at Williams College,—five miles distant. At the tavern were students with ribbons, pink or blue, fluttering from their button-holes, these being the badges of rival societies. There was a considerable

The Williams College campus in 1846.

gathering of people, chiefly arriving in wagons or buggies, some in barouches, and very few in chaises. The most characteristic part of the scene was where the pedlers, ginger-bread-sellers, etc., were collected, a few hundred yards from the meeting-house. There was a pedler there from New York State, who sold his wares by auction, and I could have stood and listened to him all day long. Sometimes he would put up a heterogeny of articles in a lot,—as a paper of pins, a lead pencil, and a shaving-box,—and knock them all down, perhaps for ninepence. Bunches of lead pencils, steel pens, pound-cakes of shaving-soap, gilt finger-rings, bracelets, clasps, and other jewelry, cards of pearl buttons, or steel ("There is some steel about them, gentlemen, for my brother stole 'em, and I bore him out in it"), bundles of wooden combs, boxes of matches, suspenders, and, in short, everything,—dipping his hand down into his wares with the promise of a wonderful lot, and producing, perhaps, a bottle of opodeldoc, and joining it with a lead pencil,—and when he had

sold several things of the same kind, pretending huge surprise at finding "just one more," if the lads lingered; saying, "I could not afford to steal them for the price; for the remorse of conscience would be worth more,"—all the time keeping an eye upon those who bought, calling for the pay, making change with silver or bills, and deciding on the goodness of banks;[1] and saying to the boys who climbed upon his cart, "Fall down, roll down, tumble down, only get down"; and uttering everything in the queer, humorous recitative in which he sold his articles. Sometimes he would pretend that a person had bid, either by word or wink, and raised a laugh thus: never losing his self-possession, nor getting out of humor. When a man asked whether a bill were good: "No! do you suppose I'd give you good money?" When he delivered an article, he exclaimed, "You're the lucky man," setting off his wares with the most extravagant eulogies.

[1] Individual banks issued their own money or banknotes, whose value rested upon the stability of the issuer.

The people bought very freely, and seemed also to enjoy the fun. One little boy bought a shaving-box, perhaps meaning to speculate upon it. This character could not possibly be overdrawn; and he was really excellent, with his allusion to what was passing, intermingled, doubtless, with a good deal that was studied. He was a man between thirty and forty, with a face expressive of other ability, as well as of humor.

A good many people were the better or the worse for liquor. There was one fellow,—named Randall, I think,—a round-shouldered, bulky, ill-hung devil, with a pale, sallow skin, black beard, and a sort of grin upon his face,—a species of laugh, yet not so much mirthful as indicating a strange mental and moral twist. He was very riotous in the crowd, elbowing, thrusting, seizing hold of people; and at last a ring was formed, and a regular wrestling-match commenced between him and a farmer-looking man. Randall brandished his legs about in the most ridiculous style, but proved himself a good wrestler, and finally threw his antagonist. He got up with the same grin upon his features,—not a grin of simplicity, but intimating knowingness. When more depth or force of expression was required, he could put on the most strangely ludicrous and ugly aspect (suiting his gesture and attitude to it) that can be imagined. I should like to see this fellow when he was perfectly sober.

There were a good many blacks among the crowd. I suppose they used to emigrate across the border, while New York was a slave State. There were enough of them to form a party, though greatly in the minority; and, a squabble arising, some of the blacks were knocked down, and otherwise maltreated. I saw one old negro, a genuine specimen of the slave negro, without any of the foppery of the race in our part of the State,[2]—an old fellow, with a bag, I suppose of broken victuals, on his shoulder, and his pockets stuffed out at his hips with the like provender; full of grimaces and ridiculous antics, laughing laughably, yet without affectation; then talking with a strange kind of pathos about the whippings he use to get while he was a slave;—a singular creature, of mere feeling, with some glimmering of sense. Then there was another gray old negro, but of a different stamp, politic, sage, cautious, yet with boldness enough, talking about the rights of his race, yet so as not to provoke his audience; discoursing of the advantage of living under laws, and the

[2] Hawthorne was from Salem, in the eastern end of the State.

wonders that might ensue, in that very assemblage, if there were no laws; in the midst of this deep wisdom, turning off the anger of a half-drunken fellow by a merry retort, a leap in the air, and a negro's laugh. I was interested—there being a drunken negro ascending the meeting-house steps, and near him three or four well-dressed and decent negro wenches—to see the look of scorn and shame and sorrow and painful sympathy which one of them assumed at this disgrace of her color.

The people here show out their character much more strongly than they do with us; there was not the quiet, silent, dull decency of our public assemblages, but mirth, anger, eccentricity,—all manifesting themselves freely.

There were many watermelons for sale, and people burying their muzzles deep in the juicy flesh of them. There were cider and beer. Many of the people had their mouth half opened in a grin, which, more than anything else, I think, indicates a low stage of refinement. A low-crowned hat—very low—is common. They are respectful to gentlemen.

ENGAGING LOOK INTO A BUSY FARMHOUSE

THIS FAITHFUL description of a rural New York farmer's home in 1848, and its industrious occupants was written by the eldest daughter of James Fenimore Cooper (*The Deerslayer, The Last of the Mohicans, The Spy*, etc.).

Susan Fenimore Cooper (1813–94) was devoted to her father, traveling with him and acting as his secretary. She lived and absorbed her country knowledge in the Cooper home in Cooperstown, New York, which was founded by her grandfather.

Rural Hours (1850) deals with the common things of life, especially with Nature, in a manner marked by knowledge, simplicity and clarity. The book, which passed through at least nine editions—and won praise from Washington Irving and William Cullen Bryant—was in general subject and treatment forerunner of Henry Thoreau's *Walden* (1854). James Fenimore Cooper (1789–1851) arranged the publication of his daughter's book and was very proud of its success.

Miss Cooper wrote three or four other books, including another on Nature and one composed of extracts from her father's works, and after his death furnished introductions to many of his books. In 1873 she founded in Cooperstown the Orphan Home of the Holy Savior.

From Rural Hours. *By A Lady.*

From the window of the room in which we were sitting, we looked over the whole of Mr. B——'s farm; the wheat-field, corn-field, orchard, potato-patch, and buckwheat-field. The farmer himself, with his wagon and horses, a boy and a man, were busy in a hay-field, just below the house; several cows were feeding in the meadow, and about fifty sheep were nibbling on the hillside. A piece of woodland was pointed out on the height above, which supplied the house with fuel. We saw no evergreens there; the trees were chiefly maple, birch, oak, and chestnut; with us, about the lake, every wood contains hemlock and pine.

Finding we were interested in rural matters, our good friend offered to show us whatever we wished to see, answering all our many questions with the sweet, old smile peculiar to herself. She took us to the little garden; it contained potatoes, cabbages, onions, cucumbers, and beans; a row of current-bushes was the only fruit; a patch of catnip, and another of mint, grew in one corner. Our farmers, as a general rule, are proverbially indifferent about their gardens. There was no fruit on the place besides the apple-trees of the orchard; one is surprised that cherries, and pears, and plums, all suited to our hilly climate in this county, should not receive more attention; they yield a desirable return for the cost and labor required to plant and look after them.

Passing the barn, we looked in there also; a load of sweet hay had just been thrown into the loft, and another was coming up the road at the moment. Mr. B—— worked his farm with a pair of horses only, keeping no oxen. Half a dozen hens and some geese were the only poultry in the yard; the eggs and feathers were carried, in the fall, to the store at B—— Green, or sometimes as far as our own village.

This busy barnyard scene appeared in 1850, the same year in which Susan Fenimore Cooper published her book, Rural Hours.

They kept four cows; formerly they had had a much larger dairy; but our hostess had counted her threescore and ten, and being the only woman in the house, the dairy-work of four cows, she said, was as much as she could well attend to. One would think so; for she also did all the cooking, baking, washing, ironing, and cleaning for the family, consisting of three persons; besides a share of the sewing, knitting, and spinning. We went into her little buttery; here the bright tin pans were standing full of rich milk; everything was thoroughly scoured, beautifully fresh, and neat. A stone jar of fine yellow butter, whose flavor we knew of old, stood on one side, and several cheeses were in press. The wood-work was all painted red.

While our kind hostess, on hospitable thought intent, was preparing something nice for tea, we were invited to look about the little sitting-room, and see "farm ways" in that shape. It was both parlor and guest-chamber at the same time. In one corner stood a maple bedstead, with a large, plump feather bed on it, and two tiny pillows in well-bleached cases at the head. The walls of the room were whitewashed, the wood-work was unpainted, but so thoroughly scoured, that it had acquired a sort of polish and oak color. Before the windows hung colored paper blinds. Between the windows was a table, and over it hung a small looking-glass and a green and yellow drawing in watercolors, the gift of a friend. On one side stood a cherry bureau; upon this lay the Holy Bible, and that its sacred pages had been well studied, our friend's daily life could testify. Near the Bible lay a volume of religious character from the Methodist press, and the Life of General Marion. The mantel-piece was ornamented with peacocks' feathers, and brass candlesticks, bright as gold; in the fireplace were fresh sprigs of asparagus. An open cupboard stood on one side, containing the cups and saucers, in neat array, a pretty salt-cellar, with several pieces of cracked and broken crockery, of a superior quality, preserved for ornament more than use.

Such was the "square room," as it was called. It opened into the kitchen, and as our dear hostess was coming and going, dividing her time between her biscuits and her guests, very impartially, at last we asked permission to follow her, and sit by her while she was at work, admiring the kitchen quite as much as we did the rest of her neat dwelling. The largest room in the house, and the one most used, it was just as neat as every other corner under the roof. The chimney was very large, according to the approved old custom, and it was garnished all about with flatirons, brooms, brushes, holders, and cooking utensils, each in its proper place. In winter, they used a stove for cooking, and in the very coldest weather, they kept two fires burning, one in the chimney, another in the stove. The walls were whitewashed. There was a great deal of wood-work about the room—wainscoting, dressers, and even the ceiling being of wood— and all was painted dark red. The ceiling of a farm-kitchen, especially if it be unplastered, as this was, is often a pretty rustic sight, a sort of store-place, all kinds of things hanging there on hooks or nails driven into the beams; bundles of dried herbs, strings of red peppers and of dried apples hanging in festoons, tools of various kinds, bags of different sorts and sizes, golden ears of seed-corn ripening, vials of physic and nostrums for man and beast, bits of cord and twine, skeins of yarn and brown thread just spun, and lastly, a file of newspapers. The low red ceiling of Farmer B——'s kitchen was not quite so well garnished in July as we have seen it at other times, still, it was by no means bare, the festoons of apples, red peppers, and Indian corn being the only objects wanting. By the window hung an ink bottle and a well-fingered almanac, witty and wise, as usual. A year or two since, an edition of the almanac was printed without the usual prognostics regarding the winds and sunshine, but it proved a complete failure; an almanac that told nothing about next year's weather nobody cared to buy, and it was found expedient to restore these important predictions concerning the future snow, hail, and sunshine of the county. Public opinion demanded it.

A great spinning-wheel, with a basket of carded wool, stood in a corner, where it had been set aside when we arrived. There was a good deal of spinning done in the family; all the yarn for stockings, for flannels, for the cloth worn by the men, for the colored woolen dresses of the women, and all the thread for their coarse toweling, etc., etc., was spun in the house by our hostess, or her granddaughter, or some neighbor hired for the purpose.

PALENESS OF AMERICAN WOMEN EXPLAINED

Ivan Golovin was exiled from Russia by the reactionary Czar Nicholas I in 1843, and became a naturalized Englishman. He was author of a number of books, including his popular *Russia Under The Autocrat, Nicholas I*. During his visit to this country in 1855 he wrote letters for the New York *Tribune* and the *National Intelligencer* of Washington. In this book about the U.S. in 1855 both his English and his observations are his own, and both are unhackneyed.

From Stars and Stripes, or American Impressions. *By Ivan Golovin*.

The American ladies well deserve the name given to them by the Indians of *pale faces*, their paleness being excessive indeed. This is owing to rocking chairs, to sexual excesses producing consumption, but particularly to absence of vegetation in the cities.

THE CAKE MANIA IN INDIANA

BACK OF all the antagonisms and alarms of the world, home life goes on. With interruptions so brief that they do not count in the span of the years, there is cooking and visiting and the amenities of social intercourse. The cake mania grappled Indiana around 1870.

Mrs. Sarah Smith Pratt (1853–1943) brings back that page of history. Her recalling is conscientious and factual and her book is the more illuminating for its unpretention. By the "Old Crop" she means "those fine ancestors who were born during the first half of the past century, some a little earlier, some a little later."

She, herself, was born in Delphi, Indiana, the daughter of Nicholas and Catherine Armor Smith who came to that state in the early 1840s. She married William Dudley Pratt who published the Logansport *Daily Journal*. Mrs. Pratt assisted in the editorial work, and for a few years edited the weekly *Sunday Critic*, a publication of her husband's. She had contributions in several eastern magazines, including the *Atlantic Monthly*. Mrs. Pratt's lifelong interest in church affairs involved editorship of the *Church Chronicle*, a diocesan monthly magazine, the conduct of a department in the *Living Church*, Episcopal weekly, and her book, *Episcopal Bishops in Indiana*. In 1896 the family moved to Indianapolis where her husband established a printing business that is now carried on by two sons.

From The Old Crop in Indiana. *By Sarah S. Pratt.*

The Pound Party succeeded the donation party; the Shower evolved from the Pound Party. The Mite Society, combining money and sociability, the Housewarming, the Infair, which followed a wedding, were all ancestors of social affairs which now appear in more elegant form and with new names. Hospitality was more spontaneous because getting around was more difficult. Nobody made calls but everybody visited. To stay to a meal or over night was almost a necessity.

The style of entertainment called a party was of epidemic nature then. Perhaps it has always been so. Weeks of social quietude

Parlor in an Indiana home of the 1870's.

would be broken by someone's having a party. This was the outbreak, the preliminary rash of the party epidemic.

These hostesses vied with each other in the supper which was
called a lap-supper (now, a buffet) and was an elaborate feast. When
Mrs. Bringhurst, who hated food, ventured early in the seventies,
to serve only coffee, cake and ices at her party, and to introduce a
guessing game, society took sides in discussing it; the people who
liked to guess, approved the innovation; the people who liked to
eat, condemned it; and I think the latter carried the day.

"If you don't have your party soon the celery will be gone and
what will you do for chicken-salad?" With all respect for the
OLD CROP, it must be admitted that they were gourmands—an unpleasant word, but one well expressing the stuffing process of the
supper hour.

Succeeding the privations attending the Civil War, came the
cake mania. Sweetening coffee with molasses, using substitutes and
doing without rich things to eat, culminated in the post-war hostess
letting herself go in a great food revel. These women, all over the

Mid-West, at the behest of the Sanitary Commission, sent boxes, bales and barrels to hospitals and camps and this food orgy was a reaction from this war state of mind. It took the form of a gastronomic indulgence in which cake was supreme.

Catharine Beecher, sister of Henry Ward Beecher, had written a cook-book in the forties. Her distinguished brother had been or was to be a preacher in Indianapolis and his preaching, joined to his sister's cookery, must have been a perfect combination.

Mrs. Rabb's Mother used this cook-book and she has told me that in her childhood the favorites were pound cake, gold and silver cake, marble, jelly in layers, lemon, black cake—now called fruit cake—and cocoanut. Of all the cakes ever devised, the rich pound cake stood at the head. The first item of its composition, a pound of butter, insured a richness almost surfeiting. When to this was added the other ingredients, brandy, sugar and eggs, the result was a large loaf cake that was moist, kept well for company and was carefully conserved. . . .

. . . But there was still something to come, and when Angel's Food appeared there was a perfect furore over it. Women yearned to taste the wondrous confection, so suggestive of heavenly joys. Legends passed from lip to lip about it:

"A new pan, ungreased." "The whites of fifteen eggs." "No one must walk across the kitchen floor while the cake was baking." "The over door must be carefully opened and shut that there be no jarring." . . .

. . . At once this new cake, when mastered, joined or rather led the procession of cakes at all parties. The Angel cake, as its name was shortened, whitish brown, un-iced, light, spongy, something like a huge mushroom had the place of honor over the easier-made, better-known cake. And as I rather resentfully think of it, I am reminded of a big good-looking woman who was elected to an exclusive club only because she could afford to wear white clothes in winter. New uses of chocolate were started by the Chicago Exposition. Chocolate *Menier* or "manure" as it was artlessly called by some women, chocolate in every form of confection, new preparations for cakes and for drink were welcomed. Chocolate began to be served more as a drink. When Darius Baldwin, who had lived in South America, was given a cup of this at a reception, he stirred it rather contemptuously. "Do you ladies call this chocolate—in South America chocolate has to be eaten with a spoon—you can't drink it."

Chocolate cake had been one of the standards but there came new forms of it; devil's food, drops, melting cookies; there were sticky sky-scrapes; there were low solid loaves, spice, marshmallow, pink, white, yellow and even green cakes iced with pistachio. There were sand tarts, jelly drops.

"Can you suggest a new cake?" was the despairing cry of intending hostesses. It was not unusual to serve twenty different kinds of cake at a party and at Julia Merriam's wedding, there were twenty-two.

At a party in the early seventies the hostess drew me aside and asked if I would accept an uncut cake as I was to entertain on the following evening. I had sufficient but could not refuse so gracious a proffer. The next morning Mrs. Eversole's butler drove up in her carriage, bringing seven entire, beautiful cakes—an almost overwhelming and embarrassing gift.

And what was going on in Indiana was going on in the whole Mid-West. Women, to this day, from the different states, compare notes and laugh over this great cake riot, when a hostess felt unappreciated if every guest at her party did not taste every kind of cake.

The beginning of the end of this age of fine food came when cold chicken and turkey gave place to veal-loaf as the main meat dish. This loaf was said to be something hated by men and especially by some of the clergy who held chicken and turkey to be their inalienable rights. But rich salads, schmier-kase dressed with nuts and cream, pickles, slaw—olives came in later—helped atone for the loss of the favorites. Floating Island, or Float, and Blanc-mange were the end-of-the-feast dishes. When ices of varied sorts became commercialized and the freezer became available for home use, frozen dainties began to have the place they now fill.

ADVANCE CLEARANCE FOR SUICIDE

JACQUES OFFENBACH (1819–80), a musical conductor and composer— *Tales of Hoffmann* is his—came to this country from Paris in 1876 to conduct orchestras in New York and Philadelphia. Like other visitors to these shores he absorbed some interesting facts. Below he throws new light on suicides.

From Offenbach in America. *By Jacques Offenbach.*

Nor has anybody the right to hang himself in America.

A drunkard tries to hang himself, but fails, and is brought back to life after a few hours. When he has recovered his senses he is taken before the judge, who sentences him to six months' imprisonment. Usually it is only three months, but in this case it was an old offender, who had tried it once before. The third time he will be condemned to death. In order to take one's own life the previous authorization of the Governor is required.

THE ILL-TIMED BALL OF THE PLUTOCRATS

THE GILDED AGE, that phrase given circulation by Mark Twain, has been taken to mean the last quarter of the nineteenth century, when big fortunes were being made and advertised amid a social consciousness that tranquilly accepted vast disparities in wealth and health. The historians, Charles and Mary Beard, said in *The Rise of American Civilization* that the famous Bradley Martin ball of 1897 came "as if to put a climax to lavish expenditure"; that "this grand ball of the plutocrats astounded the country, then in the grip of a prolonged business depression with its attendant unemployment, misery and starvation."

This historic ball is here described and defended by Bradley Martin's brother. Not least in interest is the latter's inability to comprehend the criticisms; the ball helped retail trade, he declared.

Frederick Townsend Martin (1849–1914), idly rich and enamored of any sort of royalty all his life—his class went in much for European stays—claimed in his later years he conducted a "crusade against the

*"The Splendour of Versailles." The Bradley Martin
ball as seen by the artist who covered the event for* Harper's Weekly.

idle rich," and according to his lights he did. This crusade apparently
included support of certain charity projects, talks to the poor in London
and New York, and assertion of the theory that wealth should be shared.
He wrote *The Passing of The Idle Rich* (1911) and three other books—
including the one quoted here—of a reminiscent nature.

From Things I Remember. *By Frederick
Townsend Martin.*

Every year my brother Bradley and his wife spent their winters
in New York, when they entertained largely. One morning at
breakfast my brother remarked——

"I think it would be a good thing if we got up something; there
seems to be a great deal of depression in trade; suppose we send out
invitations for a concert."

"And pray, what good will that do?" asked my sister-in-law, "the money will only benefit foreigners. No, I've a far better idea; let us give a costume ball at so short notice that our guests won't have time to get their dresses from Paris. That will give an impetus to trade that nothing else will."

Directly Mrs. Martin's plan became known, there was a regular storm of comment, which arose in the first instance from the remarks made by a clergyman who denounced the costume ball from the pulpit.

"Yes," he raged, "you rich people put next to nothing in the collection plate, and yet you'll spend thousands of dollars on Mrs. Bradley Martin's ball."

The newspapers then took up the subject, and we were besieged by reporters, but my brother and his wife invariably refused to discuss the matter. Threatening letters arrived by every post, debating societies discussed our extravagance, and last, but not least, we were burlesqued unmercifully on the stage.

I was highly indignant about my sister-in-law being so cruelly attacked, seeing that her object in giving the ball was to stimulate trade, and, indeed, she was perfectly right, for, owing to the short notice, many New York shops sold out brocades and silks which had been lying in their stock-rooms for years.

The ball was fixed for February 10, 1897, and a day or two before Mrs. Martin met Theodore Roosevelt[1] in the street. "I'm very pleased that you and Mrs. Roosevelt are coming to the ball," she said.

"Oh," he replied, "my wife's going because she's got her costume, but, as one of the commissioners, I shall be outside looking after the police!"

I think every one anticipated a disturbance, but nothing of the kind took place, and the evening passed without any untoward incident.

The best way I can describe what is always known as the "Bradley Martin Ball," is to say that it reproduced the splendour of Versailles in New York, and I doubt if even the Roi Soleil himself ever witnessed a more dazzling sight. The interior of the Waldorf-

---

[1] He was then president of the New York City Police Board.

Bradley Martin.

Astoria Hotel was transformed into a replica of Versailles, and rare
tapestries, beautiful flowers and countless lights made an effective
background for the wonderful gowns and their wearers. I do not
think there has ever been a greater display of jewels before or since;
in many cases the diamond buttons worn by the men represented
thousands of dollars, and the value of the historic gems worn by
the ladies baffles description.

My sister-in-law personated Mary Stuart, and her gold embroidered gown was trimmed with pearls and precious stones. Bradley,
as Louis XV, wore a Court suit of brocade, and I represented a
gentleman of the period. The whole thing appealed most strongly to
my imagination, and my mind constantly reverted to the friend of

my childhood, the dear grandmother who would have been so keenly interested in it all. I remember that Mrs. James Beekman, as Lady Teazle, wore a lovely dress, which formerly belonged to an ancestress, and Mrs. Henry Burnet's satin petticoat was another family heirloom which left the scented seclusion of a cedar-wood chest for this interesting occasion.

Anne Morgan lent a touch of barbaric colour with her wonderful Pocahontas costume which had been made by Indians, and the suit of gold inlaid armour worn by Mr. Belmont was valued at ten thousand dollars. The power of wealth with its refinement and vulgarity was everywhere. It gleamed from countless jewels, and it was proclaimed by the thousands of orchids and roses, whose fragrance that night was like incense burnt on the altar of the Golden Calf.

I cannot conceive why this entertainment should have been condemned. We Americans are so accustomed to display that I should have thought the ball would not have been regarded as anything very unusual. Every one said it was the most brilliant function of the kind ever seen in America, and it certainly was the most talked about.

After the ball the authorities promptly raised my brother's taxes quite out of proportion to those paid by any one else, and the matter was only settled after a very acrimonius dispute. Bradley and his wife resented intensely the annoyance to which they had been subjected, and they decided to sell their house in New York and buy a residence in London.

TRAVEL AND HARDSHIPS

LAFAYETTE AND MADISON TRAVEL
INFORMALLY

UNCONVENTIONALITIES OF the great are matter of ceaseless interest to the rest of us. In 1784, the Marquis de Lafayette, James Madison, the future president, and the Marquis de Barbé-Marbois, chargé d'affaires of the French legation, found themselves members of a small party traveling through the wilds of western New York to observe a conference with the Indians at Fort Schuyler.

Madison, in letters to Thomas Jefferson, indicated that Lafayette—here for a visit after his Revolutionary services—furthered prospects of a satisfactory treaty. The Indians always inclined more to the French than to the Americans or English, and Lafayette addressed the Indian chiefs, "who denoted the highest reverence for him," wrote Madison.

Francois, Marquis de Barbé-Marbois (1745–1837) came to this country in 1779 as secretary of the French legation, later becoming consul-general and then chargé d'affaires, till in 1785 he was named governor of San Domingo. He married the socially prominent Elizabeth Moore of Philadelphia. Questions from him produced Thomas Jefferson's *Notes on Virginia*. He negotiated for France the Louisiana Purchase, securing over 50 percent more than the price named to him by Napoleon. Barbé-Marbois wrote several books and found his convictions able to serve all French governments, from Louis XVI to Louis Philippe. General Winfield Scott met Barbé-Marbois and his wife in Paris in 1815 and received from him "many anecdotes" of our "Congressional Government."

In listing the half-serious assignment of duties to the principal members of this little expedition, the author advertises the pleasant good fellowship prevailing, and presents Lafayette in unceremonious garb.

From Our Revolutionary Forefathers: The Letters of Francois, Marquis de Barbé-Marbois During His Residence in the United States as Secretary of the French Legation, 1779–1783. *Translated and Edited by Eugene Parker Chase.*

We continued our journey across superb country, but where everything recalled the war to us. We had divided up the duties. M. de Lafayette was in charge of the cavalry, M. de Caraman[1] was in charge of lodging, Mr. Madison directed the march, and I was cook for the troop. We had a bag of corn meal which was a great resource, tea, and chocolate. They[2] furnished us with butter in abundance, and if we asked for milk, great wooden pails of it were immediately filled and brought. We used to make a soup which became famous throughout the region, and often our hosts, instead of feeding us were fed by us. Cloaks and rugs were one of our great resources. I except, to be sure, M. de Lafayette, who seemed to be immune to the extremes of the seasons. He had taken, to protect himself from the rain, a cloak of gummed taffeta, which had been sent him from France wrapped up in newspapers. The papers had stuck to the gum, and there had not been time to get them off, so that the curious could read, on his chest or on his back, the *Journal de Paris*, the *Courier de l'Europe*, or news from other places.

In spite of the devastation to which the two banks of the Mohawk were a prey, the population there makes rapid growth. We found families of ten or twelve children, large and small, all in one bed. We were new sights for them, in a region where it is very rare to see strangers traveling for curiosity. Little Indians served us as domestic servants, and there was nothing which they refused to do. If we asked for a candlestick, an urchin four or five years old was placed near us with a candle in his hand. If we seemed discommoded by the heat, another took the place of screen for us. Often the honor of turning a wooden spit, which we had invented to cook our meat, troubled the peace of the family and made a division between brothers.

We began to meet savages more frequently, and everything told

[1] Maurice Riquet, *Chevalier* de Caraman, one of LaFayette's party in this country.
[2] The scattered settlers.

us that we were about to leave the white man's settlements to enter the territory of the Indians. All the scattered houses were still surrounded by stockades, with which, during the late war, they had been protected against the barbarians, and which had not always been sufficient to stop their ravages.

We found the roads worse than we could have imagined. After having traveled miles in the carriage, we were forced to give it up, on account of the continual danger of upsetting and the extreme fatigue of the horses. I left my phaeton at the "German flats"[3] and turned my two large carriage horses into riding horses. The coverings with which I had fortunately provided myself served me as a saddle, and in that half-savage equipage we made the rest of the journey to Fort Schuyler.[4] That is the place determined upon for negotiations between three commissioners sent by the Congress, and the chiefs and warriors of the six savage nations who live in the neighborhood of the Great Lakes which separate the United States from Canada. We found a great number of them assembled, but the commissioners had not yet arrived. The Indians had hurriedly built cabins in which they lodged with the families; some even, in spite of cold and frost, had merely shelters of branches of trees whose dried leaves protected them against neither wind nor rain. One of these cabins was filled with presents intended for the Indians. The other served as lodging for Mr. Kirkland, a missionary established amongst them for about twenty years. We shared his room, which was prepared for the commissioners from the Congress.

ORDEAL BY STAGECOACH

TRAVEL BY stagecoach was, take it by and large, a dismal business. Not a foreigner neglected to bestow upon it a warm and excited attention and, as to unexpected experiences he could do without, seemed to rank it along with our tobacco-spitting and our mosquitoes. Our own citizens,

---

[3] Fifteen miles southeast of the present Utica, New York.
[4] Located where Rome, New York, now stands.

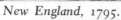

New England, 1795.

Midwest, 1825.

Concord, 1848 (in the National Museum).

Baltimore-Washington, 1830.

Californian Concord, 1860.

American Stagecoaches.

more accustomed to this lingering unease, have conveyed to us abundant evidence of delays and disasters.

Truth is, stage-coaching was an endured infliction because nothing better was available to the vast majority. The bad roads were bad beyond today's imagining, the stagecoaches were built to crowd in customers, not for pleasure; the horses were a very mixed lot and some of the drivers unreliable when sober. To book for the stagecoach was to invest in an ordeal, full of interest, but barren of comfort and a dubious insurance risk.

Two examples are provided here, one in New York State in 1848 and the other in our southwest a dozen years later.

Susan Fenimore Cooper, eldest daughter of novelist James Fenimore Cooper, lived in the family home at Cooperstown, sixty miles west of Albany. Earlier in this book she described a farmhouse in her home locality.

From Rural Hours. *By A Lady.*

The roads are at their worst just now; the stage-coach was ten hours yesterday coming the twenty-two miles from the railroad. That particular route, however, crossing the hills to the railway and canal, is the worst in the county. In the summer, our roads are very good; but for two or three weeks, spring and autumn, they are in a terrible state. And yet they have never been quite so bad as those in the clay soils of the western part of the State; the year before the railroad was completed between Geneva and Canandaigua, a gentle-man of the first village having business of consequence at the latter town early in the spring, was anxious to keep his appointment on a particular day, but he was obliged to give it up; the road, only six-teen miles, was so bad, that no carriage would take him. He made a particular application to the stage-coach proprietors; they were very sorry, but they could not accommodate him; it was quite out of the question: "We have twelve stage-coaches, at this very moment, sir, lying in the mud on that piece of road!" Now we never heard of a coach being actually left embedded in the mud on this road of ours, bad as it is; the passengers are often obliged to get out, and walk over critical spots; the male passengers are often requested to get out "and hold up the stage for the ladies"; often the coach is upset; frequently coach, passengers, and all sink into the slough to an alarming depth, when rails are taken from the fences to "pry the stage out"; but, by dint of working with a good will, what between the efforts of coachman, horses, and passengers, the whole party generally contrives to reach its destination, in a better or worse condition, somewhere within eighteen hours. They sometimes, however, pass the night on the road.

TRIP OF SIXTEEN DAYS BRINGS DELIRIUM

RAPHAEL PUMPELLY (1837–1923) was a colorful geologist and explorer. When approaching seventy, he organized and conducted—under auspices of the Carnegie Institution—an expedition into Central Asia to study ancient civilization and geology. His journey to Arizona, given below, was followed, the next two years, by work as geologist to the Japanese government; from Japan he continued geological observations in China and thence, in 1865, journeyed through Siberia to St. Petersburg. He became an expert on copper and iron ores of the Lake Superior region. Pumpelly did considerable work in his field for our government. He wrote several books on his travels.

From Across America and Asia. *By Raphael Pumpelly.*

In the autumn of 1860 I reached the westernmost end of the railroad in Missouri, finishing the first, and, in point of time, the shortest stage in a journey, the end of which I had not even attempted to foresee. My immediate destination was the silver mines of the Santa Rita, in Arizona, of which I was to take charge, as mining engineer, for a year, under the resident superintendent.

*An Overland Mail coach. Sixteen days in one of these
did Mr. Pumpelly in.*

Having secured the right to a back seat in the overland coach
as far as Tucson, I looked forward, with comparatively little dread,
to sixteen days and nights of continuous travel. But the arrival of a
woman and her brother, dashed, at the very outset, my hopes of an
easy journey, and obliged me to take the front seat, where, with my
back to the horses, I began to foresee the coming discomfort. The
coach was fitted with three seats, and these were occupied by nine
passengers. As the occupants of the front and middle seats faced
each other, it was necessary for these six people to interlock their
knees; and there being room inside for only ten of the twelve legs,
each side of the coach was graced by a foot, now dangling near the
wheel, now trying in vain to find a place of support. An unusually
heavy mail in the boot, by weighing down the rear, kept those of us
who were on the front seat constantly bent forward, thus, by taking
away all support from our backs, rendering rest at all times out of
the question.

My immediate neighbors were a tall Missourian, with his wife and two young daughters; and from this family arose a large part of the discomfort of the journey. The man was a border bully, armed with revolver, knife, and rifle; the woman, a very hag, ever following the disgusting habit of dipping[1]—filling the air, and covering her clothes with snuff; the girls, for several days overcome by sea-sickness, and in this having no regard for the clothes of their neighbors; —these were circumstances which offered slight promise of comfort on a journey which, at the best, could only be tedious and difficult.

For several days our road lay through the more barren and uninteresting parts of Missouri and Arkansas; but when we entered the Indian territory, and the fertile valley of the Red river, the scenery changed, and we seemed to have come into one of the Edens of the earth. Indeed, one of the scenes, still bright in my memory, embraced the finest and most extensive of natural park.

Before reaching Fort Smith[2] every male passenger in the stage had lost his hat, and most of the time allowed for breakfast at that town was used in getting new head-coverings. It turned out to be a useless expense, however, for in less than two days we were all again bareheaded. As this happens to the passengers of every stage, we estimated that not less than fifteen hundred hats were lost yearly by travellers, for the benefit of the population along the road.

After passing the Arkansas river, and travelling two or three days through the cultivated region of northeastern Texas, we came gradually to the outposts of population. The rivers became fewer, and deeper below the surface; the rolling prairie-land covered with grass gave way to dry gravelly plains, on which the increasing preponderance of species of cacti, and of the yucca, warned us of our approach to the great American desert. Soon after our entrance into this region we were one morning all started from a deep sleep by the noise of a party coming up at full gallop, and ordering the driver to halt. They were a rough-looking set of men, and we took them for robbers until their leader told us that they were "regulators," and were in search of a man who had committed a murder the previous day at a town we had passed through.

"He is a tall fellow, with blue eyes, and red beard," said the leader. "So if you have got him in there, stranger, you needn't tote him any further, for the branch of a mesquit tree is strong enough

[1] Chewing snuff.
[2] Arkansas.

for his neck." As I was tall, and had blue eyes and a red beard, I did not feel perfectly easy until the party left us, convinced that the object of their search was not in the stage.

One can scarcely picture a more desolate and barren region than the southern part of the Llano Estacado between the Brazos and Pecos rivers. Lying about 4,500 feet above the sea, it is a desert incapable of supporting other plant or animal life than scattered cacti, rattlesnakes, and lizards. Our route winding along the southern border of this region, kept on the outskirts of the Camanche country.

Here we were constantly exposed to the raids of this fierce tribe, which has steadily refused to be tamed by the usual process of treaties and presents. They were committing serious depredations along the route, and had murdered the keepers at several stations. We consequently approached the stockade station houses with considerable anxiety, not knowing whether we should find either keepers or horses. Over this part of the road no lights were used at night, and we were thus exposed to the additional danger of having our necks broken by being upset.

The fatigue of uninterrupted travelling by day and night in a crowded coach, and in the most uncomfortable positions, was beginning to tell seriously upon all the passengers, and was producing a condition bordering on insanity. This was increased by the constant anxiety caused by the danger from Camanches. Every jolt of the stage, indeed any occurrence which started a passenger out of the state of drowsiness, was instantly magnified into an attack, and the nearest fellow-passenger was as likely to be taken for an Indian as for a friend. In some persons, this temporary mania developed itself to such a degree that their own safety and that of their fellow-travellers made it necessary to leave them at the nearest station, where sleep usually restored them before the arrival of the next stage on the following week. Instances have occurred of travellers jumping in this condition from the coach and wandering off to a death from starvation upon the desert.

Over the hard surface of this country, which is everywhere a natural road, we frequently travelled at great speed, with only half-broken teams. At several stations, six wild horses were hitched blindfolded into their places. When everything was ready, the blinds were removed at a signal from the driver, and the animals started off at a run-away speed, which they kept up without slackening till the next station, generally twelve miles distant. In these cases the driver had no further control over his animals than the ability to guide them; to stop, or even check them, was entirely beyond his power; the frightened horses fairly flying over the ground, and never stopping till they drew up exhausted at the next station. Nothing but the most perfect presence of mind on the part of the driver could prevent accidents. Even this was not always enough, as was proved by a stage which we met, in which every passenger had either a bandaged head or an arm in a sling.

At El Paso we had hoped to find a larger stage. Being disappointed in this, I took a place outside, between the driver and conductor. The impossibility of sleeping had made me half delirious, and we had gone but a few miles before I nearly unseated the driver by starting suddenly out of a dream.

I was told that the safety of all passengers demanded that I should keep awake; and as the only means of effecting this, my neighbors beat a constant tatoo with their elbows upon my ribs. During the journey from the Rio Grande to Tucson my delirium increased, and the only thing I ever remembered of that part of the route was the sight of a large number of Indian campfires at Apache pass. My first recollection after this, is of being awakened by the report of a pistol, and of starting up to find myself in a crowded room, where a score or more of people were quarrelling at a gaming table. I had reached Tucson and had thrown myself on the floor of the first room I could enter. A sound sleep of twelve hours had fully restored me, both in mind and body.

THEY SURVIVED TO NAME IT— DEATH VALLEY

THE OVERLAND journey to the California gold fields in 1849 was companioned by suffering and tragedy. William Lewis Manly (1820–1903) became familiar with both, as a member of a party that deviated from the regular Salt Lake City–Los Angeles trail, seeking the illusory short cut, and eventually found itself—men, women and children—helpless in Death Valley, that forsaken, barren waste just over the Nevada line, in California.

Manly and John Rogers—two of the youngest men of the small group—set out to seek rescue. It was an undertaking of imposing proportions. They did not know the way and, incessantly anguished by thirst and hunger, they had around 250 miles of desert and rock and rugged mountains to overcome. They conquered the Panamint Mountains and the Argus and the Slate ranges, and the Mojave Desert and the San Bernardino chain, among other obstacles, emerging at a point not far north of Los Angeles, about New Year's Day 1850.

Manly and his companions were "responsible for the application of the name 'Death Valley,'" declared Prof. Owen Cochran Coy, director of the California State Historical Association, in *The Great Trek*.

William Lewis Manly and his family moved from Vermont to Michigan when he was about ten years old. Soon he became a roamer in the woods and rivers of that Middle West. After he reached California —during the trip he kept a diary that was later lost—he tried mining and merchandising for a while and then, in 1859, bought a farm near San Jose. He married and lived near or in San Jose the rest of his life, attending reunions of California pioneers, and apparently content with the quietude of civilization. His book, following some years of reminiscences contributed to newspapers, first appeared in 1894.

The initial portion of the following excerpts furnishes a hint of the adversities encountered by Manly and Rogers in their quest for succor; the last part depicts their return to those awaiting them in Death Valley.

From Death Valley in '49. *By William Lewis Manly.*

We turned now west again, making for a cañon, up which we passed in the hope that we should find at some turn a little basin of rain water in some rock. We traveled in it miles and miles, and our mouths became so dry that we had to put a bullet or a small smooth stone in and chew it and turn it around with the tongue to induce a flow of saliva. If we saw a spear of green grass on the north side of a rock, it was quickly pulled and eaten to obtain the little moisture it contained.

We were so nearly worn out that we tried to eat a little meat, but after chewing a long time, the mouth would not moisten it enough so we could swallow, and we had to reject it. It seemed as if we were going to die with plenty of food in our hand, because we could not eat it.

We tried to sleep but could not. After a little rest we noticed a bright star two hours above the horizon, and from the course of the moon we saw the star must be pretty truly west of us. We talked a little, expressing fear that we could not endure the terrible thirst much longer. The thought of the women and children waiting for our return made us feel more desperate than if we were the only ones concerned. We thought we could fight to the death over a water hole if we could only secure a little of the precious fluid. No one who has never felt the extreme of thirst can imagine the distress, the despair, which it brings. I can find no words, no way, to express it so others can understand.

The moon gave us so much light that we decided we would start on our course, and get as far as we could before the hot sun came out; so we went on slowly and carefully in the partial darkness, the only hope left to us being that our strength would hold out till we could get to the shining snow on the great mountain before us. We reached the foot of the range we were descending about sunrise. There was here a wide wash from the snow mountain, down which some water had sometime run after a big storm and divided into little rivulets, only reaching out a little way before they had sunk into the sand. . . .

. . . In order not to miss a possible bit of water we separated and agreed upon a general course; if either one should find water he was to fire his gun as a signal. After I had gone about a mile or so I heard Rogers' gun and went in his direction. He had found a little ice that had frozen under the clear sky. It was not thicker than window glass. After putting a piece in our mouths we gathered all we could and put it into the little quart camp kettle to melt. We gathered just a kettleful, besides what we ate as we were gathering, and kindled a little fire and melted it.

I can but think how providential it was that we started in the night for in an hour after the sun had risen that little sheet of ice would have melted and the water would have sunk into the sand. Having quenched our thirst we could now eat, and found that we were nearly starved also. In making this meal we used up all our little store of water, but we felt refreshed and our lives were renewed so that we had better courage to go on.

. . . We were some seven or eight miles along the road[1] when I stopped to fix my moccasin while Rogers went slowly along. The little mule went on ahead of both of us, searching all around for little bunches of dry grass, but always came back to the trail again, giving us no trouble. When I had started up again I saw Rogers ahead leaning on his gun and waiting for me, apparently looking at something on the ground. As I came near enough to speak I asked what he had found and he said, "Here is Captain Culverwell,[2] dead." He did not look much like a dead man. He lay upon his back with arms extended wide, and his little canteen, made of two powder flasks, lying by his side. This looked indeed as if some of our saddest forebodings were coming true. How many more bodies should we find? Or should we find the camp deserted, with never a trace of the former occupants?

One hundred yards now to the wagons and still no sign of life, no positive sign of death, though we looked carefully for both. We feared that perhaps there were Indians in ambush, and with nervous, irregular breathing we counseled what to do. Finally Rogers suggested that he had two charges in his shotgun and I seven in the Colt rifle, that I fire one of mine and await results before we ventured any nearer, and if there were any of the red devils there we could kill some of them before they got to us. And now both closely watching the wagons I fired the shot. Still as death and not a move for a moment, and then as if by magic a man came out from under a wagon and stood up looking all around, for he did not see us. Then he threw up his arms high over his head and shouted, "The boys have come! The boys have come!" Then other bare heads appeared, and Mr. Bennett and wife and Mr. Arcane came toward us as fast as ever they could. The great suspense was over. Our hearts were first in our mouths, then the blood all went away and left us almost

[1] Near the end of their return trip, to those waiting in Death Valley.
[2] Captain Culverwell had remained with the party in Death Valley.

fainting as we stood and tried to step. Some were safe, perhaps all of those nearest us, and the dark shadow of death that had hovered over us, and cast what seemed a pall upon every thought and action, was lifted and fell away, a heavy oppression gone. Bennett and Arcane caught us in their arms and embraced us with all their strength, and Mrs. Bennett when she came fell down on her knees and clung to me like a maniac in the great emotion that came to her, and not a word was spoken. If they had been strong enough they would have carried us to camp upon their shoulders. As it was they stopped two or three times, and turned as if to speak, but there was too much feeling for words; convulsive weeping would choke the voice.

All were a little calmer soon, and Bennett soon found voice to say, "I know you have found some place, for you have a mule." Mrs. Bennett through her tears looked staringly at us, as she could hardly believe our coming back was a reality, and then exclaimed: "Good boys! O, you have saved us all! God bless you forever! Such boys should never die!" It was some time before they could talk without weeping. Hope had almost died within them, and now when the first bright ray came it almost turned reason from its throne. A brighter, happier look came to them than we had seen and then they began to ply us with numberless questions, the first of which was, "Where were you?"

We told them it must be two hundred and fifty miles yet to any part of California where we could live. Then came the question, "Can we take our wagons?" "You will have to walk," was our answer, for no wagons could go over that unbroken road that we had traveled. As rapidly and carefully as we could we told them of our journey and the long distance between the water holes; that we had lost no time and yet had been twenty-six days on the road; that for a long distance the country was about as dry and desolate as the region we had crossed east of this camp.

There was no end to the questions about the road we had to answer, for this was uppermost in their minds, and we tried to tell them and show them how we must get along on our return. We told them of the great snow mountains we had seen all to the north of our road, and how deep the snow appeared to be, and how far west it extended. We told them of the black and desolate ranges and buttes to the south, and of the great dry plains in the same direction. We told them of the Jayhawkers' trail,[3] of Fish's dead body, of the salt lake and slippery alkali water to which we walked, only to turn away in disappointment, of the little sheets of ice which saved our lives, of Doty's camp and what we knew of those gone before, of the discouraged ones who gave us their names to send back to friends, of the hawk and crow diet, of my lameness, of the final coming out into a beautiful valley, in the midst of fat cattle and green meadows, and the trouble to get the help arranged on account of our not knowing the language to tell the people what we needed. They were deeply impressed that my lameness had been a blessing in disguise, or we would have gone on to the coast and consumed more time than we did in walking slowly to favor the crippled knee. Our sad adventures and loss of the horses in returning were sorrowfully told and we spoke of the provisions we had been able to bring on the little mule which had clambered over the rocks like a cat; that we had a little flour and beans, and some good dried meat with fat on it which we hoped would help to eke out the poorer fare and get them through at last.

They said they had about given up our coming back a week before, and had set about getting ready to try to move on themselves.

They had taken off the covers of the wagons to make them into houses for the oxen, so they could be used as pack animals. The strong cloth had been cut into narrow strips and well made into breast straps and breeching, for the cattle were so poor and their hide so loose it was almost impossible to keep anything on their backs. They had emptied the feathers out of the beds to get the cloth to use, and had tried to do everything that seemed best to do to get along without wagons. . . .

. . . When Mrs. Bennett was ready to show me what to do on the cloth harness, we took a seat under the wagon, the only shady place, and began work. The great mountain I have spoken of as the snow mountain has since been known as Telescope Peak, reported to be eleven thousand feet high. It is in the range running north and south which has no other peak so high. Mrs. Bennett questioned me closely about the trip, and particularly as to whether I had left

[3] A group, calling themselves the Jayhawkers, had started on the alleged short-cut with the Manly company, but had left the latter at Death Valley. Manly and Rogers, in their trek for help, had overtaken some of the Jayhawkers. Both Fish and Doty belonged to this group.

anything out which I did not want her to know. She said she saw her chance to ride was very slim, and she spoke particularly of the children, as it was impossible for them to walk. She said little Martha had been very sick since we had been gone, and for many days they had expected her to die. They had no medicine to relieve her and the best they could do was to select the best of the ox meat and make a little soup of it and feed her. They had watched her carefully for many days and nights, expecting they would have to part with her any time and bury her little body in the sands. Sometimes it seemed as if her breath would stop, but they had never failed in their attentions; at last they were rewarded by seeing her improve slowly, and even relish a little food, so that if no relapse set in they had hopes of bringing her through. They brought the little one and showed her to me, and she seemed quite different from what she had been when we went away. Then she could run about camp, climb out and in the wagons, and move about so spryly that she reminded me of a quail. Now she was strangely misshapen. Her limbs had lost all the flesh and seemed nothing but skin and bones, while her body had grown corpulent and distended, and her face had a starved, pinched and suffering look, with no healthy color it.[4]

NON-SKED STEAMBOATING WITH NO HOLDS BARRED

STEAMBOATING ON the Mississippi and its tributaries, around 1846, was often picturesquely haphazard, as Charles Edward Pancoast bears witness. Trips were improvised to catch a paying load. Passengers took their chances on safety and on eventual arrival at destination. Encounters with sandbars were common to most trips and, occasionally, sterner trouble, such as the hit-and-run steamboat, was met. Pancoast and his friend, using St. Louis as headquarters, did business up the Osage and Missouri rivers.

Pancoast (1818–1906) left Philadelphia for the West in 1840 and after many adventures on the way—including those given here—and a

---

[4] Martha survived the trip to civilization.

stay in California, returned in 1854. In 1862–75 he was an alderman in Philadelphia, where he was in the real estate business. His memoirs, written after the event, were completed in 1890.

From A Quaker Forty-Niner, The Adventures of Charles Edward Pancoast on the American Frontier. *Edited by Anna Paschall Hannum.*

About this time my Old Friend Abram Skinkle conceived the idea of purchasing a Steam Boat to run up the Osage in the Spring, when the Water was high, and in the dry season to run up the Missouri; and knowing me to be out of business, he proposed to me to join him in the Adventure. As his proposition appeared to me to have in it the elements of success, I assented, and we went to St. Louis to purchase a suitable Boat. Many were offered for sale, but they were adapted, either not to the Trade, or not to our Purse; but we finally purchased an old Boat called the *Otter*, of about 350 tons capacity, drawing (light) about eighteen inches of water. As Skinkle's purchasing ability was limited, I had to take a two-thirds interest in her, and he the other third. It was agreed that he should be Captain, and I Clerk. Of course we were both Novices at the business, but Skinkle had a good business capacity (a very important thing in Steam Boating) and we secured good offers.

By the first of March we had her fitted up and at the Levee. We put up our Sign for the Osage River, and soon secured a number of Passengers and as much Freight as we could carry. We made two trips to Warsaw without any serious interruption, clearing about $1000 on each, and made a third trip with more delay and less profit.

Although the Osage generally became so low by the middle of June that it could not be navigated with any certainty of success, we put up for another trip. When we arrived at the mouth of the Osage, we observed that the water was low, but continued on our Journey; but we were delayed at every Bar.

When we arrived at Linn Creek, we had already consumed ten days on our trip; and Capt. Burgess (our Pilot) informed us we could go no further until there was a rise in the River. The Pas-

St. Louis about 1850.

sengers deserted us and took to land Travel, with no method of con-
veyance except what Nature afforded them. We lay at Linn Creek
for several days at an expense of $75.00 per day. Then there came a
heavy shower, which raised the River enough to permit us to run up
to Warsaw; but the River fell so rapidly that we met with great
difficulty and delay in getting out.

The Osage River had now become too low for navigation, and
we had to look elsewhere for business. We raised our Sign for St.
Joseph[1] on the Missouri River, although we had grave doubts in regard to our success, as there were many finer and faster Boats in the
Missouri River Trade. We had to engage almost an entire new Crew.
The Pilots were the highest-priced and most independent Fellows
we had to deal with. We succeeded in obtaining two at the low price
of $200 for the Chief (an Irishman) and $100 for his Indian Assistant. We had to pay the Chief Engineer $125 and his Assistant
$75. (The larger Boats paid $400 per month for their two Pilots, and

[1] Warsaw and St. Joseph are both in Missouri.

It was this type of steamboat, probably somewhat smaller in size, that Pancoast and his partner, starting from St. Louis, ran up the Missouri and Osage rivers.

$300 for two Engineers; and some of the largest had four Engineers.) We soon engaged all the Freight we desired, but could not obtain the prices we received on the Osage River.

We left St. Louis in the evening with about 170 tons of Freight, 75 Cabin Passengers, and about 50 Deck Passengers, which was more encouraging than we had anticipated. We pursued our passage to St. Joseph without interruption, sparring[2] over only a few Bars, and made the trip in less than twelve days, with a profit of about $350.

This trip proving fairly profitable, we concluded to make another, and in a few days we were loaded with Freight and a goodly number of Passengers. We had on board five Catholic Priests, and on the evening we were to start a number of Rats were seen going ashore. About half of our Crew, regarding these as ill omens, refused to go with us, and we were delayed in consequence of having to ship other men. We put off, however, with good cheer, until we approached the mouth of the Missouri River, about twenty miles

[2] Assisting a vessel over a bar by use of poles.

above St. Louis, when we saw a large Mississippi Boat bearing toward us. Our Pilot was hugging the center of the River, in order to avoid the strong Current on the Illinois side, which was our proper place. We thought the other Boat was out of her course, and would give way toward the shore, where there was abundance of room; but she came rapidly on, striking us near the Bow, and trimmed off every timber to the Stem, letting our Wheel House, Shaft, and Cook House down into the River, and leaving one side of the Hull completely bare. In consequence of the large amount of weight removed from that side, we lay over on the other, and it took active work to keep us from turning over and sinking. Two Deck Passengers and one of the Priests were thrown overboard and drowned, and several others made narrow escapes. The other Boat did not deign to stop to see what damage had been done. We cast Anchor and repaired the Hull so that we could right her up, and in the morning managed to run down on one Wheel to St. Louis, where the Boat lay on the Docks for three weeks at a cost of over $1000.

When we came off the Docks we put up our Sign for Iowa Point, a Landing above St. Joseph. This was further up the Missouri than Boats usually ran, but we were induced to go there by a Merchant who had a large invoice of Goods for that point, and was willing to pay a good price for the Freight. (At that time St. Joseph was the extreme northwestern Town of any importance on the Missouri River; Kansas City consisted of a few Houses under the hill, and there were no Towns at Leavenworth, Atchison, Omaha, Iowa Point, or Council Bluffs.) We proceeded on our trip with no uncommon interruptions until we came to a Wood Pile about twenty miles above St. Joseph, where we lay up for the night in a country occupied by Kickapoo Indians. During our suspension of business we had lost our Mate, and had employed a burly Irishman by name of Dodd, who shipped an Irish Crew. As soon as we had put on the Wood and paid the old Indian who claimed it, the Crew left for the Indian Village (about a mile inland) and did not return until the next morning, some of them in a very besotted condition. Capt. Skinkle sharply reproved the Mate for his conduct, whereupon Dodd, with the whole Crew, marched to the Office and demanded their Wages. We refused to pay them, and they marched ashore, leaving us in the Wilderness without Mate or Crew. But we were not to be outdone that way, and the Officers and a Passenger took turns as Firemen until we reached Iowa Point. Here our Shipper went into the country and returned with a dozen men to unload his Freight. We induced three of them to act as Firemen as far as St. Joseph, where we procured half a dozen green "Pukes"[2] to ship with us until we could pick up better qualified men. The trip was made in fourteen days, with some profit to us.

After another trip up the Missouri with indifferent success, we found in St. Louis several Merchants from Warsaw and one from Osceola, forty miles further up the River; and with them Capt. Burgess, our Osage River Pilot. They all wanted us to make a trip up the Osage, the Osceola man offering us round prices if we succeeded in getting there. As the Pilot reported the River high, we agreed to make the trip. Our load was soon on, and we set off with flying colors, running up to Warsaw in four and a half days. The River kept up well, and we announced that we would continue our trip to Osceola, upon which a number of Warsaw Merchants made up an Excursion Party to go with us, and the Town was ransacked for good things to eat and drink.

We arrived at Osceola before night. Our Freight was soon discharged to the delight of our Merchant, who saw himself $500 the gainer through getting his Freight by Boat; otherwise he should have had to haul it a hundred miles from Boonville by Wagon, after paying Freight and Storage. It was now about the fifth of December, and the weather had suddenly become very cold. Ice was forming, and it was snowing; and as the River was falling an inch an hour, Capt. Burgess advised us to return to Warsaw that night. We turned our Boat downstream about nine o'clock with all the jolly Party on board. Neither Burgess nor his Assistant, Smoot, was very familiar with the River above Warsaw, and both were apprehensive of missing the Channel; but we went on merrily for about twenty miles, when the Pilots made a great blunder and ran us full length on a Bar in the middle of the River, with a good Channel on either side. After working with the Spars for two hours we threw up the Sponge, and settled in our minds that this lonely Sand Bar was to be our home for the Winter. Such of the Crew as were not willing to stay for their board were discharged with an allowance for Stage Fare to Jefferson City, and left immediately, leaving only Skinkle and myself, the Engineer, the Bar Keeper, the Watchman, the Carpenter and the Cook.

[2] Colloquial name for Missourians.

On the second morning the Bar was dry land, with several acres for our Playground. As we were so elegantly docked, we concluded to make the best of our position, and spend our time in painting and repairs.

EMIGRANTS TO A CITY THAT WASN'T THERE

SALE OF distant real estate, guaranteed to confer economic disaster upon the purchaser, is a time-honored racket. The settlement of new territory has always been harvest time for the handlers of plats and maps and fast talk. The calamitous case of Rollingstone, illumined at its conclusion but not in its beginning, was unusual but in all probability not unique.

Another manifestation of the frontier was the insecurity of a town's future. Some waxed fast and flourished busily and importantly, only to subside soon into ruins, their very names a fading remembrance. The author recalls three such.

Charles Edward Russell (1860–1941), newspaperman, author and politician, goes back to his youth for reminiscence of the Great River. He was born on it, in Davenport, Iowa. Later he held executive newspaper positions in New York and Chicago, was Socialist candidate for senator and governor and mayor in New York, wrote many books on many subjects, and held federal appointments in the First World War period, including membership on our 1917 diplomatic mission to Russia.

From A-Rafting On The Mississip'. *By Charles Edward Russell.*

Of the good ship *Dr. Franklin No. 2*, Captain Russell Blakely was at one time the master, and that reminds me of the tragic story of Rollingstone, which on many a night in the pilot-house I have heard recounted and wondered over.

As the flood of emigrants poured west and the new empire began to take shape out of the prairie waste, the river[1] hummed with traffic and new towns sprang up about every five miles of its course. Of some of these not a trace now remains. It is odd to reflect on this reversal of the ordinary process of development on the Western Hemisphere, and to view long stretches of silent corn-fields or empty meadow where within the memory of living men were busy streets and thriving industry.

Rockingham, Iowa—did you ever hear of Rockingham, Iowa? I doubt if diligent search now would reveal so much as a brick of an old foundation wall of Rockingham, Iowa. Yet it was in its time the future great metropolis of the upper Mississippi. It stood on the right bank of the main stream directly opposite the mouth of Rock River, and what made its importance was the transfer of traffic between the Mississippi and the Rock. There were warehouses and stores and a hotel and a fair array of dwellings in Rockingham. Once it aspired to be the county seat and perhaps the state capital. And now it is like the city of Petra in Edom.

Read's Landing (Minnesota)—that busy, thriving, confident little city, more than two thousand inhabitants when I knew it. Twenty steamboats at a time have lain before its water-front waiting for the tardy ice to move out of Lake Pepin. Lines of stages used to start from it for St. Paul and Mankato when the navigation was interrupted. Famed for its hotels it was, in those days, its inhabitants proclaiming that in proportion to its population it had more than any other city in the country. They might have been right, for more than twenty fully equipped caravansaries were in operation. The loggers used to come down with their great log drives and then tarry for days or a week in an attempt to add color to the local landscape, usually succeeding beyond one's fondest dreams. No place on the river was more famous. Read's Landing—it used to issue bonds for public improvements that were actually made. Once it deemed itself a rival of St. Paul and would have thought scorn to be compared with St. Anthony Falls.[2] And now, I am told, it has a total population of ninety-three souls, and grass is mown in the streets that used to echo with drays and stages. The river flows past as before, out of the mystery above and into the mystery below; the old posts to which

[1] The Mississippi.
[2] Minneapolis is built around the Falls.

the steamboats used to tie up are still shown to the curious; and a row of old houses are the ghosts of a dead and gone traffic.

Cassville, Wisconsin—did you ever hear of Cassville? Once it was the prize boom town of the upper river and with complacency saw its future as Wisconsin's capital. The people even went so far as to build the statehouse in readiness for the glad event. They certainly did. In my time we used to go ashore at Cassville to look at it as a curiosity—one end used as a hotel, a great and imposing structure of brick, not at all ill-planned nor ill-built. Reasonably, Cassville cherished this prospect; it was the liveliest city in the State and the best located. The river was the great highway. Cassville was the river entrepot for all the region around and always would be. Handsomely it grew and throve. In anticipation of its coming glory, it was well laid out even into the pathless jungle of bottom undergrowth beyond and beyond. Cassville—it is still on the maps, or on some maps. Persons still live there, the railroad has a station and a station agent. But if the ghost of Captain Russell Blakely should come up from the old abandoned and weed-grown steamboat-landing, he would never believe that he was looking upon Cassville.

All this as a necessary prologue to Rollingstone.

It was in the boom year of 1852. The *Dr. Franklin* was then running regularly between Galena[3] and St. Paul, loaded on her up trips to her utmost capacity with emigrants moving northwest.

One afternoon she had just pulled out of Galena, when a gentleman of port and circumstance came to the clerk's office, with an air of business drew forth his wallet, and said:

"I want a ticket to Rollingstone."

"It gathers no moss," said the clerk, who had a facetious turn. "Where would you like to go to?"

"I said Rollingstone," said the traveler with dignity.

"Say it again," said the clerk. "You ain't thinking of Prairie du Chien, are you?"

"No, sir," said the traveler, stiffly. "Not being crazy, I'm not thinking of any place except the place I want to go to, which is Rollingstone."

"There isn't any such place," said the clerk, beginning in his turn to be annoyed. "What ails you?"

"That so?" said the traveler. "Cast your eye over that," and he

[3] Galena, Illinois.

drew out an elaborate printed map, with beautiful illustrations around the border. It bore in uncompromising terms the statement that it was a map of the city of Rollingstone, situate on the Mississippi River, and to judge from documentary evidence a city of metropolitan moment. There were streets and buildings, schools, a post-office, warehouses, theatre, and at a wharf-boat on the riverfront this same good ship *Dr. Franklin* loading and unloading much freight and many passengers. The esthetic and the cultural were by no means neglected in Rollingstone. Streets there had beautiful curves and vistas; a large greenhouse provided for the growing of flowers at public expense; a large lecture-hall, a public library, churches, met every need of the panting soul of man as well as of his bodily comfort. The clerk looked and gasped. He had been sailing up and down the river for seven years and never had he suspected such magnificence.

"That's where I'm going," said the traveler. "Rollingstone City, and I want my ticket."

A consultation of the boat's officers was called and the map put down among them. Not one had ever heard of the thriving city of Rollingstone; but Captain Blakely, who knew every inch of the river, surmised from the shape of the bend shown on the map that the place was on land owned by the Sioux Indians, about three miles above the spot where the great chief Wabasha had his headquarters. There was as much of a settlement as in the crater of Vesuvius. In a radius of ten miles of the spot dwelt only one white man, and if another should appear the gentle Sioux would probably make short work of him and his hair. The streets, the warehouses, the school, the wharf-boat and alas! library, church, and flower-decked greenhouse were pure imagination.

When this had been explained to the traveler, he was still unconvinced. The previous fall, he said, a small army of artisans had left New York for Rollingstone to build the houses and the school and the library and the rest of the city, and now the colonists were on their way to take possession of the place, he being the advance courier. . . .

When the *Franklin* returned to Galena, here, sure enough, were the Rollingstone colonists, about one hundred in number, men and women, all from New York City. They took passage on the *Franklin*

*Cassville, Wisconsin, one of the boom-and-ghost towns on
the Mississippi described by author Russell.*

undeterred when the honest Captain Blakely told them about the
advance courier and what they might expect at Wabasha's prairie.
Some had brought wagons and farm implements, all had their
furniture, some of them had their canary birds and cats and gold-
fish.

When the *Dr. Franklin* reached the prairie, off piled the whole
outfit, wagons, baggage, canary birds, and all, with not a thing to
shelter them bigger than the lee side of a hair trunk and not a sign
of human habitation, except that three miles away the smoke arose
lazily from the camp-fires of the great chief Wabasha.

The next boat from Galena brought another detachment of
the colony; more came on succeeding steamers until there were
about four hundred squatting helplessly on the river's edge. In those
days there was rafting of lumber from the mills above on the Mississippi and St. Croix. The colonists got boards from these rafts
and erected a few lean-tos under which they cowered. The fallacious
Moses that had led them into the wilderness never appeared. I

could never learn what became of him, nor what he gained from the cruel deception he practised. An experienced pioneer drifting by on a raft suggested to the wretched, shivering colonists that huts could be built of sod, and some of these dreary structures arose on the plain. A part of the troop lived in caves dug into the river bank.

Then came an epidemic of mysterious disease and carried off many. Perhaps mercifully. It seems that they had no physician among them and the nearest medical man was seventy-five miles away. The agricultural skill acquired in a New York lecture-room broke down early when put to the test. Many things were planted; few matured. Some of the settlers learned to fish and some to do a little hunting. The summer drifted by, the fall came on, and the disheartened survivors began to try to make their way back to New York. A few determined to stick out the winter. Brief experience with the cutting winds and driving snows of that latitude was enough, and when spring came the only traces of the city of Rollingstone, once magnificent on the map, were a few tottering shacks and a long row of graves.

ASPECTS OF RELIGION

THE INCREDIBLE RELIGIOUS "JERKS"

"THE JERKS" and other religious excesses are here described by two of
the most forceful itinerant Methodist preachers of the first quarter of
the last century, Lorenzo Dow (1772–1834) and Peter Cartwright
(1785–1872). Dow rode the countryside from 1794 to about 1820,
reaching to Alabama in the South and Natchez, Mississippi, in the West.
Cartwright exhorted in Kentucky, Tennessee, Indiana, Ohio and Illinois,
most of his daily pilgrimaging being from 1803 to around 1824.

These evangelists, fired with the quenchless zeal of the reformer,
performed mighty feats of endurance, suffered poverty, sickness and revile-
ment, and were tough and quick to meet trick and physical opposition
in kind.

The national religious climate still smelled of brimstone; emotional
releases for those on or near the frontiers were infrequent. The large
harvests for the solitary-riding preachers were gathered at the camp-
meetings—those unique, indescribable outlets for religion and delirium.
They were staged in the solemn woods, lighted by flickering pine torches,
tents and wagons and horses off on the edges, rude benches for the
many hundreds attending, up front the space for the converts; and all
hands given Hark-From-The-Tomb for days and nights by a succession of
gymnastic, thundering preachers. "The Jerks," marking the process to
conversion, were a characteristic product.

From The Dealings of God, Man, and the Devil, as exemplified in the Life, Experience, and Travels of Lorenzo Dow, in a Period of Over Half a Century: Together with His Polemic and Miscellaneous Writings, Complete. To which is added the Vicissitudes of Life, by Peggy Dow (Two volumes in one.).

I had heard about a singularity called the *jerks* or *jerking exercise* which appeared first near Knoxville,[1] in August last, to the great alarm of the people; which reports at first I considered as vague and false; but at length, like the Queen of Sheba, I set out to go and see for myself; and sent over these appointments into this country accordingly.

When I arrived in sight of this town, I saw hundreds of people collected in little bodies; and observing no place appointed for meeting, before I spoke to any, I got on a log and gave out a hymn; which caused them to assemble round, in solemn attentive silence. I observed several involuntary motions in the course of the meeting, which I considered as a specimen of the jerks.

Hence to Mary's-ville, where I spoke to about one thousand five hundred; and many appeared to feel the word, but about fifty felt the jerks; at night I lodged with one of the Nicholites, a kind of Quakers who do not feel free to wear colored clothes: I spoke to a number of people at his house that night. Whilst at tea I observed his daughter, (who sat opposite to me at the table) to have the jerks; and dropped the teacup from her hand in the violent agitation: I said to her, "Young woman, what is the matter?" she replied, "I have got the jerks." I asked her how long she had it? she observed "a few days," and that it had been the means of the awakening and conversion of her soul, by stirring her up to serious consideration about her careless state, etc.

Sunday, February 19th, I spoke in Knoxville to hundreds more than could get into the court-house, the Governor being present: about one hundred and fifty appeared to have jerking exercise,

[1] Tennessee: about 1804.

among whom was a circuit preacher, (Johnson) who had opposed them a little before, but he now had them powerfully; and I believe he would have fallen over three times had not the auditory been so crowded that he could not, unless he fell perpendicularly.

After meeting I rode eighteen miles to hold meeting at night: the people of this settlement were mostly Quakers; and they had said, (as I was informed) that Methodists and Presbyterians have the *jerks* because they *sing* and *pray* so much, but we are a still peaceable people, wherefore we do not have them; however, about twenty of them came to meeting, to hear one, as was said, somewhat in a Quaker line: but their usual stillness and silence was interrupted; for about a dozen of them had the jerks as keen and as powerful as any I had seen, so as to have occasioned a kind of grunt or groan when they would jerk. It appears that many have under-valued the great revival, and attempted to account for it altogether on natural principles; therefore it seems to me, (from the best judgment I can form,) that God hath seen proper to take this method, to convince people, that he will work in a way to show his power; and sent the *jerks* as a sign of the times, partly in judgment for the people's unbelief, and yet as a mercy to convict people of divine realities.

I have seen Presbyterians, Methodists, Quakers, Baptists, Church of England, and Independents, exercised with the *jerks*; Gentleman and Lady, black and white, the aged and the youth, rich and poor, without exception; from which I infer, as it cannot be accounted for on natural principles, and carries such marks of involuntary motion, that it is no trifling matter: I believe that those who are most pious and given up to God, are rarely touched with it; and also those naturalists, who wish and try to get it to philosophize upon it are excepted: but the lukewarm, lazy, half-hearted, indolent professor, is subject to it, and many of them I have seen, who when it came upon them, would be alarmed and stirred up to redouble their diligence with God, and after they would get happy, were thankful it ever came upon them. Again, the wicked are frequently more afraid of it than the smallpox or yellow fever; these are subject to it; but the persecutors are more subject to it than any, and they sometimes have cursed, and swore, and damned

Lorenzo Dow—exhorting.

it, whilst jerking: there is no pain attending the jerks except they resist it, which if they do, it will weary them more in an hour, than a day's labour; which shows, that it requires the *consent* of the *will* to avoid suffering.

20th. I passed by a meeting-house where I observed the undergrowth had been cut up for a camp meeting, and from fifty to one hundred saplings, left breast high; which to me appeared so slovenish that I could not but ask my guide the cause, who observed they were topped so high, and left for the people to jerk by: this so excited my attention that I went over the ground, to view it; and found where the people had laid hold of them and jerked so powerfully, that they had kicked up the earth as a horse stamping flies: I observed some emotion, both this day and night among the people; a Presbyterian minister (with whom I stayed,) observed, "yesterday whilst I was preaching some had the jerks, and a young man from N. Carolina mimicked them out of derision and soon was seized with them himself, (which was the case with many others) he grew ashamed, and on attempting to mount his horse to go off, his foot jerked about so, that he could not put it into the stirrup; some youngsters seeing this, assisted him on, but he jerked so that he could not sit alone, and one got up to hold him on; which was done with difficulty: I observing this, went to him and asked him what he thought of it? said he, 'I believe God sent it on me for my wickedness, and making so light of it in others;' and he requested me to pray for him.

I observed his wife had it; she said she was first attacked with it in bed. Dr. Nelson said, he had frequently strove to get it, (in order to philosophize upon it,) but could not; and observed they could not account for it on natural principles. . . .

And so on to Abingdon in Virginia: the last jerks that I saw was on a young woman, who was severely exercised during meeting. She followed me into the house, I observed to her the indecency and folly of such public gestures and grunts; and requested (speaking sternly to make an impression on her mind) if she had any regard for her character, to leave it off; she replied, "I will if I can." I took her by the hand, looking her in the face and said, "do not tell lies." I perceived (by the emotion) that she exerted every nerve to restrain it, but instantly she jerked as if it would have jerked her out of her skin if it were possible; I did this to have an answer to others on the subject, which I told her, that my abruptness might leave no bad impression on her mind.

From The Autobiography of Peter Cartwright, The Backwoods Preacher. *Edited by*
W. P. Strickland.

Just in the midst of our controversies on the subject of the powerful exercises among the people under preaching, a new exercise broke out among us, called the *jerks*, which was overwhelming in its effects upon the bodies and minds of the people. No matter whether they were saints or sinners, they would be taken under a warm song or sermon, and seized with a convulsive jerking all over, which they could not by any possibility avoid, and the more they resisted the more they jerked. If they would not strive against it and pray in good earnest, the jerking would usually abate. I have seen more than five hundred persons jerking at one time in my large congregations. Most usually persons taken with the jerks, to obtain relief, as they said, would rise up and dance. Some would run, but could not get away. Some would resist; on such the jerks were generally very severe.

To see those proud young gentlemen and young ladies, dressed in their silks, jewelry, and prunella, from top to toe, take the *jerks*, would often excite my risibilities. The first jerk or so, you would see their fine bonnets, caps, and combs fly; and so sudden would be the jerking of the head that their long loose hair would crack almost as loud as a wagoner's whip.

While I am on this subject I will relate a very serious circumstance which I knew to take place with a man who had the jerks at a camp meeting, on what was called the Ridge, in William Magee's congregation. There was a great work of religion in the encampment. The jerks were very prevalent. There was a company of drunken rowdies who came to interrupt the meeting. These rowdies were headed by a very large drinking man. They came with their bottles of whiskey in their pockets. This large man cursed the jerks, and all religion. Shortly afterward he took the jerks, and he started to run, but he jerked so powerfully he could not get away. He halted among some saplings, and, although he was violently agitated, he took out his bottle of whiskey, and swore he would drink the damned jerks to death; but he jerked at such a rate he could not get the bottle to his mouth, though he tried hard. At length he fetched a sudden jerk, and the bottle struck a sapling and was broken to pieces, and spilled his whiskey on the ground. There was a great crowd gathered round him, and when he lost his whiskey he became very much enraged, and cursed and swore very profanely, his jerks still increasing. At length he fetched a very violent jerk, snapped his neck, fell, and soon expired, with his mouth full of cursing and bitterness.

I always looked upon the jerks as a judgment sent from God, first, to bring sinners to repentance; and, secondly, to show professors that God could work with or without means, and that he could work over and above means, and so whatsoever seemeth him good, to the glory of his grace and the salvation of the world.

There is no doubt in my mind that, with weak-minded, ignorant, and superstitious persons, there was a great deal of sympathetic feeling with many that claimed to be under the influence of this jerking exercise; and yet, with many, it was perfectly involuntary. It was, on all occasions, my practice to recommend fervent prayer as a remedy, and it almost universally proved an effectual antidote.

There were many other strange and wild exercises into which the subjects of this revival fell; such, for instance, as what was called the running, jumping, barking exercise. The Methodist preachers generally preached against this extravagant wildness. I did it uniformly in my little ministrations, and sometimes gave great offense; but I feared no consequences when I felt my awful responsibilities to God. From these wild exercises another great evil arose from the heated and wild imaginations of some. They professed to fall into trances and see visions; they would fall at meetings and sometimes at home, and lay apparently powerless and motionless for days, sometimes for a week at a time, without food or drink; and when they came to, they professed to have seen heaven and hell, to have seen God, angels, and devil and the damned; they would prophesy, and, under the pretense of Divine inspiration, predict the time of the end of the world, and the ushering in of the great millennium.

This was the most troublesome delusion of all, it made such

an appeal to the ignorance, superstition, and credulity of the people, even saint as well as sinner.

EVEN NEW ENGLAND FUNCTIONED ON HARD LIQUOR

HERE REVEREND LYMAN BEECHER and Horace Greeley bear testimony to the accepted ubiquity of strong drink in New England in the first quarter of the last century. It was in hearty usage at virtually every social occasion, from a gathering of Connecticut Congregational ministers down.

Horace Greeley (1811–1872), the nationally influential editor of the New York *Tribune*, spent his first nineteen years in his native New England and it is the drinking habits of this region he describes. He was the presidential candidate of the Independent Republicans and the Democrats in 1872.

Lyman Beecher (1775–1863), two of whose children, Henry Ward Beecher and Harriet Beecher Stowe, were more renowned than their father, was a Congregational minister at Litchfield, Connecticut, during most of his preaching life. From 1832 to 1850 he was head of Lane Theological Seminary, Cincinnati.

From Autobiography, Correspondence, Etc., of Lyman Beecher, D.D. *Edited by Charles Beecher.*

Soon after my arrival at Litchfield I was called to attend the ordination at Plymouth of Mr. Heart,[1] ever after that my very special friend. . . .

Well, at the ordination at Plymouth, the preparation for our

[1] This was about 1811.

creature comforts, in the sitting-room of Mr. Heart's house, besides food, was a broad sideboard covered with decanters and bottles, and sugar, and pitchers of water. There we found all the various kinds of liquors then in vogue. The drinking was apparently universal. This preparation was made by the society as a matter of course. When the Consociation arrived,[2] they always took something to drink round; also before public services, and always on their return. As they could not all drink at once, they were obliged to stand and wait as people do when they go to mill.

There was a decanter of spirits also on the dinner-table, to help digestion, and gentlemen partook of it through the afternoon and evening as they felt the need, some more and some less; and the sideboard, with the spillings of water, and sugar, and liquor, looked and smelled like the bar of a very active grog-shop. None of the Consociation were drunk; but that there was not, at times, a considerable amount of exhilaration, I can not affirm.

When they had all done drinking, and had taken pipes and tobacco, in less than fifteen minutes there was such a smoke you couldn't see. And the noise I can not describe; it was the maximum of hilarity. They told their stories, and were at the height of jocose talk. They were not old-fashioned Puritans. They had been run down. Great deal of spirituality on Sabbath, and not much when they got where there was something good to drink.

From Recollections of a Busy Life. *By* *Horace Greeley.*

In my childhood, there was no merry-making, there was no entertainment of relatives or friends, there was scarcely a casual gathering of two or three neighbors for an evening's social chat, without strong drink. Cider, always, while it remained drinkable without severe contortions of visage; Rum at all seasons and on all occasions, were required and provided. No house or barn was raised without a bountiful supply of the latter, and generally of both. A wedding without "toddy," "flip," "sling," or "punch," with rum

[2] Consociation was a Council of neighboring Congregational Churches.

undisguised in abundance, would have been deemed a poor, mean affair, even among the penniless; while the more fortunate and thrifty of course dispensed wine, brandy, and gin in profusion. Dancing—almost the only pastime wherein the sexes jointly participated —was always enlivened and stimulated by liquor. Militia trainings— then rigidly enforced at least twice a year—usually wound up with a drinking frolic at the village tavern. Election days were drinking days, as they still too commonly are; and even funerals were regarded as inadequately celebrated without the dispensing of spirituous consolation; so that I distinctly recollect the neighborhood talk, in 1820, after the funeral of a poor man's child, that, if he had not been mean as well as poor, he would have cheered the hearts of his sympathizing friends by treating them to at least *one* gallon of rum. I have heard my father say that he had mowed through the haying season of thirty successive years, and never a day without liquor; and the account of an Irishman who mowed and pitched throughout one haying, drinking only buttermilk, while his associates drank rum, yet accomplished more, and with less fatigue, than any of them was received with as much wondering incredulity as though it had been certified that he lived wholly on air. Nay: we had an ordination in Amherst[1] nearly fifty years ago,[2] settling an able and popular clergyman named Lord (I believe he is now the venerable ex-President of Dartmouth College) to the signal satisfaction of the great body of our people; and, according to my recollection, strong drink was more generally and bountifully dispensed than on any previous occasion: bottles and glasses being set on tables in front of many farmers' houses as an invitation to those who passed on their way to or from the installation to stop and drink freely. We have worse liquor now than we had then; and delirium tremens, apoplexy, palsy, etc., come sooner and oftener to those who use it; but our consumers of strong drink are a class; whereas they were then the whole people. The pious probably drank more discreetly than the ungodly; but they all drank to their own satisfaction, and, I judge, more than was consistent with their personal good.

My resolve not to drink was only mentioned by me at our own fireside; but it somehow became known in the neighborhood,

[1] New Hampshire.
[2] Greeley's recollections were published in 1868.

where it excited some curiosity, and even a stronger feeling. At the annual sheep-washing, in June following, it was brought forward and condemned; when I was required to take a glass of liquor, and, on my declining, was held by two or three youngsters older and stronger than I, while the liquor was turned into my mouth, and some of it forced down my throat. That was understood to be the end of my foolish attempt at singularity.

It was not, however. I kept quiet, but my resolution was unchanged; and, soon after my removal to Poultney,[3] I "assisted" in organizing the first Temperance Society ever formed in that town, —perhaps the first in the county. It inhibited the use of distilled liquors only; so that I believe our first president died of intemperance some years afterward; but a number still live to rejoice that they took part in that movement, and have since remained faithful to its pledge and its purpose. I recollect a story told at that time by our adversaries of a man who had joined the Temperance Society just organized in a neighboring township, and, dying soon afterward, had been subjected to an autopsy, which developed a cake of ice weighing several pounds, which had gradually formed and increased in his stomach, as a result of his fanatical devotion to cold water. Alas that most of our facetious critics have since died, and no autopsy was needed to develop the cause of *their* departure! A glance at each fiery proboscis, that irradiated even the cerements of the grave, was sufficient.

THE MELODRAMA OF A CAMP MEETING

FRANCES TROLLOPE's book on American manners aggravated us no end and, in the course of fashioning a lasting fame for itself, created the Americanism, "to trollope," meaning to perform an act condemned in the book. Her judgments, to be sure, were highly disapproving but the author seems to have written honestly and—she covered much more than manners in her volume—was reasonably just.

[3] Vermont.

*Emotion at a camp meeting. Mrs. Trollope was
repelled.*

She brought no glad and worshiping mind to her task. With a son
and two daughters she had journeyed to the Western town of Cincinnati
to recoup the family resources by establishing a bazaar or store for the
sale of fancy goods—a venture which failed. Her stay here of almost four
years, 1827–31, was largely in Cincinnati, so far removed from English
drawing rooms. Incidentally much of her writing talent, displayed also
in her subsequent volumes, lay in depicting "the more vulgar aspect
of things."

Her writing on the U.S. done when Mrs. Trollope (1780–1863)
was past fifty years of age, gave her the first money she ever earned.
It was followed by a series of paying travel books and novels. In the
following quotation she stirringly traces one of the dividend periods of
the itinerant preachers, the camp meeting. She locates the scene "on
the confines of Indiana," probably near the Ohio line.

Those camp meetings repelled others beside Mrs. Trollope. Mark
Twain, giving directions in 1884 concerning the illustrations for *Huckle-*

berry Finn, wrote: "But you must knock out one of them—the lecherous old rascal kissing the girl at the campmeeting. . . . Let's not make *any* pictures of the campmeeting. The subject won't *bear* illustrating. It is a disgusting thing, & pictures are sure to tell the truth about it too plainly."

From Domestic Manners of The Americans.
By Mrs. Trollope.

We reached the ground about an hour before midnight, and the approach to it was highly picturesque.[1] The spot chosen was the verge of an unbroken forest, where a space of about twenty acres appeared to have been partially cleared for the purpose. Tents of different sizes were pitched very near together in a circle round the cleared space; behind them were ranged an exterior circle of carriages of every description, and at the back of each were fastened the horses which had drawn them thither. Through this triple circle of defence we distinguished numerous lights flickering from the trees that were left in the enclosure. The moon was in meridian splendour above our heads.

We left the carriage to the care of a servant, who was to prepare a bed in it for Mrs. B. and me, and entered the inner circle. The first glance reminded me of Vauxhall,[2] from the effect of the lights among the trees, and the moving crowd below them; but the second showed a scene totally unlike any thing I had ever witnessed. Four high frames, constructed in the form of altars, were placed at the four corners of the enclosure; on these were supported layers of earth and sod, on which burned immense fires of blazing pine-wood. On one side a rude platform was erected to accommodate the preachers, fifteen of whom attended this meeting, and with very short intervals for necessary refreshment and private devotion, preached in rotation, day and night, from Tuesday to Saturday.

When we arrived, the preachers were silent; but we heard issu-

---

[1] The year is 1830.
[2] Vauxhall Gardens, London pleasure resort.

ing from nearly every tent mingled sounds of praying, preaching, singing, and lamentation. . . .

Great numbers of persons were walking about the ground, who appeared like ourselves to be present only as spectators; some of these very unceremoniously contrived to raise the drapery of this tent, at one corner, so as to afford us a perfect view of the interior.

The floor was covered with straw, which round the sides was heaped in masses, that might serve as seats, but which at that moment were used to support the heads and the arms of the close-packed circle of men and women who kneeled on the floor.

Out of about thirty persons thus placed, perhaps half a dozen were men. One of these, a handsome-looking youth of eighteen or twenty, kneeled just below the opening through which I looked. His arm was encircling the neck of a young girl who knelt beside him, with her hair hanging dishevelled upon her shoulders, and her features working with the most violent agitation; soon after they both fell forward on the straw, as if unable to endure in any other attitude the burning eloquence of a tall grim figure in black, who, standing erect in the centre, was uttering with incredible vehemence an oration that seemed to hover between praying and preaching; his arms hung stiff and immovable by his side, and he looked like an ill-constructed machine, set in action by a movement so violent, as to threaten its own destruction, so jerkingly, painfully, yet rapidly, did his words tumble out; the kneeling circle ceased not to call, in every variety of tone, on the name of Jesus; accompanied with sobs, groans, and a sort of low howling inexpressibly painful to listen to.

At midnight a horn sounded through the camp, which, we were told, was to call the people from private to public worship; and we presently saw them flocking from all sides to the front of the preachers' stand. Mrs. B. and I contrived to place ourselves with our backs supported against the lower part of this structure, and we were thus enabled to witness the scene which followed, without personal danger. There were about two thousand persons assembled.

One of the preachers began in a low nasal tone, and, like all other Methodist preachers, assured us of the enormous depravity of man as he comes from the hands of his Maker, and of his perfect sanctification after he had wrestled sufficiently with the Lord to get hold of him, *et cetera.* The admiration of the crowd was evinced by almost constant cries of "Amen! Amen!" "Jesus! Jesus!" "Glory! Glory!" and the like. But this comparative tranquillity did not last long: the preacher told them that "this night was the time fixed upon for anxious sinners to wrestle with the Lord"; that he and his brethren "were at hand to help them" and that such as needed their help were to come forward into "the pen."

"The pen" was the space immediately below the preacher's stand; we were therefore placed on the edge of it, and were enabled to see and hear all that took place in the very center of this extraordinary exhibition.

The crowd fell back at the mention of the *pen,* and for some minutes there was a vacant space before us. The preachers came down from their stand and placed themselves in the midst of it, beginning to sing a hymn, calling upon the penitents to come forth. As they sang they kept turning themselves round to every part of the crowd, and, by degrees, the voices of the whole multitude joined in chorus. . . .

The exhortation nearly resembled that which I had heard at "the Revival," but the result was very different; for, instead of the few hysterical women who had distinguished themselves on that occasion, above a hundred persons, nearly all females, came forward, uttering howlings and groans, so terrible that I shall never cease to shudder when I recall them. They appeared to drag each other forward, and on the word being given, "let us pray," they all fell on their knees; but this posture was soon changed for others that permitted greater scope for the convulsive movement of their limbs; and they were soon all lying on the ground in an indescribable confusion of heads and legs. They threw about their limbs with such incessant and violent motion, that I was every instant expecting some serious accident to occur.

But how am I to describe the sounds that proceeded from this strange mass of human beings? I know no words which can convey an idea of it. Hysterical sobbings, convulsive groans, shrieks and screams the most appalling, burst forth on all sides. I felt sick with horror. As if their hoarse and overstrained voices failed to make noise enough, they soon began to clap their hands violently.

Many of these wretched creatures were beautiful young females. The preachers moved about among them, at once exciting and soothing their agonies. I heard the muttered "Sister! dear sister!" I saw the insidious lips approach the cheeks of the unhappy girls; I heard the murmured confessions of the poor victims, and I watched their tormentors, breathing into their ears consolations that tinged the pale cheek with red. . . .

After the first wild burst that followed their prostration, the moanings, in many instances, became loudly articulate; and I then experienced a strange vibration between tragic and comic feeling.

A very pretty girl, who was kneeling in the attitude of Canova's Magdalene immediately before us, amongst an immense quantity of jargon, broke out thus: "Woe! woe to the backsliders! hear it, hear it Jesus! when I was fifteen my mother died, and I backslided, oh Jesus, I backslided! take me home to my mother, Jesus! take me home to her, for I am weary! Oh John Mitchel! John Mitchel!" and after sobbing piteously behind her raised hands, she lifted her sweet face again, which was as pale as death, and said, "Shall I sit on the sunny bank of salvation with my mother? my own dear mother? oh Jesus, take me home, take me home!"

The stunning noise was sometimes varied by the preachers beginning to sing; but the convulsive movements of the poor maniacs only became more violent. At length the atrocious wickedness of this horrible scene increased to a degree of grossness, that drove us from our station: we returned to the carriage at about three o'clock in the morning, and passed the remainder of the night in listening to the ever increasing tumult at the pen. To sleep was impossible. At day-break the horn again sounded, to send them to private devotion; and in about an hour afterwards I saw the whole camp as joyously and eagerly employed in preparing and devouring their most substantial breakfasts as if the night had been passed in dancing; and I marked many a fair but pale face, that I recognised as a demoniac of the night, simpering beside a swain, to whom she carefully administered hot coffee and eggs. The preaching saint and the howling sinner seemed alike to relish this mode of recruiting their strength.

THE SUNDAY SCHOOL VERSE-MASTERING ORGY

THE MEMORIZING of Bible and other churchly verses was an infliction that cast a gloom over generations of otherwise happy children. Conspicuous success was usually rewarded by a staid book or other suitable gift from the Sunday School teacher. The leading scores achieved by pupils of the Framingham, Massachusetts, Sabbath School in 1818, as reported by the school's superintendent, recall this long learning-by-heart era.

From History of the First Sabbath School in Framingham, Mass., from 1816 to 1868; with A Sketch of The Rise of Sabbath Schools. *By J. H. Temple.*

Framingham Sabbath School.—The Sabbath school commenced for the season on the 20th of May, under the direction of a Superintendent and ten teachers, and closed the 20th of October, thus continuing in session twenty-three Sabbaths. During this time there were committed to memory and recited, answers in Doctrinal Catechism, 1,676; Historical Catechism, 1,646; Assembly's Shorter Catechism, 4,166; Wilbur's Catechism, 242; Baldwin's Catechism, 92; Cumming's Questions, 8,409; verses of Scripture, 5,984; stanzas of Hymns, 13,242,—amounting in all to 35,457. Whole number of scholars, 142; average in attendance, 70. One girl, Nancy Hill, recited 1,048 verses of Scripture, 142 answers in Wilbur's Catechism, and 558 stanzas of Hymns. Another, Emily Conant, recited 2,018 answers in Cumming's Questions, 223 verses of Scripture, and 491 Hymns. Another, Fanny Underwood, recited 1,871 answers in Cumming's Questions, and 194 verses of Scripture. One girl, Helen C. Bell, recited 1,461 Hymns. Six little girls, Mary F. Hemenway, Arethusa Underwood, Nancy Hemenway, Almira Hemenway, Mary Bailey and Sally Belknap, recited 3,344 Hymns.

UNCOMMON
GLIMPSES OF AUTHORS

WEIRD EXPERIENCE WITH
EDGAR ALLAN POE

ONE OF Edgar Allan Poe's friends toward the end of that genius' largely joyless life was John Sartain of Philadelphia. The two had met through *Graham's* magazine; Poe wrote and Sartain engraved for it. Sartain's *Union Magazine of Literature and Art* was launched in 1849 and to it Poe contributed one of his best-known poems, *The Bells*. When submitted to Sartain it contained eighteen lines, but revisions by Poe ran it to fifty-eight lines when it was published in November 1849. Poe (1809–49) had died October 7 of that year.

About a month before his death, Poe, in one of his mental unsettlements, had come to his friend, Sartain, to receive material and psychological help. This eerie episode is presented below.

John Sartain arrived in this country from England in 1830 and fast became known in the art and literary circles of Philadelphia and beyond. A sizable measure of the success of *Graham's* magazine (1841–53) rose from its introduction of original illustrations, and these engravings were done by Sartain. He produced the first important mezzotint in this country, did some portrait painting and designed public memorials. His periodical ventures — he was interested in four such — were generally not so fortunate, even though Poe, Longfellow, John Howard Payne and Harriet Martineau were contributors to the four-year existence of Sartain's *Union Magazine of Literature and Art*.

From The Reminiscences of A Very Old
Man, 1808–1897. *By John Sartain.*

The last time I saw Mr. Poe was late in that same year, 1849,
and then under such peculiar and almost fearful conditions that the
experience can never fade from my memory. Early one Monday afternoon he suddenly entered my engraving room, looking pale and
haggard, with a wild and frightened expression in his eyes. I did
not let him see that I noticed it, and shaking him cordially by the
hand invited him to be seated, when he began, "Mr. Sartain, I have
come to you for a refuge and protection; will you let me stay with
you? It is necessary to my safety that I lie concealed for a time."
I assured him that he was welcome, that in my house he would be
perfectly safe, and he could stay as long as he liked, but I asked
him what was the matter. He said it would be difficult for me to believe what he had to tell, or that such things were possible in this
nineteenth century. I made him as comfortable as I could, and
then proceeded with my work, which was pressing. After he had had
time to calm down a little, he told me that he had been on his
way to New York, but he had overheard some men who sat a few
seats back of him plotting how they should kill him and then throw
him off from the platform of the car. He said they spoke so low
that it would have been impossible for him to hear and understand
the meaning of their words, had it not been that his sense of hearing
was so wonderfully acute. They could not guess that he heard them,
as he sat so quiet and apparently indifferent to what was going on,
but when the train arrived at the Bordentown station he gave them
the slip and remained concealed until the cars moved on again. He
had returned to Philadelphia by the first train back, and hurried to
me for refuge.

I told him that it was my belief the whole scare was the crea-
tion of his own fancy, for what interest could those people have in
taking his life, and at such risk to themselves? He said, "It was
for revenge." "Revenge for what?" said I. He answered, "Well, a
woman trouble."

Now and then some fragmentary conversation passed between
us as I engraved, and shortly I began to perceive a singular change

*Schuylkill Water Works, Philadelphia. It was in this area that
John Sartain kept Edgar Allen Poe's attention from suicide.*

in the current of his thoughts. From such fear of assassination his
mind gradually veered round to an idea of self-destruction, and his
words clearly indicated this tendency. After a long silence he said
suddenly, "If this mustache of mine were removed I should not be
so readily recognized; will you lend me a razor, that I may shave it
off?" I told him that as I never shaved I had no razor, but if he
wanted it removed I could readily do it for him with scissors. Accordingly I took him to the bathroom and performed the operation
successfully.

After tea, it being now dark, I saw him preparing to go out;
and on my asking him where he was going, he said, "To the
Schuylkill." I told him I would go too, it would be pleasant in the
moonlight later, and he offered no objection. He complained that
his feet hurt him, being chafed by his shoes, which were worn down
on the outer side of the heel. So for ease and comfort he wore my
slippers, which he preferred to my shoes as less ill-fitting. When we
had reached the corner of Ninth and Chestnut Streets we waited for

an omnibus some minutes, which were passed in conversation, and among the many things he said was that he wished I would see to it after his death that the portrait Osgood had painted of him should go to his mother (meaning Mrs. Clemm[1]). I promised that as far as I could control it that should be done. After getting the omnibus we rode to its stopping-place, a little short of Fairmount, opposite a tavern on the north side of Callowhill Street, at the bend it makes to the northwest to reach the bridge over the river. At that spot a bright light shone out through the open door of the tavern, but beyond all was pitchy dark. However, forward into the darkness we walked. I kept on his left side, and on approaching the foot of the bridge guided him off to the right by a gentle pressure, until we reached the lofty flight of steep wooden steps which ascended almost to the top of the reservoir. There was a landing with seats, and we sat down to rest. All this time I had contrived to hold him in conversation, except while we were labouring breathless up that long, breakneck flight of stairs.

There he told me his late experiences, or what he believed to be such, and the succession of images that his imagination created he expressed in a calm, deliberate, measured utterance as facts. These were as weird and fantastic as anything to be met with in his published writings. Of course it is altogether beyond me to convey even a faint idea of his wild descriptions. "I was confined in a cell in Moyamensing Prison,"[2] said he, "and through my grated window was visible the battlemented granite tower. On the topmost stone of the parapet, between the embrasures, stood perched against the dark sky a young female brightly radiant, like silver dipped in light, either in herself or in her environment, so that the cross-bar shadows thrown from my window were distinct on the opposite wall. From this position, remote as it was she addressed to me a series of questions in words not loud but distinct, and I dared not fail to hear and make apt response. Had I failed once either to hear or to make pertinent answer, the consequences to me would have been something fearful; but my sense of hearing is wonderfully acute, so that I passed safety through this ordeal, which was a snare to catch me. But another was in store.

"An attendant asked me if I would like to take a stroll about

[1] Poe's mother-in-law; his wife had died.
[2] The new Philadelphia jail.

the place, I might see something interesting, and I agreed. In the course of our rounds on the ramparts we came to a cauldron of boiling spirits. He asked me if I would not like to take a drink. I declined, but had I said yes, what do you suppose would have happened?" I said I could not guess. "Why, I should have been lifted over the brim and dipped into the hot liquid up to the lip, like Tantalus." "Yes," said I, "but that would have killed you." "Of course it would," said he, "that's what they wanted; but, you see, again I escaped the snare. So at last, as a means to torture me and wring my heart, they brought out my mother, Mrs. Clemm, to blast my sight by seeing them first saw off her feet at the ankles, then her legs to the knees, her thighs at the hips, and so on." The horror of the imagined scene threw him into a sort of convulsion. This is but a very faint sample of the talk I listened to up there in the darkness. I had been all along expecting the moon to rise, forgetting how much it retarded every evening, and the clouds hid the light of the stars. It came into my mind that Poe might possibly in a sudden fit of frenzy leap freely forth with me in his arms into the black depth below, so I was watchful and kept on my guard. I asked him how he came to be in Moyamensing Prison.

He answered that he had been suspected of trying to pass a fifty-dollar counterfeit note. The truth is, he was there for what takes so many there for a few hours only—the drop too much. I learned later that when his turn came in the motley group before Mayor Gilpin, some one said, "Why, this is Poe, the poet," and he was dismissed without the customary fine.

I suggested at last that as it appeared we were not to have the moon we might as well go down again. He agreed, and we descended the steep stairway slowly and cautiously, holding well to the handrails. Being down I kept this time, on our return walk, on his right side, and did not suffer the conversation to flag. On arriving at the omnibus waiting for passengers at the tavern door I pressed gently against him and he raised his foot to the step, but instantly recollecting himself drew back. I urged him in, and being seated beside him said "You were saying?" The conversation was resumed, I got him safe home, and gave him a bed on a sofa in the dining-room, while I slept alongside him on three chairs, without undressing.

On the second morning he appeared to have become so much

like his old self that I trusted him to go out alone. Rest and regular meals had had a good effect, although his mind was not yet entirely free from the nightmare. After an hour or two he returned, and then told me he had come to the conclusion that what I said was true, that the whole thing had been a delusion and a scare created by his own excited imagination. He said his mind began to clear as he lay on the grass, his face buried in it and his nostrils inhaling the sweet fragrance mingled with the odour of the earth. While he lay thus, the words he had heard kept running in his thoughts, but he tried in vain to connect them with the speaker, and so the light gradually broke in upon his dazed mind and he saw that he had come out of a dream. Being now all right again he was ready to depart for New York. He borrowed what was needful, and I never saw him again.

A HAPPY RECALLING OF
MARK TWAIN HUMOR

AN EXCELLENT recapturing of Mark Twain's humor is presented in these anecdotes by Mrs. Thomas Bailey Aldrich, wife of the poet, author and *Atlantic Monthly* editor. The art here displayed is rare, as readers of the usual dismal misfires in that field will testify, and the source is unexpected since records indicate that Mrs. Aldrich had no experience in writing save this autobiography of hers. This memorable visit to the Twain home can be set down as in the spring of 1874.

Much of entertainment value could be written on the reaction of Mark Twain and Mrs. Aldrich, one upon the other. They first met two or three years before this Hartford occasion when Aldrich brought Twain home to supper and Mrs. Aldrich, not knowing who it was and concluding from his unconventional dress, swaying walk and slow speech that the visitor was drunk, forced her husband to turn Twain away supperless. It ended, for the public, after the humorist's death when in *Mark Twain in Eruption*, Mark gives Mrs. Aldrich a comprehensive and colorful scorching. But none of these adverse reactions are hinted in the good-fellowship of that Hartford house party.

Mr. and Mrs. Aldrich—she was born Lillian Woodman—were married in Boston in 1865 and made that their home till the end. They were given forty-two years of married life, he dying in 1907 and she in 1927. After his death she published a book of selections from his poems.

From Crowding Memories. *By Mrs. Thomas Bailey Aldrich.*

On the arrival at Hartford we were met by the same carriage and coachmen that Mr. Clemens, after he had entered the enchanted land, described to Mr. Redpath, who was urging lecture engagements: "I guess I am out of the field permanently. Have got a lovely wife, a lovely house, a lovely carriage and a coachman whose style and dignity are simply awe-inspiring—nothing less." Patrick McAleer was accompanied by "George," who was both butler and guardian spirit of the house. George had been the body servant of an army general, and was of the best style of the Southern negro of that day. With much formality we were presented to him by Mr. Clemens, who said: "George came one day to wash windows; he will stay for his lifetime. His morals are defective; he is a gambler—will bet on anything. I have trained him so that now he is a proficient liar —you should see Mrs. Clemens's joy and pride when she hears him lying to the newspaper correspondent, or the visitor at the front door."

The next morning, as were dressing and talking of the pleasant plans of the day, there was a loud and rather authoritative knock at the bedroom door, and Mr. Clemens's voice was heard, saying, "Aldrich, come out, I want to speak to you." The other occupant of the room wrapped her kimono round her more closely, and crept to the door, for evidently something of serious import was happening, or about to happen. The words overhead were most disquieting. Twain's voice had its usual calmness and slowness of speech, but was lacking in the kindly, mellow quality of its accustomed tone, as he said: "In Heaven's name, Aldrich, what are you doing? Are you emulating the kangaroos, with hob-nails in your shoes, or trying the jumping-frog business? Our bedroom is directly under yours, and poor 'Livy and her headache—do try to move more quietly, though 'Livy would rather suffer than have you give up your game on her account." Then the sound of receding footsteps.

Our consternation was as great as our surprise at the reprimand, for we had been unconscious of walking heavily, or of making unnecessary noise. The bedroom was luxurious in its appointments, the rugs soft on the floor; we could only surmise that the floor boards had some peculiar acoustic quality that emphasized sound. On tiptoe we finished our toilets, and spoke only in whispers, much disturbed in mind that we had troubled our hostess, and hoped she knew that we would not willingly have added to her headache even the weight of a hummingbird's wing. When the toilets were finished, slowly and softly we went down the stairs and into the breakfast room, where, behind the larger silver coffee urn, sat Mrs. Clemens. With sorrowful solicitude we asked if her headache was better, and begged for forgiveness for adding to her pain. To our amazement she answered, "I have no headache." In perplexed confusion we apologized for the noise we inadvertently made. "Noise!" Mrs. Clemens replied. "We have not heard a sound. If you had shouted we should not have known it, for our rooms are in another wing of the house." At the other end of the table Mark Twain sat, looking as guileless as a combination of cherubim and seraphim—never a word, excepting with lengthened drawl, more slow than usual, "Oh, do come to your breakfast, Aldrich, and don't talk all day."

It was a joyous group that came together at the table that morning, and loud was the laughter, and rapid the talk, excepting Mrs. Clemens, who sat rather quiet, and with an expression of face as if she were waiting. Suddenly Mr. Clemens brought the laughter to a pause with his rap on the table, and then, with resonant and deep-toned voice, speaking even more slowly than usual, he asked God's blessing and help for the day. The words were apparently sincere, and spoken with reverent spirit, but we who listened were struck with the same surprised wonder as was the companion of his rougher days, Joe Goodman,[1] who came East to visit them, and was dumfounded to see Mark Twain ask a blessing and join in family worship. Nothing could have so clearly shown his adoration of Mrs. Clemens as this. He worshipped her as little less than a saint, and

---

[1] Joseph T. Goodman, editor and owner of the Virginia City *Enterprise*, Nevada Territory, on which Twain worked.

Mark Twain at fifty.

would have "hid her needle in his heart to save her little finger from a scratch."

Out of those far-off days are two indelible pictures in my memories of the last morning and evening of our happy visit; the assembling of the guests at the breakfast table, and while we waited the entrance of our hostess, Mr. Clemens, with sober face and his inimitable drawl, telling his night experience, with the orders for the next day. The evening before, Mrs. Clemens had been speaking of her consternation in finding she had misspelled a word in a formal note, and said it had always been a great mortification to her that she could not spell; that the sound of a word left her helpless as to the spelling of it, and that, for Mr. Clemens's sake, she should not be allowed to write even the simplest note unless he looked it over. While she was speaking there glimmered and twinkled in Mr. Clemens's eye a laughing imp that boded mischief. Mr. Clemens said, "I had just fallen into 'the first sweet sleep of dawn,' when this mumur reached my ear: 'Mark, do tell me how to spell sardines,' I replied, 'Livy, for God's sake, don't let them think down in the city that you are destitute of general information in regard to spelling. How did you spell sardines?' And she told me. Then I got up and opened the window and picked up her poor little scrap of paper, which she left on the ledge for the market-boy to take in the morning, on which she had written her wish for extra milk, and a small box of sardines. I brought the bit of paper to the bedside and said, 'Here, Love, is your pen and ink. Just put an "h" at the end of your sardines, then we can both lie down in peace to sleep, and in the morning when the marketman reads your paper, he will know you know how to spell the fish, although the "h" is always silent.' And God forever bless her! she wrote it. But if she ever discovers that in that spelling I was wrong, why, the china and I will fly."

It was voted at dinner that the company would not disband until the genial morn appeared, and that there should be at midnight a wassail brewed. The rosy apples roasted at the open fire, the wine and sugar added, and the ale—but at this point Mrs. Clemens said, "Youth,[2] we have no ale." There was a rapid exit by Mr. Clemens, who reappeared in a moment in his historic sealskin coat and cap, but still wearing his low-cut evening shoes. He said he wanted a walk, and was going to the village for the ale and should shortly return with the ingredient. Deaf, absolutely deaf, to Mrs. Clemens's earnest voice, that he should at least wear overshoes that snowy night, he disappeared. In an incredibly short time he reappeared, excited and hilarious, with his rapid walk in the frosty air—

[2] A name Mrs. Clemens used for her husband.

very wet shoes, and no cap. To Mrs. Clemens's inquiry, "Youth, what have you done with your cap?" there was a hurried search in all his pockets, a blank and surprised look on his face, as he said: "Why, I am afraid I have thrown it away. I remember being very warm and taking it off, carrying it in my hand, and now I do remember, at such a turn in the road, my hand feeling a strain of position, opening it and throwing away in the darkness something in my hand that caused the sensation." Then, in real anxiety, "Livy, do you think it could have been my cap?"

Mr. Clemens was sent for George, with Mrs. Clemens's instruction that George should carefully retrace Mr. Clemens's footsteps in the quest for the mislaid cap, and also to see that Mr. Clemens put on dry shoes. When the culprit returned, the wet low shoes had been exchanged for a pair of white cowskin slippers, with the hair outside, and clothed in them, with most sober and smileless face, he twisted his angular body into all the strange contortions known to the dancing darkies of the South. In this wise the last day of the joyous, jubilant visit came to the close. Untroubled by the flight of time I still can hear a soft and gentle tone, "Youth, O Youth!" for so she always called him.

A GREAT ILLUSTRATOR'S DRAWINGS OFFEND

THE CONFINING influence that editors and advertisers can exert upon authors and illustrators forms the theme of these diverting references to Mark Twain and two of his books.

Illustrator Dan Beard implies that the offensive "Connecticut Yankee" drawings had a connection with the subsequent failure of Mark Twain's publishing house of Webster & Company. The implication is interesting but unproved. *"The Yankee"* was produced by Webster in late 1889. It was in 1892 that Webster & Company's situation became alarming; it failed in 1894.

Presumably the particular illustrations that displeased pertained to the English Church and its servants of King Arthur's reign. Dan Beard illustrated several Twain books, though none so freshly as A *Connecticut Yankee in King Arthur's Court.*

Tom Sawyer Abroad is the other Twain book mentioned in the Beard reminiscences. Here the watchful editors of the *St. Nicholas* magazine for young people banned depiction of barefoot characters. The story ran in St. Nicholas 1893–94.

Daniel Carter Beard (1850–1911)—he is the same Dan Beard who was known to a later generation as founder and national commissioner of the Boy Scouts of America—was artist, author, magazine editor, and always the lover of the outdoors. His life was varied and busy. His books, mainly dealing with outdoor life for boys, totaled about a dozen and a half. His illustrations characterized numerous magazines and volumes. He taught the first organized class in animal drawing. Mt. Beard, the peak adjoining Mt. McKinley, was named for him. He received the first State of Kentucky medal for outstanding citizenship.

From Hardly A Man Is Now Alive. *The Autobiography of Dan Beard.*

Mr. Fred Hall, Mark Twain's partner in the publishing business, came to my studio in the old Judge Building and told me that Mark Twain wanted to meet the man who had made the illustrations for a Chinese story in the *Cosmopolitan* and he wanted that man to illustrate his new book, *A Connecticut Yankee in King Arthur's Court.* The manuscript was sent to me to read. I read it through three times with great enjoyment. Then I met Mr. Clemens by appointment in his little office on Fourteenth Street, not far from the corner of Fifth Avenue.

Fourteenth Street was then the abode of artists, writers and illustrators, whose studios seemed to be the pioneer fringe which pushed ahead of the business houses as they moved uptown. There was no elevator in this building. When I climbed to Mark Twain's office, if I was a little short of breath, it was not from the exercise so much as the awe I felt in the presence of a man who stood so high in my esteem. I stood before this shaggy-headed man, first on one foot and then on the other, not knowing how to open the conversation. He did not rise but turned his head slowly toward me, drawling, "Sit down. In regard to the illustrations you are to make," he said, "I only want to say this. If a man comes to me and wants

Tom and Huck wearing shoes by order of St. Nicholas *in one of Dan Beard's illustrations for* Tom Sawyer Abroad.

me to write a story, I will write one for him; but if he comes to me and wants me to write a story and then tells me what to write, I say, 'Damn you, go hire a typewriter,'" meaning a stenographer. In saying this, he did not blow the smoke from his mouth, but it seemed to roll out slowly like round, bulbous clouds, in perfect rhythm with his words, with which the smoke was so intimately connected that I remember it as if what he said were vocalized cumulus clouds of tobacco smoke. If the building had been burning down it would not have hurried him a bit. He would have leisurely arose and, while complaining of the interruption, just as leisurely have found his way downstairs.

In making the illustrations for his book I referred to a collection of photographs of people of note. When I wanted a face or a figure to fit a character in the story I looked over this collection of photographs and made free use of them, not as caricatures or portraits of the people themselves, but for the dress, pose, or their whole figure

and features as best fitted the character I was to depict. The captain
of our boat club, holding a halberd in his hand, posed for one of the
initial letters as a sentry dressed with a sealskin. For the Yankee himself I used George Morrison, a real Connecticut Yankee who was
experimenting in a photoengraving establishment adjoining my
studio. The charming actress Annie Russell appears in the pages as
Sandy, the heroine. Sarah Bernhardt is there as a page. In fact no
one held too lofty a position to escape my notice if I thought he or
she possessed the face or figure suited to the character I wished to
draw. I had more fun making the drawings for that book than any
other book I ever illustrated.

I made about four hundred illustrations in seventy working days.
The first illustration was that of a knight with lance set charging
on the Yankee, who was climbing a tree. This pleased Mr. Clemens
very greatly. In the corner of the illustration there is a helmet as a
sort of decoration with the visor partly open, of which Mark said,
"The smile on that helmet is a source of perennial joy to me." When
I finished the book he wrote:

Dear Mr. Beard—
*Hold me under everlasting obligations. There are a hundred
artists who could have illustrated any other of my books, but
only one who could illustrate this one. It was a lucky day I went
netting for lightning bugs and caught a meteor. Live forever.*

Sad to say, the illustrations which so pleased Mark Twain and
delighted people all over the world grievously offended some big
advertisers. The offending illustrations were removed from further
editions. Not only did the book feel the force of the displeasure of
this group, but it is significant that after its publication Mark Twain
was ruined financially and my work was boycotted for many years
by the prominent magazines, with the exception of *Life* and *Cosmopolitan*. I, too, went practically broke, but Mark Twain died a
wealthy man and I lived to find my work in great demand. . . .

. . . When Mark Twain sent the manuscript of *Tom Sawyer
Abroad* to *St. Nicholas* there was a part of it which the editor
thought might be improved, and the wording was consequently
changed. Mark Twain was a gentle soul, but if Theodore Roosevelt
stood for civic righteousness, Mark stood for the unalienable rights

of the author to his own statements. When Mark read the proof he was exceedingly wroth and, entering the sanctum sanctorum, the holy of holies, or the editorial department of *St. Nicholas*, he shocked the gentle creatures and terrified the associate editors by exclaiming, "Any editor to whom I submit my manuscripts has an undisputed right to delete anything to which he objects but"—and his brows knit as he cried—"God Almighty Himself has no right to put words in my mouth that I never used!"

After smelling salts were administered to the whole editorial staff, and the editor in chief was resuscitated, the mistake was remedied, the error rectified and things went smoothly. I was not present, but some of the editorial staff themselves with great glee told me of the shocking incident as a profound secret. What prompted them to give this confidential information was that my illustrations of Huck Finn, Tom Sawyer and Nigger Jim had been returned to me, the editor ruling that it was excessively coarse and vulgar to depict them with *bare feet*! I was asked to cover their nakedness with shoes. Of course I was working for *St. Nicholas* and it was only right that I should conform to *St. Nicholas*' idea of propriety, so I pinched the toes of those poor vagabonds with shoes they never wore in life, mentally asking their forgiveness as I did so.

A SHOCKING PICTURE OF
STEVENSON'S LAST YEARS

THIS IS an uncustomary glimpse of Robert Louis Stevenson (1850–94), author of *Treasure Island, Kidnapped, Dr. Jekyll and Mr. Hyde* and others. Traveling in the South Seas for his health, Stevenson had just occupied his home on Upolu, in the Samoan Islands, when Henry Adams saw him.

Stevenson's wife, unflatteringly described by Adams, had been neither unattractive nor considered uncultured in earlier days. Born in Indianapolis, Fanny Van de Grift (1840–1914) came of a well-to-do family. Her first marriage in 1857 (to Sam Osbourne of Kentucky) was not a lasting success, and in 1875 she and her daughter went to

France to study art. She met Stevenson there. They were married in California in 1880.

Stevenson continued writing in his mountain home, Vailima, where Adams visited him and where he was soon to die. The small building Adams saw was replaced by a larger one. Stevenson's household in that wild remoteness usually included—besides his wife—his stepson, his stepdaughter and his mother.

Henry Adams, great grandson of one President of the U.S. and grandson of another, wrote in several fields but is remembered for his introspective, finely-wrought autobiography, *The Education of Henry Adams*. He sought a perfection in his mental development and was always self-criminatory and annoyed when perfection failed to arrive. In his quest for it, he traveled much.

John La Farge (1835–1910), mentioned here, was a mural painter and designer of stained glass who was accompanying Adams in the South Seas. Harold Marsh Sewall (1860–1924) was the American consul at Apia, Upolu.

From Letters of Henry Adams (1858–1891). *Edited by Worthington Chauncey Ford.*

October 17 (1890). Yesterday afternoon Sewall took La Farge and me to call on Robert Louis Stevenson. We mounted some gawky horses and rode up the hills about an hour on the native road or path which leads across the island. The forest is not especially exciting; not nearly so beautiful as that above Hilo in Hawaii, but every now and again, as Captain Peter, or Pito, used to say, we came on some little touch of tropical effect that had charm, especially a party of three girls in their dress of green leaves, or *titi*, which La Farge became glowing about. The afternoon was lowering, with drops of rain, and misty in the distance. At last we came out on a clearing dotted with burned stumps exactly like a clearing in our backwoods. In the middle stood a two-story Irish shanty with steps outside to the upper floor, and a galvanized iron roof. A pervasive atmosphere of dirt seemed to hang around it, and the squalor like a railroad navvy's board hut. As we reached the steps a figure came out that I cannot do justice to. Imagine a man so thin and emaciated that he looked like a bundle of sticks in a bag, with a head and eyes morbidly intelligent and restless. He was costumed in a dirty striped cotton pyjamas, the baggy legs tucked into coarse knit woollen stockings, one of which was bright brown in color, the other a purplish dark tone. With him was a woman who retired for a moment into the house to reappear a moment afterwards, probably in some change of costume, but, as far as I could see, the change could have consisted only in putting shoes on her bare feet. She wore the usual missionary nightgown which was no cleaner than her husband's shirt and drawers, but she omitted the stockings. Her complexion and eyes were dark and strong, like a half-breed Mexican. They received us cordially enough, and as soon as Stevenson heard La Farge's name and learned who he was, they became very friendly, while I sat by, nervously conscious that my eyes could not help glaring at Stevenson's stockings, and wondering, as La Farge said, which color he would have chosen if he had been obliged to wear a pair that matched. We sat an hour or more, perched on his verandah, looking down over his field of black stumps, and the forest beyond, to the misty line of distant ocean to the northward. He has bought a hundred acres or more of mountain and forest so dense that he says it costs him a dollar for every foot he walks in it. To me the place seemed oppressively shut in by forest and mountain, but the weather may have caused that impression. When conversation fairly began, though I could not forget the dirt and discomfort, I found Stevenson extremely entertaining. He has the nervous restlessness of his disease, and, although he said he was unusually well, I half expected to see him drop with a hemorrhage at any moment, for he cannot be quiet, but sits down, jumps up, darts off and flies back, at every sentence he utters, and his eyes and features gleam with a hectic glow. He seems weak, and complains that the ride of an hour up to his place costs him a day's work; but, as he describes his travels and life in the South Seas, he has been through what would have broken me into a miserable rag. For months he has sailed about the islands in wretched trading schooners and stray steamers almost worse than sailing vessels, with such food as he could get, or lived on coral atolls eating bread-fruit and yams, all the time working hard with his pen, and of course always dirty, uncomfortable and poorly served, not to speak of being ill-clothed, which matters little in these parts. He has seen more of the island than any literary or scientific man ever did before, and knows all he has seen. His talk is most entertaining, and of course interested us peculiarly. He says that the Tahitians are by far finer men than the Samoans, and that he does not regard the Samoans as an especially fine race, or the islands here as specially beautiful. . . . Stevenson is about to build a house, and says he shall never leave the island again, and cannot understand how any man who is able to live in the South Seas, should consent to live elsewhere.

Vaiale,[1] 15 December, 1890. We found Stevenson and his wife just as they had appeared at our first call, except that Mrs. Stevenson did not think herself obliged to put on slippers, and her nightgown costume had apparently not been washed since our visit. Stevenson himself wore still a brown knit woollen sock on one foot, and a greyish purple sock on the other, much wanting in heels, so that I speculated half my time whether it was the same old socks, or the corresponding alternates, and concluded that he must have worn them ever since we first saw him. They were evidently his slippers for home wear. He wore also, doubtless out of deference to us, a pair of trousers, and a thin flannel shirt; but, by way of protest he rolled up the sleeves above his shoulders, displaying a pair of the thinnest white arms I ever beheld, which he brandished in the air habitually as though he wanted to throw them away. To La Farge and me, this attitude expressed incredible strength, and heroic defiance of destiny, for his house swarmed with mosquitoes which drove us wild, though only our heads and hands were exposed. Of course it was none of our business, and both Stevenson and his wife were very friendly, and gave us a good breakfast—or got it themselves —and kept up a rapid talk for four hours, at the end of which I was very tired, but Stevenson seemed only refreshed. Both La Farge and I came round to a sort of liking for Mrs. Stevenson, who is more human than her husband. Stevenson is an *a-itu*—uncanny. His fragility passes description, but his endurance passes his fragility. I cannot conceive how such a bundle of bones, unable to work on his writing without often taking to his bed as his working place, should have gone through the months of exposure, confinement and bad nourishment which he has enjoyed. Their travels have broken his

[1] The correct name for Stevenson's home was Vailima.

wife up; she is a victim of rheumatism which is becoming paralysis, and, I suspect, to dyspepsia; she says that their voyages have caused it; but Stevenson gloats over discomforts and thinks that every traveller should sail for months in small cutters rancid with cocoa-nut oil and mouldy with constant rain, and should live on coral atolls with nothing but cocoa-nuts and poisonous fish to eat. Their mode of existence here is far less human than that of the natives, and compared with their shanty a native house is a palace; but this squalor must be somehow due to his education. All through him, the education shows. His early associates were all second-rate; he never seems by any chance to have come in contact with first-rate people, either men, women or artists. He does not know the difference between people, and mixes them up in a fashion as grotesque as if they were characters in his New Arabian Nights.

WESTERN WRITER BRET HARTE DIES AN ENGISH DANDY

STRANGE AND incongruous is this likeness of Bret Harte, portrayer of the rough, early days in California and the Pacific Slope, author of "The Luck of Roaring Camp," "The Outcasts of Poker Flat," "The Heathen Chinee" and similar tales and poems. Francis Bret Harte (1839–1902) went to California in the 1850s, struggled and made his fame there through the 1860s, and so was properly part of that rude day and place.

But in 1878 he went abroad, to live no more in the land of his birth. He held consular posts in Germany and Scotland, and in 1885 took residence in England, to die there seventeen years later, "an elderly fop," as Hamlin Garland saw him.

Hamlin Garland (1860–1940), born in Wisconsin, was a product of the Middle West, whose earlier days and ways he finely and conscientiously reclaimed in his "Middle Border" series of autobiographical writings. Garland's progress to recognition was more laborious than Harte's and his identification with toil and soil was closer. He wrote many novels dealing with the Middle West and Rocky Mountain regions; also memories touching on those he knew in later life.

From Roadside Meetings. *By Hamlin Garland.*

One afternoon as Zangwill[1] and I were having tea at Joseph Hatton's house, my attention was drawn to a man whose apperance was almost precisely that of the typical English clubman of the American stage. He was tall, and his hair parted in the middle was white. He wore gray-striped trousers, a cutaway coat over a fancy vest, and above his polished shoes glowed lavender spats. In his hand he carried a pair of yellow gloves.

"Who is that?" I asked of Zangwill.

"Don't you know who that is?" he asked. "That is your noble compatriot, Francis Bret Harte."

"Bret Harte!" I stared at him in amazement. Could that dandy, that be-monocled, be-spatted old beau be the author of "The Luck of Roaring Camp" and "Two Men of Sandy Bar"? As I stared, I recalled Joaquin Miller in his little cottage high on the hills above Oakland, and marveled at the changes which the years had wrought in his expatriate fellow. I said to Zangwill, "I have a letter to Harte from Howells[2]—present me."

Zangwill led me over to Harte and introduced me as an American writer with a note from Howells. Harte was politely interested. "Come and see me on Thursday," he said, and gave me his address which was near Lancaster Gate.

Although courteous, his manner was not winning and I hesitated about making the call. However, it was easier to go than to excuse myself, and on the afternoon he had named, I found my way to his "bachelor apartments" in Lancaster Gate. They seemed to me very ladylike, spic and span, and very dainty in coloring, with chairs of the gilded, spindle-legged perilous sort which women adore; and when Harte came in to greet me he was almost as aristocratic as the room. He was wearing the same suit with the same fancy vest but with a different tie, and from his vest dangled an English eyeglass. His whole appearance was that of an elderly fop whose life had been one of self-indulgent ease. His eyes were clouded with yellow, and beneath them the skin was puffed and wrinkled. Al-

---

[1] Israel Zangwill, British author; the time, 1899.
[2] William Dean Howells, American novelist and editor.

Bret Harte, sartorially resplendent, in 1896.

though affable and polite he looked and spoke like a burned-out London sport. I was saddened by this decay of a brilliant and powerful novelist.

Taking the letter which I handed him he asked me to be seated. Seating himself he read its two short pages slowly. At the close of it he sat for a few moments in silence. Then raising his glance he dropped his eyeglass and his English accent at the same time and said, "Tell me about Howells. Tell me of Tom Aldrich[1] and all the rest of the boys."

My heart warmed to him. He was wholly the American. His voice and his words were not even Bostonian—they were Californian. Howells' words and something in my voice had not only awakened youthful memories but had strengthened a secret desire. His eyes as I talked became dreamy and his voice wistful, and at last I said, "When are we to see you again?"

"Never again, I fear. I *can't* go back now."

"You would have a splendid reception in California," I urged.

"I'm not so sure of that," he replied, a note of sadness in his voice. "I couldn't find *my* California. *My* California is gone. My friends are gone. The men who represented California to me are gone. No, I shall never go back. Sometimes I wish I had never come away."

In his mind, as in mine, he was an exile, an expatriate, old and feeble and about to die, estranged from his family and from all his American friends. He was poor and the subject of gossip. His books were no longer in demand. He had lived here too long, working over his memories of California, and it was reported that he was living on the bounty of a patron.

JULIAN STREET—AN AUTHOR AND A RED-LIGHT DISTRICT

JULIAN STREET (1879–1947) wrote a number of books but the one that Cripple Creek, Colorado, remembers is his *Abroad At Home*. Mr. Street did not detail the town of Cripple Creek as he did other towns and regions in 1913–14, but contented himself with observing and writing up its red-light district. It seemed to him, he said "that Cripple Creek must be the most awful looking little city in the world."

The reactions of Cripple Creek were on schedule and as to be

[1] The Aldriches' visit to Mark Twain is described by Mrs. Aldrich earlier in this book.

anticipated—but with this constructive addition: The city officially named its red-light thoroughfare Julian Street.

The whole episode is told below. First comes Mr. Street's unhappy summation of Cripple Creek. Next, from a little book booming Cripple Creek, that bears the printed seal of the "Cripple Creek District Press Club," is chronicled the resourceful rejoinder of the city council.

Mr. Street produced a sequel to *Abroad At Home*, both books of value for their sketches of America and its people in the early years of this century. His other work embraces a play, *The Country Cousin*, in collaboration with Booth Tarkington, a volume on Japan and books on French dining and wining. In 1935 France awarded him the "Cross of Chevalier, Legion of Honor, for work on wines and gastronomy"— which located Julian Street a long step from Cripple Creek.

From Abroad At Home. American Ramblings, Observations, and Adventures of Julian Street.

However, we did get to Cripple Creek, and for all its mountain setting, and all the three hundred millions of gold that it has yielded in the last twenty years or so, it is one of the most depressing places in the world. Its buildings run from shabbiness to downright ruin; its streets are ill paved, and its outlying districts are a horror of smokestacks, ore-dumps, shaft-houses, reduction-plants, gallows-frames and squalid shanties, situated in the mud. It seemed to me that Cripple Creek must be the most awful looking little city in the world, but I was informed that, as mining camps go, it is unusually presentable, and later I learned for myself that that is true.

Cripple Creek is not only above the timber-line; it is above the cat-line. I mean this literally. Domestic cats cannot live there. And many human beings are affected by the altitude. I was. I had a headache; my breath was short, and upon the least exertion my heart did flip-flops. Therefore I did not circulate about the town excepting within a radius of a few blocks of the station. That, however, was enough.

After walking up the main street a little way, I turned off into a side street lined with flimsy buildings, half of them tumbledown and abandoned. Turning into another street I came upon a long row of tiny one story houses, crowded close together in a block. Some of them were empty, but others showed signs of being occupied. And instead of a number, the door of each one bore a name, "Clara," "Louise," "Lina," and so on, down the block. For a time there was not a soul in sight as I walked slowly down that line of box-stall houses. Then, far ahead, I saw a woman come out of a doorway. She wore a loose pink wrapper and carried a pitcher in her hand. I watched her cross the street and go into a dingy building. Then the street was empty again. I walked on slowly. As I passed one doorway it opened suddenly and a man came out—a shabby man with a drooping mustache. He did not look at me as he passed. The window-shade of the crib from which he had come went up as I moved by. I looked at the window, and as I did so, the curtains parted and the face of a negress was pressed against the pane, grinning at me with a knowing, sickening grin.

I passed on. From another window a white woman with very black hair and eyes, and cheeks of a light orchid-shade, showed her gold teeth in a mirthless automatic smile, and added the allurement of an ice-cold wink.

The door of the crib at the corner stood open, and just before I reached it a woman stepped out and surveyed me as I approached. She wore a white linen skirt and a middy blouse, attire grotesquely juvenile for one of her years. Her hair, of which she had but a moderate amount, was light brown and stringy, and she wore gold-rimmed spectacles. She did not look depraved but, upon the contrary resembled a highly respectable, if homely, German cook I once employed. As I passed her window I saw hanging there a glass sign, across which, in gold letters, was the title, "Madam Leo."

"Madam Leo," she said to me, nodding and pointing at her chest. "That's me. Leo, the lion, eh?" She laughed foolishly. . . .

"Well," she returned, "when you go back send some nice boys up here. Tell them to see Madam Leo. Tell them a middle-aged woman with spectacles. I'm known here. I been here four years. Oh, things ain't so bad. I manage to make two or three dollars a day."

As I passed to leeward of her on the narrow walk I got the smell of a strong, brutal perfume.

"Have you got to be going?" she asked.

"Yes," I answered. "I must go to the train."

"Well, then—so long," she said.

"So long."

"Don't forget Madam Leo," she admonished, giving utterance, again, to her strident, feeble-minded laugh.

"I won't," I promised.

And I never, never shall.

From Yellow Gold of Cripple Creek. Romances and Anecdotes of The Mines, Mining Men and Mining Properties. *By Harry J. Newton.*

There used to be a low down nigger dance hall under the Midland trestle, to mark the changing of the gulch into the red light street of dance halls, gambling dens, saloons, cribs and other "sporting houses," and this salacious thoroughfare was named after Julius A. Myers, one of the owners of the homestead upon which most of the town was built—a respected, honored and prominent Coloradoan. . . .

The old Short Line depot was on the south side of Myers Avenue, which had to be crossed to reach the main part of the town, and when innocent tourists would catch a glimpse of Myers Avenue in all its red blinds, and red lights, and other markings of the honkitonk, they would return to the depot and wait for the next train back, not even venturing to the main business street, in case of further jeopardy to their morals.

Then along came Julian Street, the eminent writer and author, and he "wrote up" Cripple Creek solely from the aspect of its red light district, and greatly to the disgust of the better element of the community which constituted the majority of the citizenry. These people resented the picturing of their city in such lurid colors and by vote of the city council officially changed Myers Avenue into Julian Street, and it is so known today.

A VARIETY
OF HAPPENINGS

BANK STOCK SALES BRING TOLL OF INJURED

THE BANK of Penn Township, Philadelphia, had been chartered by the state legislature in 1827. The next step was to sell stock to the public.

"So great was the demand for shares of the stock that when the subscription books were opened in February 1828, at Commissioners Hall on Vine Street, tickets of admission were required, and resolutions were passed 'to deny the subscription from anyone who shall come to a window over the heads of or on the shoulders of persons who may be standing under same,' " according to Holdsworth's *History of Banking in Pennsylvania.*

Violence, often accompanied by physical injury, was the rule in these frantic efforts to buy stock in state banks that issued their own banknotes and paid expansive dividends. In 1834 the Pennsylvania auditor-general found these banks showed: banking capital, $17,061,000; circulating notes, $10,336,000; deposits, $7,708,000; specie on hand, $2,898,000; discounts, $29,965,000; real estate, $1,216,000. In the panic of 1837 an anti-bank meeting in Harrisburg, the state capital, where a new state constitution was being framed, laid all the troubles to "an unchecked and uncontrolled banking system."

The following eyewitness account of one of these mob scenes is taken from *A Subaltern's Furlough* by an English officer, Lieutenant E. T. Coke, who visited North America in 1832. His book appeared the following year in Waldie's Select Circulating Library, published in Philadelphia.

Equally significant as the narrative of Lieutenant Coke are the supporting footnotes appended to his reporting by the editor of Waldie's, John Jay Smith. The latter was a collector of historical material, author, editor of several literary publications and for over twenty years librarian of the Library Company of Philadelphia, established by Benjamin Franklin. Waldie's Select Circulating Library was the first successful venture—international copyright had not arrived—to republish important foreign books in an inexpensive weekly. Editor Smith testifies to the savage bank-stock pandemonium.

From A Subaltern's Furlough: descriptive of scenes in the United States, Upper and Lower Canada, New Brunswick and Nov*.*. Scotia During the Summer and Autumn of 1832. *Dedicated to the Duke of Rutland by E. T. Coke, Lieutenant of the 45th Regiment.*

On my way to the office of a railroad, which was opened on the 7th of June between the city and Germantown, six miles distant, I witnessed a most extraordinary mode of selling the stock in some new bank. It was a scene worthy of St. Giles's or Billingsgate; and such as I should never have expected to see in the quiet city of Philadelphia.

The manner in which it was disposed of was as follows: the sellers were in a house, with a small aperture in a window-shutter, only sufficiently large to admit a man's hand, and through which he delivered his money; but having received his scrip, after a lapse of some time, it was impossible for him to withdraw through the crowd of purchasers; no one would make way, lest he should thereby lose his chance of ever gaining the window.

The only plan then was, that one of his friends threw him the end of a rope, which he fastened round his body, and part of the mob, who came as mere lookers-on, dragged him out by main strength, frequently with the loss of the better half of his apparel. Many had, however, come prepared for the worst, by leaving their coats, shirts, and hats, at home.

It was here that the strongest went to the wall, and various were the schemes adopted to keep possession. One fellow had very knowingly brought a gimlet with him, and, boring it into the shutter, held on with one hand, while he fought most manfully with the other.

[At this point, Editor Smith, in a footnote, supplements this description as follows: "In another instance a strong man lashed himself to the window-shutter.—Ed."]

A bystander told me that a large party had leagued together for mutual support, and taken possession of the window the proceeding evening; but that a stronger one attacked them in the morning, and drove them from their position, though not without several heads, arms, and legs being broken in the affray. It appeared, therefore, that the only chance a peaceable citizen had of obtaining any stock was to hire the greatest bully he could find to fight his battles for him.

This scene continued throughout three days; and besides many dangerous and severe wounds which were inflicted in the contest, one man was killed.

[Here the editor of Waldie's enters another footnote to give general confirmation and to state such a scene was not unique: "We are not sure as to the killing, but the scene described is not otherwise exaggerated, and to the disgrace of our city there were several repititions. A gentleman of property lost the best part of his ear, which was hacked off by a butcher knife; he was one of a party dislodged from the windows which had been taken possession of before daylight. These scenes, it is hoped, will not occur hereafter, as experience has proved the necessity of a sale of the stock of newly incorporated banks at auction.—Ed."]

In consequence, however, of this and similar disturbances meetings of respectable citizens were held, to discuss means to prevent a recurrence of them on like occasions; and, as an additional proof that they were ashamed of these proceedings, one of them expressed a hope "that I had not witnessed a sale of bank stock." Pursuing my way to the rail-road, I overheard a bricklayer call out from his kiln to another at some distance, "I say, Jem, Bob'll have a blow out tomorrow." "Why? how?" "He's gone to buy stock, and he'll work his way amongst them, I know."

FLASHBACK TO THE BOSTON OF 1837

THIS IS the Boston of 1837, the Boston of runaway omnibuses and hit-and-run chaises, of financial panic and cannon-celebrated Whig victories, of highwaymen and rattlesnakes at its doors. It was a year of balloon ascensions and fire company riots and of New England's first mechanics fair, the latter recognizable by its myriad exhibits of Yankee ingenuity and by its pickpockets. A time when travel in that novelty, the railroad train—called "the cars" then and long afterwards—could prove colder than a sleighride. The Semaphoric Telegraph, with one "repeating station on the cupola of the old State House," was signaling news from incoming ships to State Street.

Samuel N. Dickinson (1801–1848), compiler of this "Boston Almanac," which with its varied information is actually a Boston guide, declared with wisdom as well as business acumen: "The general utility and interest of these local events cannot be doubted. When they are read collectively as here presented, they are not only interesting, but they also contain instruction, and present hints and cautions to reflecting persons, which are seldom gathered from reading them in a cursory manner in the daily papers."

From The Boston Almanac, For the Year 1838.

MEMORANDA OF EVENTS IN BOSTON, DURING THE YEAR 1837.

JANUARY

12. The Ocean Insurance Company declare a dividend of 14 per cent. for the last six months. This dividend made 64 per cent. or $128,000 which this company have paid for the last 18 months, on a capital of $200,000.

FEBRUARY

13. Several passengers in the cars from Providence severely frost bitten while detained on the road, from freezing of the water.

18. A woman knocked down by a stage coach in Water Street. Pieces of an earthern vessel she had in her hand cut the jugular vein, and she died in a few moments.

MARCH

2. Great excitement at Amory Hall in consequence of an intended lecture to ladies, exclusively, on physical education. Many women were present, but so great was the tumult made by persons adverse to Graham and his lecture, that his object was defeated.

15. John Merrill, commonly called the *honey and butter man,* sentenced at the Municipal Court on six several indictments for cheating. His method was to call at a gentleman's store and say, the gentleman's lady had purchased a pot of honey of him at the house, and sent him to the store for pay, when in fact he had not seen house, lady or honey. He succeeded in this game 7 or 8 times.

MAY

11. The New York Banks suspend specie payments. On the following day the Banks in Boston adopt the same measure.[1] A meeting of Bank Delegates was held at the hall of the Tremont Bank, at which it was voted "That the Banks in this city and vicinity do suspend specie payments for the present." The banks throughout the whole country suspend specie payments.

11. Cooke's Equestrian Company arrive from New York, and open at the Lion Theatre.

12. Since November last there have been one hundred and sixty-eight failures in Boston, in consequence of the severity of the times.

JUNE

6. A lady in a chaise, (on the crossbridge leading from Craigie's to Charlestown, the Cambridge omnibus and horses coming furiously towards her, having run away.) had the presence of mind to stop her horse and step out, which she had barely done, when the omnibus struck the chaise, and dashed it to pieces.

[1] 1837 was a panic year, virtually all banks suspending specie payment in May.

Boston's State Street in 1837.

11. Great Riot in Broad street. It commenced between an engine company, returning from a fire, and an Irish funeral procession. It has not been satisfactorily ascertained which party were the aggressors. The tumult increased to such a degree, that nearly a thousand persons, at one time, were supposed to be engaged in a brawl, the most desperate that ever occurred in this city. Several houses were broken into, the furniture shattered, and cast into the street. Beds ripped open, and their contents given to the winds. Sticks, stones, bricks, and all manner of missiles, were discharged by the combatants, at each other, with the utmost ferocity—and yet, strange to tell, no one was killed in the affray. The military were called out, and in a strong body marched to the scene of action, and in a short time the rioters were dispersed or captured. Crowds were sent off to the Police Court; and, at length, after the proper

authorities had sifted the whole affair, it resulted in sending John Whaley *for four months*, and John Welsh and Barney Fanning, each *two months*, at hard labor, in the House of Correction.

19. Christopher Jones, an Englishman, undertook to perform a novel feat on South Boston bridge, where the water was about 8 feet deep, by jumping over in the garb of a man, and coming up in female attire. With a stone weighing about 25 lbs., and a rope about six feet long, fastened to his body, he sprung into the water, and while under, trying to arrange his dress, he became entangled and was drowned.

21. Mr. Lauriat made a very fine ascension from Chelsea, about five o'clock. After mounting to a very great height, in a direction about north, he alighted in Lynn. One of the ferry-boats, in returning, after the balloon had gone off, came nigh sinking, in consequence of the great number of passengers she had on board. She was relieved by the boat coming from the opposite side of the Ferry.

21. Since the first of May the Fire Department have been called out sixty-three times, sixteen of which were on false alarms.

JULY

7. Three boys detected in laying stones on the Boston and Worcester Railroad. They were committed to jail in Lowell.

8. Patrick Mahony, the boy sentenced to be hung for setting fire to the Cambridge Alms House, had his sentence commuted to imprisonment for life, by the Governor.

19. A Rattlesnake, 4 feet long, with 8 rattles, killed on the Dedham turnpike, by Daniel Barker. The snake darted at him twice. Several rattlesnakes have been killed in this vicinity this summer, one of which measured about 9 feet, and had 20 rattles.

AUGUST

7. A book thief detected in Cornhill; he had been stealing books from Burnham's Antiquarian Bookstore. He made free to bolt out the back way, and up Franklin Avenue, not stopping long enough to have it ascertained who he was.

Model of the Boston & Worcester's Meteor engine and its train. The three boys "detected in laying stones on the Boston and Worcester Railroad" in July 1837 were trying to derail a train like this.

SEPTEMBER

1. A salute of one hundred guns was fired at one o'clock from Bunker Hill, in honor of the Whig victory in Rhode Island.

18. The first Mechanics Fair in New England, opened this day in Faneuil and Quincy Halls, at 12 o'clock, announced by the firing of cannon and the ringing of a large bell placed among the articles for exhibition. The number of articles of various kinds was estimated at fifteen thousand, including specimens of the most finished workmanship, from a steam-engine down to a pair of scissors and a pen-knife, both made of one five cent piece. The throng of visitors was very great during the exhibition.

19. Mr. Cyrus Lothrop robbed, while at the Fair, of $30,000 in notes and $2000 in bank bills. Mr. Josiah Dunham robbed of $400 and many valuable papers. Two other persons were also robbed of their pocket books.

NOVEMBER

8. Mr. Gustin, a drover, was robbed on the Mill Dam of a small sum of money by a highwayman.

13. The Maverick House at East Boston was brilliantly illuminated, in honor of the Whig triumphs, and a salute of 100 guns fired. On the same occasion a splendid entertainment was given by Mr. John W. Fenno, at which addresses were made by Mr. Webster, and others.

19. Another deputation of Indians arrived from Washington, belonging to the Pawnees, Ottoways, and Upper Mississippi tribes; they staid at Concert Hall, visited the Navy Yard, Theatres, Faneuil Hall, Armories, etc. They staid but one day.

DECEMBER

9. A teamster was run against on Warren bridge by a chaise, and thrown under the wheels ot his own vehicle, where his head was crushed in a most shocking manner. The men in the chaise, regardless of the accident, drove on as fast as possible.

THE HUGE CONGREGATIONS OF WILD PIGEONS

INCREDIBLE but true is this testimony (1847–48) respecting the wild pigeons of the United States. Other writers have borne like witness as to their unbelievable numbers, the thunderous noise they made, the great branches broken by their weight, the guano and the easy and wholesale killing of them by guns, sulphur smoke, poles and other simple means.

Speaking of this phenomenon as he saw it in the 1840s near Florida, Missouri, Mark Twain wrote: "I remember the pigeon seasons, when the birds would come in millions and cover the trees and by their weight break down the branches. They were clubbed to death with sticks; guns were not necessary and were not used." As late as 1870, in Iowa, Hamlin Garland, the author, saw "enormous flocks of pigeons, in clouds which almost filled the sky."

Our wild or passenger pigeon—now vanished—is described as a large slender bird with a small head, short strong legs, long tapering tail and long, pointed and powerful wings; a beautiful and graceful bird, about sixteen inches long, colored bluish above and reddish-brown underneath.

Benedict Henry Revoil (1816–82) was connected with the Ministry of Public Instruction and the Bibliotèque Nationale before he left France, in 1841, to spend a few years in the U.S. Here he put on three comedies, written in English, did some correspondence for a newspaper, and hunted in different regions of the land to produce his book on hunting in North America. Back in France he continued to translate German and English and American books.

From The Hunter and Trapper in North America. *By Benedict Revoil. Translated by* W. H. Davenport Adams.

Along the waters of the Green River, in Kentucky, I saw the most magnificent roosting-place which came across my notice during my residence in the United States. It was situated on the threshold of a forest, whose trees were of immense height; trunks upright, tall, and isolated, starting up straight from the soil. A company of sixty hunters had just installed themselves in the environs, escorted by vehicles loaded with provisions and warlike munitions. They had raised their tents, and a couple of negro cooks were preparing the dinner. Among them were two Glasgow farmers, who had brought a herd of three hundred pigs to fatten upon pigeons, and thus, in a very short time, fit them for the market. On my arrival in the camp I was astonished, nay, stupified, by the quantity of slaughtered pigeons which strewed the ground. Fifteen women were engaged in plucking them, cleansing and salting them, and packing them in barrels. What surprised me most was to learn from the hunters that, though the roosting-place was empty through the day, every night it was covered with myriads of pigeons returning from Indiana, where they had spent the day in the vicinity of the village of Coridon, thus accomplishing a flight of one hundred leagues. It is useless to say that next morning they resumed the same route at early dawn. The ground over the whole area of the roosting place was covered with guano, one or two inches thick. At your first view of this gray-coloured soil, these denuded trees—their branches leafless and without sap—you would have supposed that it was already the middle of winter, or that some tornado had devastated the forest and withered the surrounding scenery.

The hunters began their sport in the evening, and lost no time in making the necessary preparations. Some packed up sul-

A passenger pigeon.

phur in small iron pots; others armed themselves with long poles,
like bakers' peels; some carried torches made of resin and branches
of pine; others—and these the leaders of the troop—were armed
with single and double-barrelled guns, loaded almost to the muzzle
with powder and shot.

At sunset each man took up his position in silence, though
not a bird was yet visible on the horizon. Suddenly, I heard these
words repeated by every hunter:—"Here they come!"

In fact, the horizon grew dark; and the noise made by the
pigeons resembled that of the terrible mistral of Provence as it
plunges into the gorges of the Apennines.

When the column of pigeons swept above my head, I experienced a shudder, the effect partly of astonishment and partly
of cold; for the displacement of air occasioned an unusual at

mospheric current. Meantime, the poles were waving to and fro, bringing down thousands of pigeons. The fires had all been kindled as if by magic. I was witness of an admirable spectacle. The pigeons arrived by millions, rushing headlong one upon another, pressing close together like the bees in a swarm which has escaped from its hive in the month of May. The lofty tops of the overloaded roosting-place cracked, and, falling to the ground, carried down with them the pigeons which had perched upon the branches. So great was the noise, that you could not hear your neighbor speak, though he exerted himself with all his strength. It was with difficulty you could distinguish an occasional shot, though you saw hunters constantly reloading their weapons. We all kept to the edge of the wood, out of the reach of the falling branches; and thus the massacre continued throughout the night, though after eleven o'clock the passage of the pigeons had wholly ceased.

At daybreak the whole army of pigeons sprung into the air to fly in search of their daily food. The noise was then indescribable and truly frightful. It could only be compared to the simultaneous discharge of a battery of cannon.

The hunters levied their tithe, and out of this mass of dead and dying selected the plumpest pigeons, with which they loaded their waggons, leaving the young fry to the dogs and pigs of the association.

Two months after this memorable hunt, of which I have preserved a very lively recollection, I found myself, one morning, on the quay of East River, at New York, when my eyes were attracted by the following inscription, painted in black letters on a strip of sail-cloth: *"Wild Pigeons for Sale."* I proceeded on board a small coasting-vessel, and was shown by the captain several baskets of dead pigeons, which had been killed inland, and which he offered for sale at *three cents* a piece.

A Tennessee planter once assured me, that in a single day he had caught, with a net, four hundred dozen pigeons. His negroes, twenty in number, were thoroughly worn out in the evening with knocking down the birds that had traversed his estate.

In the month of October 1848, the flights of pigeons in the state of New York were so considerable, that these birds were sold on the quays and in the principal markets at the rate of a penny a piece.

One morning, in this same month of October 1848, on the heights of the village of Hastings, which stretches along the Hudson River, I fired some thirty times into a swarm of pigeons, securing a booty of one hundred and thirty-nine birds. This number included about eighty enormous birds, fat and plump as young chickens.

A HAPPY EVENING FOR THEATER AUDIENCE

JOSEPH JEFFERSON (1829–1905) and Edwin Forrest (1806–72) were distinguished American actors of the last century. Jefferson, whose fame is linked with his portrayal of Rip Van Winkle, came of a line of actors and had long success in the theatre. He was a personality in his own right. He achieved money and the friendship of the great, including President Grover Cleveland, a fishing companion. Jefferson, who landscape-painted as a recreation, wrote a fine autobiography.

Forrest, in contrast to Jefferson, was a tragedian. He owned great physical strength and voice but lacked much pliability and humor. His talent marshaled big audiences until his death. The personal rivalry and enmity between Forrest and the English actor, William Macready, led to the Astor Place Opera House (New York) riot of 1849, when a pro-Forrest mob attacked the theater where Macready was performing. The 7th regiment was called out, fired, and twenty-two were killed and thirty-six wounded.

From The Autobiography of Joseph Jefferson.

During the engagement of which I am about to speak, and on occasion while we were rehearsing "Damon and Pythias," Edwin Adams, who was cast for *Pythias*, was going through the exciting scene in which that character parts with *Calanthe*. Forrest took exception to the business arrangements of the stage; but as this was one of his quiet, dignified mornings, he made his objections with respectful deference, saying that if Mr. Adams would allow him he would suggest some new business that might improve the scene. Adams expressed himself as quite willing to receive any instruction; so Forrest went through the parting with *Calanthe*, giving some new and very good suggestions. Adams tried but failed to catch Forrest's idea. It was tried over and over till finally Forrest became impatient. Again taking Adam's place, he rushed towards the fainting form of *Calanthe*, and as he dropped upon his knee, throwing his head tragically forward, his hat fell off. Now it is always a comical thing to see a man's high black-silk hat tumble from his head, but especially when he is going through a tragic scene. Forrest for a moment hesitated whether he should pause and pick up the hat or not; at last he made a savage grab for it, but it eluded his grasp, and, slipping through his fingers rolled round the stage, he pursuing it with tragic passion. The company, one by one, turned their heads away, quietly enjoying his discomfiture. At last he secured it, and fixing it firmly on his head, he proceeded with the action of the scene. He felt we had been laughing at him, and became furious. Rushing upon *Calanthe*, he embraced her again and again. "Farewell, my love," cried he in dire woe. He then tore himself from her embrace, and madly careering up the stage ran head first into a scene that the carpenters were moving across the stage, mashing the unlucky hat over his eyes. He struggled manfully to get it off, but with no effect till Adams and I came to the rescue. We were now all in a roar of laughter. For a moment he looked bewildered and even angry, but as the absurdity of the scene dawned upon him he joined in the merriment, and declared it was the most ridiculous thing that had ever occurred.

At the conclusion of the Richmond engagement[1] the company journeyed to Washington, where we were to open with Forrest as *Metamora*—a character that he detested, and one that the public admired. Forrest was always in a state of intense irritation during the rehearsal and performance of this drama. Irregularities

[1] This was in 1854 or 1855.

that he would have overlooked under ordinary circumstances were now magnified to an enormous size, so that when he donned the buckskin shirt, and stuck the hunting-knife of the American savage in his wampum belt, he was ready to scalp any offending actor who dared to cross his path. The copper-colored liquid with which he stained his cheeks might literally have been called "war paint."

At the rehearsal the poor property man, old Jake Search, got in a dreadful state of nervousness, and everything went wrong. The tragedian naturally held me, as stage-manager, responsible for these accidents, particularly as the unlucky Jake would conceal himself behind set pieces, or mysteriously disappear through traps as each mishap occurred. In the midst of this dreadful confusion, principally brought about by his own ill humor, Forrest turned on me, saying he would not act that night, and strode out of the theater. I hurried through the front of the house, and heading him off in the alley addressed him, as nearly as I can remember, in the following words:

"Mr. Forrest, before you decide upon this step let me state an important fact, that perhaps has not crossed your mind." He saw I was in earnest, and stopped short to listen, as I resumed: "Mr. Ford, the manager, is absent, so I must take his responsibility to the public on myself. The blunders on the stage this morning have been unfortunate, perhaps culpable, but you must pardon me for saying that your excited manner and somewhat unreasonable demands have contributed not a little to confuse the company and bring about the disorder. But be that as it may, there is another and still more important matter to consider. Every seat in the theater is taken for to-night; the audience will crowd the house in expectation of a great dramatic treat, to which they have been looking forward for some time. If you decline to act, and so break your contract with the public, what course is left for me? Why, only this: I must wait for the vast concourse of people to assemble, and then go before them and explain the reason of your non-appearance. I shall have to make a clear statement of the case, and say that you have refused to act because there were some slight discrepancies and irregularities in the rehearsal. The public are, you know, quite unreasonable when their diversion is checked, and it is likely that they will be indignant at the disappointment, fail-

Edwin Forrest as Metamora. Lithograph, from a photograph by Mathew Brady.

ing to see the reason as clearly as you may have done. Now consider for a moment: under these circumstances will it not be more magnanimous in you to overlook the shortcomings and go on with the rehearsal?"

He paused for a moment and said: "I will not go back to the rehearsal. I am too much excited, and my presence on the stage now will only make matters worse; but if you will see that details are attended to, I will act tonight."

I promised to do so, and we parted. I was only too glad to get rid of him on those terms, in his then intemperate state of mind. I went back to the stage and dismissed the rehearsal, cautioning the actors to do what they could to render the night's performance creditable. I now began to hunt up the delinquent and frightened property man, Jake Search,—an appropriate name for a fellow who needed so much looking after,—and discovered him hiding under a pile of old scenery. "Is he gone?" said Search. "Yes," I answered, "but he will return tonight; so see that your properties are in good condition, or he will be the death of you."

The night came and matters progressed favorably until the council scene. One of the characters here, being overcome with nervousness, reversed his questions to *Metamora*, giving the wrong lines, and of course receiving an absurd answer. The audience, recognizing the confusion of the dialogue, began to laugh, and of course this made matters worse. The act terminates with the Indian's great speech, "From the east to the west, from the north to the south, the loud cry of vengeance shall be heard," and here he hurls his knife into the center of the stage, where it quivers a defiance as the curtain falls. In his anger and excitement the blade failed to stick in the stage and bounded into the orchestra, the handle hitting the double-bass player on the top of his head, which was as innocent of hair as a billiard-ball, so as the curtain came down the old fellow was stamping about and rubbing his bald pate to the delight of the audience.

I realized now that the storm had burst in earnest, and that a total wreck would soon follow. Knowing that I could not avert the catastrophe, and having no desire to face the tragedian's wrath, like a politic but disloyal captain I deserted the ship and went in front to see it go down. Byron says of a battle, "Oh, what a sight to him who has no friend or brother there!" to which Prentice adds, "and is not there himself." The latter was now my case. I was not there myself, and I did not intend to be, so from the secure corner of an upper private box I watched the progress of the most disastrous performance I had ever seen.

As the curtain rises on the last act the tribe of *Metamora* should rush through the woods as their leader calls them; but by this time the braves were so frightened that they had become demoralized, and as the foremost rushed through the opening in the woods his long bow got crosswise between two trees. This not only precipitated the redskin over it, but the entire tribe followed, tumbling head over heels into the middle of the stage. I trembled now lest the "big Injun" would refuse to put in an appearance. At last, to my relief, the audience quieted down, and Forrest strode upon the stage. If I remember the story, at this point *Metamora*'s wife and children had been stolen away and murdered. His pathos was fine, and by his magnificent acting he reduced his audience to attention and enthusiasm. All was now going well, and I looked forward to a happy termination of the play, which I was thankful to know had nearly reached its climax.

A funeral pile of burning fagots was then brought on, at which some pale-face was to be sacrificed. The two Indians in charge of this mysterious-looking article set it down so unsteadily that a large sponge, saturated with flaming alcohol, tumbled off and rolled down the stage, leaving a track of fire in its wake. "Put it out!" said Forrest, "put it out!" whereupon the two Indians went down on their knees and began to blow alternately in a seesaw way, singeing each other's eyebrows at every puff. The audience could not stand this comical picture, and began to break forth in laughter. "Let the theater burn!" roared Forrest. At last one tall Indian, supposed to be second in command, majestically waved off the two who were blowing, and stamped his foot with force and dignity upon the flaming sponge, at which a perfect fountain of burning alcohol spouted up his leather legs. He caught fire, tried to put himself out, rubbing and jumping about frantically, and at last danced off the stage in the most comical agony. Forrest made a furious exit; the curtain was dropped, and the public, in perfect good nature, dispersed. I mingled with the crowd as it went forth, and I never saw the faces of an audience, at the end of a five-act comedy, wreathed in such smiles.

BUSINESSLIKE HANGINGS IN MONTANA TERRITORY

THIS is authentic history of lawlessness and frontier law by a man who witnessed at least some of it and who was in the midst of all of it. As editor of *The Montana Post* of Virginia City, a headquarters of the Vigilantes, and a friend of some of the organizers and leaders of that organization, Thomas J. Dimsdale knew whereof he wrote.

The man himself and his background contrast with the stern and cheerful satisfaction that colors his recital of these hangings. Dimsdale, described by his Montana friends as bashful and unskilled with firearms, was an Englishman, destined by his parents for the Church, who wandered to Montana Territory where he became its first superintendent of public instruction and editor of its first newspaper.

His narrative of the Vigilantes in 1863–64 ran as a serial in his paper, from August 1865 to March 1866; in the latter year it sold as a book, at $2.00 a copy for gold dust and $2.25 for greenbacks. Mark Twain quoted from it, inaccurately, in *Roughing It* (1872). Do not confuse Virginia City, Montana Territory, with the more famed mining town, Virginia City, Nevada Territory.

Here are presented some scattered incidents of that grim interval when the Vigilantes operated against the "road agents," or highwaymen, and their fraternity of thieves and murderers.

From The Vigilantes of Montana, or Popular Justice in the Rocky Mountains: Being a Correct and Impartial Narrative of the Chase, Trial, Capture and Execution of Henry Plummer's Road Agent Band, Together with Accounts of the Lives and Crimes of Many of the Robbers and Desperadoes, the Whole Being Interspersed with Sketches of Life in the Mining Camps of the "Far West." *By Prof. Thos. J. Dimsdale.*

At dusk, three horses were brought into town, belonging severally and respectively to the three marauders so often mentioned,

Early book advertising in the Wild West. The cost of the book in gold dust or in greenbacks can be made out at the bottom of the poster.

Plummer, Stinson and Ray. It was truly conjectured that they had determined to leave the country, and it was at once settled that they should be arrested that night. Parties were detailed for the work. Those entrusted with the duty performed it admirably. Plummer was undressing when taken at his house. His pistol (a self-cocking weapon) was broken and useless. Had he been armed, resistance would have been futile; for he was seized the moment the door was opened in answer to the knocking from without. Stinson was arrested at Toland's, where he was spending the evening. He would willingly have done a little firing, but his captors were too quick for him. Ray was lying on a Gambling table when seized. The three details marched their men to a given point, en route to the gallows. . . . A rope taken from a noted functionary's bed had been mislaid and could not be found. A nigger boy was sent off for some of that highly necessary but unpleasant remedy for crime, and the bearer made such good time that some hundreds of feet of hempen necktie were on the ground before the arrival of the party at the gallows. On the road Plummer heard the voice and recognized the person of the leader. He came to him and begged for his life; but was told, "It is useless for you to beg for your life; that affair is settled and cannot be altered. You are to be hanged. You cannot feel harder about it than I do; but I cannot help it if I would." Ned Ray, clothed with curses as with a garment, actually tried fighting, but found that he was in the wrong company for such demonstrations; and Buck Stinson made the air ring with the blasphemous and filthy expletives which he used in addressing his captors. Plummer exhausted every argument and plea that his imagination could suggest, in order to induce his captors to spare his life. He begged to be chained down in the meanest cabin; offered to leave the country forever; wanted a jury trial; implored time to settle his affairs; asked to see his sister-in-law, and, falling on his knees, with tears and sighs declared to God that he was too wicked to die. He confessed his numerous murders and crimes, and seemed almost frantic at the prospect of death.

The first rope being thrown over the cross-beam, and the noose being rove, the order was given to "Bring up Ned Ray." This desperado was run up with curses on his lips. Being loosely pinioned, he got his fingers between the rope and his neck, and thus prolonged his misery.

Buck Stinson saw his comrade robber swinging in the death agony, and blubbered out, "There goes poor Ed Ray." Scant mercy had he shown to his numerous victims. By a sudden twist of his head at the moment of his elevation, the knot slipped under his chin, and he was some minutes dying.

The order to "Bring up Plummer" was then passed and repeated; but no one stirred. The leader went over to this perfect gentleman, as his friends called him, and was met by a request to "give a man time to pray." Well knowing that Plummer relied for a rescue upon other than Divine aid, he said briefly and decidedly, "Certainly; but let him say his prayers up here." Finding all efforts to avoid death were useless, Plummer rose and said no more prayers. Standing under the gallows which he had erected for the execution of Horan,[1] this second Haman slipped off his necktie and threw it over his shoulder to a young friend who had boarded at his house, and who believed him innocent of crime, saying as he tossed it to him, "Here is something to remember me by." In the extremity of his grief, the young man threw himself weeping and wailing upon the ground. Plummer requested that the men would give him a good drop, which was done, as far as circumstances permitted, by hoisting him up as high as possible, in their arms, and letting him fall suddenly. He died quickly and without much struggle.

It was necessary to seize Ned Ray's hands, and by a violent effort to draw his fingers from between the noose and his neck before he died. Probably he was the last to expire of the guilty trio.

The weather was intensely cold, but the party stood for a long time round the bodies of the suspended malefactors, determined that rescue should be impossible.

On the evening of the 13th of January, 1864, the Executive Committee,[2] in solemn conclave assembled, determined on hanging six of them forthwith.

While the Committee were deliberating in secret, a small party of men who were at that moment receiving sentence of death, were gathered in an upper room at a gambling house, and engaged in betting at faro. Jack Gallagher suddenly remarked, "While we are here betting, those Vigilante sons of —— are passing sentence on us." This is considered to be the most remarkable and most truth-

[1] Plummer, "chief of the road agents," had been named sheriff.
[2] Of the Vigilantes.

ful saying of his whole life; but he might be excused telling the truth once, as it was entirely accidental.

Express messengers were sent to warn the men of the neighboring towns in the gulch, and the summons was instantly obeyed.

Morning came—the last on earth that the five desperadoes should ever behold. The first rays of light showed the pickets of the Vigilantes stationed on every eminence and point of vantage round the city. The news flew like lightning through the town. Many a guilty heart quaked with just fear, and many an assassin's lip turned pale and quivered with irrepressible terror. The detachments of Vigilantes, with compressed lips and echoing footfall, marched in from Nevada,[3] Junction, Summit, Pine Grove, Highland and Fairweather, and halted in a body in Main Street. Parties were immediately detailed for the capture of the road agents, and all succeeded in their mission, except the one which went after Bill Hunter, who had escaped.

The criminals were marched into the centre of a hollow square, which was flanked by four ranks of Vigilantes, and a column in front and rear, armed with shot-guns and rifles carried at a half present, ready to fire at a moment's warning, completed the array. The pistol men were dispersed through the crowd to attend to the general deportment of outsiders, or, as a good man observed, to take the roughs "out of the wet."

At the word "march!" the party started forward, and halted, with military precision, in front of the Virginia Hotel. The halt was made while the ropes were preparing at the unfinished building, now Clayton & Hale's Drug Store, at the corner of Wallace and Van Buren streets. The logs were up to the square, but there was no roof. The main beam for the support of the roof, which runs across the center of the building, was used as a gallows, the rope being thrown over it, and then taken to the rear and fastened round some of the bottom logs. Five boxes were placed immediately under the beam, as substitutes for drops.

The nooses were adjusted by five men, and—all being ready— Jack Gallagher, as a last request, asked that he might have something to drink, which, after some demur, was acceded to. Club-Foot George looked round, and, seeing an old friend clinging to the logs of the building, said, "Good-by, old fellow—I'm gone"; and,

[3] A town in Montana Territory.

hearing the order, "Men, do your duty"—without waiting for his box to be knocked away—he jumped off, and died in a short time.

Haze stood next; but was left to the last. He was talking all the time, telling the people that he had a kind mother, and that he had been well brought up; that he did not expect that it would have come to that; but that bad company had brought him to it.

Jack Gallagher, while standing on the box, cried all the time, using the most profane and dreadful language. He said, "I hope that forked lightning will strike every strangling —— of you." The box flying from under his feet brought his ribaldry and profanity to a close, which nothing but breaking his neck would ever have done.

Boone Helm, looking coolly at his quivering form, said, "Kick away, old fellow; I'll be in hell with you in a minute." He probably told the truth, for once in his life. He then shouted, "Every man for his principles—hurrah for Jeff. Davis! Let her rip!" The sound of his words was echoed by the twang of the rope.

Frank Parish requested to have a handkerchief tied over his face. His own black necktie, fastened in the road agent's knot, was taken from his throat and dropped over his face like a veil. He seemed serious and quiet, but refused to confess anything more, and was launched into eternity. A bystander asked the guard who adjusted the rope, "Did you not feel for the poor man as you pùt the rope round his neck?" The Vigilanter, whose friend had been slaughtered by the road agents, regarded his interrogator with a stern look, and answered slowly, "Yes, I felt for his left ear!"

On the road back the guard had wormed out of Barney that a stranger was stopping at Van Dorn's, in the Bitter Root valley. "No. 84,"[4] who was leading the party who captured Shears, asked "Does Van live here?" "Yes," said the man himself. "Is George Shears in your house?" asked 84. "Yes," said Van. "Where is he?" "In the next room." "Any objection to our going in?" The man replied by opening the door of the room, on which George became visible, knife in hand. He gave himself up quietly, and seemed so utterly indifferent to death that he perfectly astonished his captors. Taking a walk with 84, he pointed out to him the stolen horses in the corral, and confessed his guilt, as a man would speak of the

---

[4] For security reasons, important members of the Vigilantes, it is indicated, went under numbers instead of names.

weather. He said, "I knew I should have to go up, some time; but I thought I could run another season." When informed of his doom, he appeared perfectly satisfied. On being taken into the barn, where a rope was thrown over a beam, he was asked to walk up a ladder, to save trouble about procuring a drop. He at once complied, addressing his captors in the following unique phraseology, "Gentlemen, I am not used to this business, never having been hung before. Shall I jump off or slide off?" Being told to jump off, he said "All right; good by," and leaped into the air with as much sang froid as if bathing.

The drop was long and the rope tender. It slowly untwisted, and Shears hung, finally, by a single strand. George's parting question was, for a long time, a byword among the Vigilantes.

On looking back at the dreadful state of society which necessitated the organization of the Vigilantes, and on reading these pages, many will learn for the first time the deep debt of gratitude which they owe to that just and equitable body of self-denying and gallant men. It was a dreadful and a disgusting duty that devolved upon them; but it was a duty, and they did it. Far less worthy actions have been rewarded by the thanks of Congress, and medals glitter on many a bosom, whose owner won them lying flat behind a hillock, out of range of the enemy's fire. The Vigilantes, for the sake of their country, encountered popular dislike, the envenomed hatred of the bad, and the cold toleration of some of the unwise good. Their lives they held in their hands. "All's well that ends well." Montana is saved, and they saved it, earning the blessings of future generations, whether they receive them or not.

THE WILD ANIMALS HAVE ESCAPED!— THE *HERALD'S* HOAX

NEWSPAPERMEN OF the 1870s never forgot the New York *Herald's* wild-animal hoax. This is understandable. On November 9, 1874, there was an extravagantly headlined announcement completely filling the

AWFUL CALAMITY.

The Wild Animals Broken Loose from Central Park.

TERRIBLE SCENES OF MUTILATION

A Shocking Sabbath Carnival of Death.

SAVAGE BRUTES AT LARGE

Awful Combats Between the Beasts and the Citizens.

THE KILLED AND WOUNDED

General Duryee's Magnificent Police Tactics.

BRAVERY AND PANIC

How the Catastrophe Was Brought About---Affrighting Incidents.

PROCLAMATION BY THE MAYOR

Governor Dix Shoots the Bengal Tiger in the Street.

CONSTERNATION IN THE CITY

Another Sunday of horror has been added to those already memorable in our city annals. The sad and appalling catastrophe of yesterday is a further illustration of the unforeseen perils to which large communities are exposed. Writing even at a late hour, without full details of the terrors of the evening and night, and with a necessarily incomplete list of the killed and mutilated, we may pause for a moment in the widespread sorrow of the hour to cast a hasty glance over what will be felt as a great calamity for many years. Few of the millions who have visited Central Park, and who, passing in through the entrance at East Sixty-fourth street, have stopped to examine the collection of birds and animals grouped around the old Arsenal building, could by any possibility have foreseen the source of such terrible danger to a whole city in the caged beasts around him, as the trivial incident of yesterday afternoon developed. The unfortunate man to whose fatal imprudence all accounts attribute the outbreak of the wild animals of the menagerie has answered with his life for his temerity, but we have a list of calamities traceable from his act which one life seems inadequate to expiate. We have a list of forty-nine killed

Shaler and Commissioner Duryee, will meet with the obedience which its gravity merits. Discipline is the only means of meeting and conquering such an untoward chain of circumstances, and we here point out that the obedience which is given by the militia to General Shaler, by the police to General Duryee, the hero of the hour, should be cheerfully rendered by the citizens at large to the proclamation of his Honor the Mayor. The deaths and mutilations are already too numerous to risk their increase, and the authorities will only serve the common cause by enforcing the law against those whose curiosity leads them to defy the mandates of the civil power.

The following is the Mayor's proclamation:—

A Proclamation.

MAYOR'S OFFICE, SUNDAY NIGHT, Nov. 1, 1874.

All citizens, except members of the National Guard, are enjoined to keep within their houses or residences until the wild animals now at large are captured or killed. Notice of the release from this order will be spread by the firing of cannon in City Hall Park, Tompkins square, Madison square, The Round and at Macomb's Dam Bridge. Obedience to this order will secure a speedy end to the state of siege occasioned by the calamity of this evening.

An account will be opened at the City Hall of the city of New York for contributions to the sufferers.

THE CATASTROPHE.

The location of the zoological collection in the Park is well known to most New Yorkers; but it appears that changes were made recently in the disposition of the various animals, and to realize the exact nature of the catastrophe it becomes necessary to indicate where the various animals were situated yesterday when the frightful event occurred that spread such terror throughout the city. If you enter the menagerie from Fifth avenue you will find on either hand, running parallel to the street, the houses where the herbivorous beasts were domiciled. In former times several bears from the northern regions occupied the right hand corner, where a few beautiful zebras lately gladdened the eye. To the extreme left were the cages of the several foreign birds formerly devoted to a large collection of monkeys. To the extreme right were the vultures and eagles, and the visitor, by making a short circuit of the large building, known in times gone by as the Arsenal, found himself in front of a handsome wooden structure, one story high, where the principal wild animals resided. Of course the residence of the sea lion was known to everybody. On the inside of the garden the stately giraffe occupied a somewhat large enclosure, and adjacent were a number of pelicans, intermingled with several specimens of the ostrich tribe. The bears were in isolated cages on the green sward, near the common pedestrian route from the Fifth avenue entrance.

THE PROMINENT ANIMALS

in the quadrangle nearest to Fifth avenue were the bison, the nylghau, the zebu, the sacred bull, cow and calf, the zebras, the young elephant, the capybara, the guanaco, the fat tailed Syrian var, the aoudad and the fallow deer. In the valuable monkey collection was the sooty mangabey, the bonnet macaque, the Toque monkey, the pigtailed monkey, the Arabian baboon, the black handed spider monkey, the brown capuchin, the Teetee and the black eared marmoset. Such was the scene before

THE TERRIBLE EVENTS

of yesterday—the bursting forth of the most ferocious of the beasts within the menagerie of the Park, the awful slaughter that ensued, the exciting conflicts between the infuriated animals, the frightful deaths that followed, the destruction of property and the fearful and general excitement, making an era in the history of New York not soon to be forgotten. How singular that Sunday, of all days in the week, should make the occasion of such great panics as mark the record of the past four years. It was a Sabbath morning that witnessed the destruction of Chicago and Boston, and a Sabbath afternoon beheld the streets of New York given up to the fury of a drove of Texan cattle. It was on a Sabbath that the Westfield exploded her boiler. But yesterday capped the climax of unthought possibilities, and it was the Sabbath, too, that deepened the significance of the great disaster.

As everybody knows, the Central Park on Sunday is the popular resort of all classes. The rich and fashionable in their carriages and the poor and humble on foot, alike sally forth to enjoy its beauties. It is safe to say that at least 20,000 people filled the various walks, drives and avenues yesterday. To nine-tenths of the pedestrian visitors the Menagerie is a chief source of attraction. That it contained

safety by this means but he was too close to the animal, for the latter, swinging his unwieldy body toward him, knocked him down with a touch of his shoulder, and an instant after had trampled him out of recognition. Backing down from the mangled body with a swiftness almost incredible from his bulk, the rhinoceros plunged his horrid horn into the dead keeper, dashing the last possible spark of life out against the walls of one of the pens, which likewise gave way. All this tragedy transpired in an instant. Horror stricken, I tried to push my way from the window, but the crowd was now dense behind me, and I could not stir. I cried:—

"For God's sake, let some one run to the police station for help!"

I struggled to get out, putting my hands against the window and my feet below it, and pushing with all my might. An accursed curiosity in the crowd, who were only vaguely conscious of what was transpiring, made my efforts useless. When I looked in through the window again the destruction at the further end had increased, the rhinoceros breaking open the dens of the animals on the left hand side.

THE KEEPER, HYLAND,

whom I had first seen standing spellbound, was advancing, pale as marble, and a navy revolver in his hand, toward the enraged rhinoceros. The animal saw him, turned and made for him in an instant. He sprang aside and fired. The ball hit the rhinoceros on the left shoulder, for he swerved over for an instant; but it can scarcely have more than hurt him a little, as he turned with a whiff, whiff, whiff snort, his head down toward the keeper. The latter, with cat-like agility, retreated toward the lions' and tigers' cages, evidently making for the space between them; but too late. The horrid horn impaled him against the corner cage, killing him instantly, tearing the cage to pieces and releasing the panther, who landed in the middle of the open space with a spring. The cries of all the animals were now joined in horrid chorus by the loud and long-sustained roar of the lion and lioness, the tigers and all the wild beasts, that doubtless had their carniverous instincts whetted by the smell of human blood and the sound and sight of the bloody struggles outside their bars.

"THE WILD ANIMALS ARE LOOSE,"

I yelled, and the savage chorus within bore out my words. At last curiosity seemed to give way. The crowd fled in all directions, women falling as they ran, and no one staying to help them out of the way of the coming danger, which was then shaping itself so swiftly. I ran to the police station in the Arsenal Building, and found that the sergeant on duty was dozing quietly. I shook him up, told him in a few words what was the matter, and ran round to the space in front of the Arsenal. There I found Keeper Miller talking to the policeman, who was just coming off duty. Miller laughed at my story.

"Come around," I said earnestly.

"Too thin, young fellow," said the policeman.

"Don't you hear?" I said, as the roaring of the animals sounded ominously in our ears. The sergeant now came running out in search of the policeman.

"Anderson and Hyland are killed," said he to Miller. "Why don't you stir yourself."

Miller is a tall, stalwart man of about thirty-three, and it is but just to say that from the moment the sergeant spoke he sprang into action. He rushed into the keeper's room and grasped a sixteen shooter rifle, which is kept loaded for such emergencies, and ran out through the central door in the rear of the Arsenal to the window the crowd had just deserted. What he saw evidently appalled him, as he let the butt of his rifle fall to the ground and continued gazing in through the window like one in a dream. From his own lips I have learned what he saw. He said:—

"An attentive glance through the window revealed the fact that

THE HUGE RHINOCEROS HAD BROKEN LOOSE.

He had apparently made no more of the massive barrier that enclosed him than of a sheet of pasteboard. I saw the dead bodies of Hyland and Anderson, the former nearer to me than the other. The panther was crouched over Hyland's body knawing horribly at his head. I recognized his body by the striped shirt which I could just see hanging tattered from the arm. It was growing dark, and this made everything look twice as fearful. I saw the rhinoceros plunge blindly forward against the double tier of cages where the black and spotted leopards, the striped hyena, the prairie wolf, the puma and the jaguar were lying. Judging from the condition of the cages the onset of the powerful and infuriated rhinoceros must have been tremendous. In some cases the bars were only bent to an elbow, but, as a rule, they snapped asunder like kindling wood before the smashing weight brought against them

THE RELEASE OF THE ANIMALS

mentioned angered still more the lions and tigers and all the rest within the building. The rhinoceros in the meantime was busy in the work of destruction. In a few moments more he had broken down the pens of the wild swine, the manatee, the American tapir, the two-toed sloth and the pair of kangaroos. Just then, too, Lincoln the Numidian lion escaped from his cage through some unfortunate oversight committed at feeding time. The bolt of his prison door was insecure, and when the raging rhinoceros butted his head against the bottom it flew wide open. Hardly had Lincoln the lion bounded into the centre aisle of the building when the three cages containing the black and spotted leopards, the tiger and tigeresses, the black wolf and the striped and spotted hyenas were sprang open by an overpowering charge from the now desperate rhinoceros. The noise of this crash might have been heard several blocks away. It was followed by a series of fights between the liberated beasts. Close by a window on the western side of the building the black wolf sprung upon the flank of the Bengal tiger. The lion stood a little distance away pawing the floor, awaiting rathe

A section of the front page of the New York Herald, *November 9, 1874.*

Herald's first news page, reporting that the beasts had escaped from Central Park Zoo.

The headlines said, in part: Awful Calamity, The Wild Animals Broken Loose From Central Park, Terrible Scene of Mutilation, Savage Brutes at Large, Awful Combat Between The Beasts and The Citizens, The Killed and Wounded, Proclamation by Mayor. The article was circumstantial to the last degree, including vivid incidents of the escape and of the bloody roamings on the streets, "incomplete" lists of the dead and wounded, tabulations of the animals shot and those still at large, and the mayor's proclamation, warning all but the National Guard off the streets.

At the bottom of the last column, under a subhead the same size as more than four dozen other subheads employed to punctuate the account, was a short explanatory paragraph beginning: "Of course the entire story given above is pure fabrication." It is not recorded that any excited citizen read down through that final paragraph.

Here, the man who wrote that panic-producing story tells how and why it was written. Joseph I. C. Clarke (1846–1925) was born in Ireland, was a leader of the Fenian movement in London, and came to this country in 1868. His speaking ability induced the Republicans to send him out campaigning for the Grant-Colfax ticket. He served the *Herald*, 1870–83, and again, 1903–6, in various capacities. During 1883–95, he was managing editor of Pulitzer's *Morning Journal* and from 1906–13, publicity chief for the Standard Oil Company. Clarke wrote half a dozen plays—and regarded himself more as a playwright than a newspaperman—some poems and ballads, and a book on Japan. He was president general of the Irish American Historical Society, 1913–23.

From My Life and Memories. *By Joseph I. C. Clarke.*

Buried at the "Night Desk," as the Night Editorship of the *Herald* was called, through 1874 and 1875, I had little chance of doing what I then longed to do, write the passing events of the world. Save for a few things accomplished, I was nailed to the cross of sifting news as it came in, ordering telegraph stories, declaring for or against "spread heads," writing them in the *Herald* vein, directing the staff, selecting the articles for the editorial page, reading proofs, seeing the forms to press, waiting for possible second editions, thus keeping astoundingly busy 7 P.M. to 4 A.M. on the following morning. I had one advantage, two nights off a week.

Some time in October, 1874, Mr. Connery[1] dropped in one evening, and disclosed to me an idea he had of making a sensational story founded on a visit he had made to the menagerie in Central Park one Sunday afternoon when he had observed the flimsy nature of the cages for the wild beasts. Suppose the animals broke loose and scattered over the city! "Spring a story like that," I thought, "and *the citizens will insist on the cages being made safe.*" Pursuing this idea, he put Harry O'Connor, one of the *Herald*'s cleverest writers, on it, but his story, humorous in places, was unconvincing and would not have deceived a ten-year-old. With this, he handed me a bundle of manuscripts saying he wanted me to take it in hand, go up to Central Park, work out the plan, and make the story as strong and realistic as I could, rewrite it to fill an entire page, using any of O'Connor's stuff I pleased, and put the whole in type. At the end I was to append a paragraph saying that the foregoing was only a hoax. Now Connery was the mildest of men, father of a large family, given at rare times to little jokes, but a great, far-seeing worker and especially learned in *Herald* traditions.

I took it in hand, carried out his instructions to the best that in me lay, and on the first Sunday in November sent it up to the composing-room after all the regular news matter was in type, and so had the proofs ready for Mr. Connery on Monday morning when he came down to the office. It made about a third of a column short of the page—enough, I thought, for the spread-head when the order came to print it. For Mr. Connery, I learned it was not only a chance to read it himself, but to submit it to Mr. Bennett[2] who was then in town. I heard no more of it until the following Sunday evening when an order came from Connery to "run it" in the Monday paper. I "ran it."

Reaching home as usual at 4 A.M., I awakened my wife and told her when she read the paper in the morning not to be frightened about the wild animals. It was the story I had been writing,

---

[1] Thomas B. Connery, managing editor.
[2] James Gordon Bennett, the son, who inherited the *Herald* on his father's death in 1872.

and whose subject I had kept from her. "Indeed?" she said shortly, and resumed her slumber.

There was, however, no indifference in New York by the time I awakened. I went out at noon. There was a public school in our street, and one after another I saw mothers presently come forth with one or more children and dash homeward dragging the little ones after them. By George! It scared me. I went some half mile up to my mother's home through almost empty streets. I found the family around the lunch table in consternation. My cousin Jennie was reading my story in a broken voice, my mother and sister were in tears. They rose up as I came in. "Thank God, you are safe!" When I told them it was not true and showed them the explanatory paragraph at the end, they were not to be quieted and denounced the writer. He must be a terrible fellow. I agreed. Their feelings, I declared, did them honor, and hurriedly made my escape.

For two weeks stories were current of the aspects of the scare.

When the *Herald* was brought up to Bennett with his coffee as he lay abed, he was said, after a gulp of coffee with a glance at the paper, to lie back and groan.

Connery came down early to find small boys selling the *Herald* along the streets shouting, "Wild Animals, ten cents a copy." Soon after he was seated in his chair, George W. Hosmer, an old Civil War correspondent, strode into the office, throwing open his coat and pointing to a huge army revolver, said: "Well, here I am!"

It was, however, in the office of the *New York Times* (then occupying the building at the corner of Park Row nearest to City Hall) that the utmost effect was wrought. George F. Williams, a Civil War Veteran of bright journalistic qualities but a very excitable man, was City Editor. He had arrived in a fury. He had hired a coach on his way down, collected every reporter he found about the office, stuffed them in the coach and drove to Police Headquarters in Mulberry Street. Entering alone, he proceeded to upbraid the officials for concealing the flagrant facts from all the papers but the *Herald*. Naturally the situation resolved itself into a dumfounded Williams and a funereal return of himself and his coachload to Park Row.

All the papers exploded in violent condemnation, but the *Times* "led all the rest." Dipping his pen in lunar caustic, the editor, now gone to his well-earned repose, "roasted" the *Herald*, its proprietor, its editor, its "too famous intellectual department." "No such carefully prepared story could appear without the consent of the proprietor or editor—always supposing that this strange newspaper has an editor, which seems rather a violent stretch of the imagination." His note throughout was that it was all intended as a joke, and aimed to be funny and laughter-provoking. Of course it was not intended as a joke, and that foolish assumption was the bit of commercialism that made his "screed" ineffective. For myself, my judgment I felt was clear of blame. It was a vivid bit of realistic writing that had shocked a couple of millions of people, written under orders. How to treat the result was not in my hands. And I may say that both Mr. Bennett and Mr. Connery failed to ride the storm as they should. In the end, however, the rumpus it made helped the *Herald's* circulation and did not perceptibly affect its advertising—and *the wild animals' cages were made secure without any stress being laid upon it.*

My share in it remained wholly unknown in the *Herald* office. As a hard worked Night Editor, I would not be suspected of such elaborate work as it involved. For months the authorship was an office topic often discussed around my desk. Harry O'Connor held his peace. Stanley McKenna, a Police Headquarters reporter, was oftenest charged with it, not that he could write, but that it made so free with the Department. To his great joy he was made drunk many times by groups of detectives thus seeking to explore his mind when he would be off his guard. He stuck to his formula, "Now, don't ask me!"

WHEN THE SETTLERS FLEECED THE EASTERN FINANCIERS

THE MORTGAGE racket, in the solitudes of sparsely settled regions, was in one respect the reverse of the real estate racket. In the latter, purchasers of poor or even nonexistent sites were the losers and prosperous sellers the winners. In the former, numerous settlers got mortgage money which they never repaid, and eastern financiers were the unsophisticated losers.

It was not so long ago—as late as 1890—when the era of the mortgage loan, advanced on settled government lands in Dakota Territory and Kansas and Nebraska, blazed its trail in history.

Seth King Humphrey (1864–1932), who tells this story of the time when he represented a Boston farm mortgage company in its endeavor to retrieve what it could from its loans in Nebraska and Dakota Territory, was born in Minnesota of New England parents. Before this adventure he was in the flour milling business and had invented an elevator. Later he wrote a number of books, two or three dealing with racial values and prospects, and including one on American Indians, and two travel volumes concerning the Pacific and Africa.

From Following the Prairie Frontier. *By Seth K. Humphrey.*

An odd twist in events took me back once more to the regions of the prairie settler.[1] All through the eighties, while the settlement of government land was going forward in Kansas, Nebraska, and Dakota Territory, farm loan companies throve enormously in the business of making first mortgage loans to settlers and selling the paper to small investors in New England, New York, and eastern Pennsylvania. The demand for these western investments often exceeded the supply, the loan companies competed with each other to get mortgages; in fact, through their local agents they would persuade settlers to borrow and borrow generously. It thus became really too easy for settlers to cash in on their western venture and "go back to their wives' folks." They borrowed more than the land was worth and fled.

Naturally the companies began to stagger under their loads of defaulted mortgages. In the same predicament as all the others was a certain farm mortgage company with headquarters in Boston and branch offices in Omaha and Kansas. Its sponsors were substantial business men of Boston; two or three of the directors had once gone West to investigate conditions. I never really believed the tales told

[1] This was in 1889.

A pioneer family poses outside its sod dugout home on the South Loup River, Custer County, Nebraska.

about their driving around the prairies in silk hats. For one thing, they returned from the settlements alive. But they saw what the local agents wanted them to see and gathered no practical information.

Now what the company wanted, according to a friend of mine who had a considerable interest in it, was a western man with some knowledge of prairie conditions and no high hat, who would go into that country and stay there until he had found out what was the matter with the farm mortgage business. Would I consider the undertaking? . . .

. . . Besides checking up delinquents I was to approve discreet loans to worthy settlers, as submitted by the company's local agents. Risky business this, loaning money on land in a country where four-fifths of it was for sale; but, as the company's officials expressed it, "How are we going to pay expenses if we don't have new mortgages to sell?"

Out through the town's collection of sleepy, false-front stores our little team patters and the worn buggy rattles—both of them ill-used leftovers from the hectic land-seeking days of three or five years before. In five minutes we are trotting along on the same sort of trail that one might travel over for a thousand miles without getting out of the county: two wheel tracks cut into the prairie, inside of which are two horse paths scuffed out of the sod by just such pattering little hoofs as are now taking us for a hundred-mile ride at the rate of six miles an hour. Road-builders could not have done the job as well on this dry, hard prairie soil. . . .

. . . Almost every vacant quarter section—the regular claim of one hundred and sixty acres—bore the marks of its settler: the crumbling walls of a sod house; a caved-in well, if one wished to look for it; and the breaking of ten acres as required by law for "proving up" the title. This breaking might run along a full half mile side of the quarter section; in that case it would be ten rods wide, since a strip one rod wide and a half mile long comprises an acre of land. But whatever its shape, a patch of prairie once broken always show up as a patch on the landscape; it goes back to grass, but not to the original prairie grass. It is darker, straighter, different, this mark of a settler gone.

I do not recall the noon stop for that day, although the place we stayed overnight I remember distinctly, because I made a loan of six hundred dollars on it; but on the basis of the multitude of noon-day stops I made during my three thousand miles of prairie driving in that first season of 1889, I should put the odds at about fifteen to two that our hostess was a bit frumpy as to person, and in her outlook on life somewhat down at the corners of the mouth; while it would be safe to bet a thousand to one that the table was next to the cookstove, that it was covered with oil-cloth, and that the food consisted of ham and eggs, coffee, and short biscuit. The chances for potatoes were about fifty-fifty. Anything else on a Dakota settler's table always put me into a stupor of surprise.

These women always seemed pleased to have wayfarers drop in for a meal, principally because they often saw nobody for days or weeks at a time, and the customary fifty cents left on the table— there was no charge made—perhaps cheered them up a bit. Good enough food for anybody, an agreeable break in the housewife's dead level, and a half hour's restful pipe for me while the horses were finishing their hay; those noonday stops on the Dakota prairie —a hundred to one—I look back upon contentedly.

A certain pride in my ability to fathom the real intentions of would-be borrowers more than once suffered injury, but on one occasion it had next to a knockout. The loan prospect for whom I fell headlong was a man who offered as security a piece of prairie quite as unpromising as any other, with only the usual ten acres broken; but on it was a house such as rarely graced a claim in that vast land of vanishing sod shacks. It was of frame and boards, evidently built by a carpenter, and it rose to the unprecedented height of a story and a half. The extra half was explained later by the size of the family.

But the man of that house! A Connecticut Yankee, so he said. This at once gave me fellow feeling for him, whereas I should have been thinking of nutmegs. He received us with a courtly manner and quietly let me do the pushing in the matter of making a loan. The agent, too, suddenly withdrew his customary pressure, much to my relief at the time. My questions were answered simply by the Yankee and without promptings from the agent.

Yes, it was a pretty good house. Cost him nearly five hundred dollars. Well, it *was* rather too much to have put into a house. All the money he had had, in fact. And the loan? Exactly—to equip the farm and set him going. Only four hundred and twenty-five dollars, that was all he wanted. No, no more—he had figured out just how much he needed—why borrow more?

And so on. It was all quite unusual. Now if he had shown an eagerness to get all he could, or even more than that odd four hundred and twenty-five dollars, or if the agent had done his usual pulling and urging, in short, if either party had given me one bit of argument on which to base a resistance, I would never have loaned a dollar on a raw piece of land with nothing to show toward the making of a farm except a frame house. They simply held off and let me do it.

A month later the whole family was off for San Francisco. Some relative there had a fruit ranch job waiting for him, it was said. The thing he had figured out so precisely was the price of the tickets.

In the middle of October, 1889, the clouds gathering over the western farm mortgage business broke violently. The failure of one of the biggest companies engaged in it revealed to the public for the first time the incredible extent to which western farms had been deserted, and carried with it the implication that the affairs of all other companies must be in the same unhappy state. Down slumped the sales of western farm mortgages, almost overnight.

One day toward noontime, when thoughts of ham and eggs were getting the better of the land business, my driver and I happened upon a little sod shack up against a hillside. Some of these benchlands—shelves part way down from the hilltops to the creeks —yielded a firm sod.

This was our only prospect of getting food. As we drove up, a young woman came around the side of the house, went in quickly, and shut the door. This was, as everywhere on the frontier, a sign that isolation had made her timid. The etiquette of the new country was as rigid in its way as that of milady's parlor. In such cases as this the rule was never to get out and go to the door, but just to sit in the buggy and shout "Good morning!" and thus give her a chance to get over the shock of seeing somebody. After a few cordial greetings sent into the air, she came out—they always did after a look through the window—and with a few careful preliminaries accepted our invitation to stay for dinner.

She was a refined, intelligent woman, alone with her two little children. Her husband was away, as so many others were, to earn money for his family. The home was exceptionally neat, but it had no floor. She explained that they had been among the earliest settlers in that part of the country—had lived here for six years, each year hoping to have enough money to buy lumber for a floor, but something had always happened to make them put off the expenditure. Now that her husband was working she really felt that the lumber could be had before winter closed in. With a touch of honest, unassumed yearning she said she had always wanted a floor.

Numberless sweepings had left the stove and the table a few inches above the rest of the clay floor level, and this made it a bit awkward with the chairs; but the universal meal was served with the quiet grace of a hostess. The boy and girl were neat in home-cut dresses. Curtains were at each of the little windows, and the two beds were screened off with calico hangings. To make a really good home that woman did not need a floor.

CARRY NATION, ROCKS AND EXCITED BARTENDERS

AT THE start of this century Carry Nation's name and deeds were newspaper headlines. Her nationwide campaign against the grog shops, starting in dry Kansas where she lived, was sincere and spectacular. The sale of her autobiography, a businesslike recital filled with unconscious humor, was one means of raising money for her crusade. She held that saloons and their contents possessed no rights; she was arrested some thirty times, mainly on the charge of disturbing the peace, a true charge.

Carry Amelia Moore Nation (1846–1911) was acquainted with vicissitudes. Her father, once a prosperous stockman, lost his money. In 1867 Carry loved and married a young doctor who died a drunkard in about a year. She married Davis Nation, lawyer, minister and educator of sorts and nineteen years her senior, in 1877; they were divorced in 1901. For many years she largely supported herself and those dependent on her, first by teaching school, and then by running hotels. In her later, more prosperous years she built a home for drunkards' wives in Kansas City, Kansas.

She is described as "a woman of commanding presence, nearly six feet tall, weighing 175 pounds, with extremely muscular arms; she dressed in a sort of black-and-white deaconess uniform." She was "afflicted with an hereditary paranoia." The inscription on her monument at Bolton, Missouri, "she hath done what she could," possesses the virtue of accuracy.

From The Use and Need of the Life of Carry A. Nation. *Written by Herself*.

On the 6th of June, before retiring, as I often did, I threw myself face downward at the foot of my bed and told the Lord to use me any way to suppress the dreadful curse of liquor. The next morning, before I awoke, I heard these words very distinctly: "Go to Kiowa,[1]

---

[1] Of the places named in this extract, Kiowa, Medicine Lodge, Wichita, Topeka, Chetopa and Barber County are in Kansas.

and" (as in a vision and here my hands were lifted and cast down suddenly.) "I'll stand by you."

I got a box that would fit under my buggy seat, and every time I thought no one would see me, I went out in the yard and picked up some brick-bats, for rocks are scarce around Medicine Lodge, and I wrapped them up in newspapers to pack in the box under my buggy seat. I also had four bottles I had bought from Southworth, the druggist, with "Schlitz-Malt" in them, which I used to smash with.

I hitched my horse to the buggy, put the box of "smashers" in, and at half past three o'clock in the afternoon, the sixth of June, 1900, I started to Kiowa.

I got there at 8:30 P.M. and stayed all night with a friend. Early next morning I had my horse put to the buggy and drove to the first place, kept by Mr. Dobson. I put the smashers on my right arm and went in. He and another man were standing behind the bar. These rocks and bottles being wrapped in paper looked like packages bought from a store. Be wise as devils and harmless as doves. I did not wish my enemies to know what I had.

I said: "Mr. Dobson, I told you last spring, when I held my county convention here (I was W. C. T. U. president of Barber County), to close this place, and you didn't do it. Now I have come with another remonstrance. Get out of the way. I don't want to strike you, but I am going to break up this den of vice."

I began to throw at the mirror and the bottles below the mirror. Mr. Dobson and his companion jumped into a corner, seemed very much terrified. From that I went to another saloon, until I had destroyed three, breaking some of the windows in the front of the building. In the last place, kept by Lewis, there was quite a young man behind the bar. I said to him: "Young man, come from behind that bar, your mother did not raise you for such a place." I threw a brick at the mirror, which was a very heavy one, and it did not break, but the brick fell and broke everything in its way. I began to look around for something that would break it. I was standing by a billiard table on which there was one ball. I said: "Thank God," and picked it up, threw it, and it made a hole in the mirror. While I was throwing these rocks at the dives in Kiowa, there was a picture before my eyes of Mr. McKinley, the President, sitting in an old arm chair and as I threw, the chair would fall to pieces.

The other dive keepers closed up, stood in front of their places and would not let me come in. By this time the streets were crowded with people; most of them seemed to look puzzled. There was one boy about fifteen years old who seemed perfectly wild with joy, and he jumped, skipped and yelled with delight. I have since thought of that as being a significant sign. For to smash saloons will save the boy.

When I reached Medicine Lodge the town was in quite an excitement, the news having been telegraphed ahead. I drove through the streets and told the people I would be at the postoffice corner to tell why I had done this. A great crowd had gathered and I began to tell them of my work in the jail here, and the young men's lives that had been ruined, and the broken hearted mothers, the taxation that had been brought on the county, and other wrongs of the dives of Kiowa. . . .

On the 27th of December, 1900, I went to Wichita, almost seven months after the raid in Kiowa. Mr. Nation went to see his brother, Mr. Seth Nation, in eastern Kansas and I was free to leave home.

I took a valise with me, and in that valise I put a rod of iron, perhaps a foot long, and as large around as my thumb. I also took a cane with me. I found out by smashing in Kiowa that I could use a rock but once, so I took the cane with me. I got down to Wichita about seven o'clock in the evening, that day, and went to the hotel near the Santa Fe depot and left my valise. I went up town to select the place I would begin at first. I went into about fourteen places, where men were drinking at bars, the same as they do in licensed places. The police standing with the others.

I finally came to the "Carey Hotel," next to which was called the Carey Annex or Bar. The first thing that struck me was the life-size picture of a naked woman, opposite the mirror.

I went back to the hotel and bound the rod and cane together, then wrapped paper around the top of it. I slept but little that night, spending most of the night in prayer. I wore a large cape. I took the cane and walked down the back stairs the next morning, and out in the alley I picked up as many rocks as I could carry under my cape. I walked into the Carey Bar-room, and threw two rocks at the picture; then turned and smashed the mirror that covered almost the entire side of the large room. Some men drinking at the bar ran at break-

Carry Nation in a moment of repose.

neck speed; the bar-tender was wiping a glass and he seemed trans-fixed to the spot and never moved. I took the cane and broke up the sideboard, which had on it all kinds of intoxicating drinks. Then I ran out across the street to destroy another one. I was arrested at 8:30 A.M., my rocks and cane taken from me, and I was taken to the police headquarters, where I was treated very nicely by the Chief of Police, Mr. Cubbin, who seemed to be amused at what I had done. This man was not very popular with the administration, and was soon put out.

At 6:30 P.M., I was tried and taken to Wichita jail; found guilty of malicious mischief. . . .

The way I happened to think of a hatchet as a souvenir, some one brought me one and told me I ought to carry them. I then selected a pattern and got a party in Providence, R. I., to make them. These have been a great financial aid to me; helped me pay my fines and expenses. People have often bought them from me, at my prison cell window. I sell them everywhere I go. . . .

From Holt I went to Topeka. I stopped with the United Brethren minister there, and spoke in his church. The saloons were all over Topeka. I went down town after dark, to see the condition of things. It was soon learned that I was on the streets, and a crowd gathered. I went to some dives and joints. I could not get in. One had his mistress stationed at the door with a broomstick. She gave me four blows before I could get away, poor creature. I met her neice after that, who told how the saloon-keeper cast her off and that she died a miserable death.

While I was there the State Temperance Union had a meeting in the First Presbyterian church. Capt. Cook, from Chetopa, got up in the meeting and said: "Here is ten dollars towards giving a medal to the bravest woman in Kansas, Carry Nation." One hundred and twenty dollars was raised.

I said: "I would prefer that the money be used to pay my lawyers, rather than be put into a medal as I did not wear gold in any way."

We held a good many meetings. I spoke in several churches and held meetings in Dr. Eva Harding's office, where we prepared to take measures to break up saloons in Topeka, where sworn officials were perjuring themselves from governor down to constable.

I passed on down to the "Senate" saloon and went in. This

was about daylight. The bartender ran towards me with a yell, wrenched my hatchet out of my hand and shot off his pistol toward the ceiling; he then ran out of the back door, and I got another hatchet from a lady with us. I ran behind the bar, smashed the mirror and all the bottles under it; picked up the cash register, threw it down; then broke the faucets of the refrigerator, opened the door and cut the rubber tubes that conducted the beer. Of course it began to fly all over the house. I threw over the slot machine, breaking it up and I got from it a sharp piece of iron with which I opened the bungs of the beer kegs, and opened the faucets of the barrels, and then the beer flew in every direction and I was completely saturated. A policeman came in and very good-naturedly arrested me. For this I was fined $100 and put in jail. . . .

I spoke in Austin, Texas, at the state university. When I arrived in the city I was met by "Uncle Tom" Murrah. "Uncle Tom" is a true type of the old fashion gentleman. Had it not been for the chivalry of this dear old friend I expect I would have had some trouble with the police of Austin.

I went into a saloon and was led out in very forcible manner by the proprietor, who was one of the city council. I stood in front of this man's man-trap and cried out against this outrageous business. The man kept a phonograph going to drown my voice. The police would have interfered but "Uncle Tom" told me to say what I pleased, and he would stand by me. I went up to the state university with students who tried to get a hall for me to speak to them but they could not. I spoke from the steps. In the midst of the speech and the cheers from the boys I heard a voice at my side. I looked and there stood the Principal, Prexley Prather. He was white with excitement, saying: "Madam, we do not allow such." I said: "I am speaking for the good of these boys." "We do not allow speaking on the campus." I said: "I have spoken to the students at Ann Arbor, at Harvard, at Yale, and I will speak to the boys of Texas." The boys gave a yell. The mail man was driving up at this time. The horse took fright, the letters and papers flew in every direction. The man jumped from the sulky; the horse ran up against a tree and was stopped. I offered to pay for the broken shafts but the mail carrier would take nothing. There was no serious damage and all had a good laugh, except, perhaps, the dignified principal.

WHEN A CITY BURNS—VIVID DETAILS

THE CHELSEA fire of 1908, which burned over 492 acres in the center of the Massachusetts city, leaving 17,450 homeless, is here graphically portrayed by one who was there. Walter Merriam Pratt served first as volunteer fireman, then on guard duty with the militia. As a description of a fire, this is one of the best.

Mr. Pratt, 28 years old at the time of the fire, went on to become a businessman and headed companies in the paper, real estate and auto fields. His goings and comings touched an uncommonly wide reach of interests; included were the writing of half a dozen books and membership in various veterans and geneological societies.

The Chelsea fire broke out just before eleven on Sunday morning, April 12, in the poorer section of the city. The scene opens with the conflagration well under way.

From The Burning of Chelsea. *By Walter Merriam Pratt.*

It seems as if every one tried first to save a mattress, which would become ignited before it was carried a block, and add to the volume of the flames. The yards and open spaces were strewn with old bedding and other inflammable material, which assisted in spreading the fire.

While the human beings were having such a hard time of it, dogs and cats were also having their sufferings. Looking out into Walnut Street one dog was seen, that had once been black, rushing madly about; its hide had been singed to a crisp, and when last seen it was headed right back into the flames. On many streets, dogs, cats, and hens were found after the fire, burned to death, and many horses also perished, as more would have, but for heroic work. In one instance Frank W. Wentworth, with some help, saved nineteen horses from a burning building by covering their eyes with blankets.

Huntington Smith of the Animal Rescue League estimates that as many as two thousand cats were burned to death. He says these figures are conservative, and gives as the reason their devotion to

These pictures of a Chelsea street, before and after the great fire of 1908, give some idea of the engulfing destruction and desolation wrought.

their homes; dogs, on the other hand, are more devoted to their masters, whom they followed, and for this reason very few perished.

The Universalist Church caught first in the steeple, as did most of the churches. The deacons had saved the communion service and had loaded a team with other church property, including valuable books and documents. On top of these they piled many pew cushions, —a fatal error. To quote Dr. Bush, "Do not ever try to save cushions under such conditions; if we hadn't tried to, we would have our books and papers today." The cushions caught fire before they had been taken two blocks and were instrumental in setting fire to several wooden houses in the vicinity of Chestnut Street and Washington Avenue.

Every one seemed to feel sure that the fire would be stopped at Broadway, as the buildings on this street were substantial structures built of stone and brick, and no one even then judged rightly the havoc which must ensue before the fury would abate.

It first reached Broadway between Third and Fourth streets. Here a heavy battery of engines was assembled to prevent its crossing, but the efforts of man and the floods of water were of no avail; the fire was beyond human control.

Up to now the flames had rushed through the foreign tenement district, but when it passed Chestnut Street it entered the business center. Before the fire had even reached Chestnut and Fifth streets awnings in Bassett Square, two and three blocks away, caught fire. The fire reached Bellingham Station about two o'clock. The sight from here, looking down Broadway and Hawthorne Street, was beyond description. The fire fairly lay across the streets in a cyclonic whirl of flame.

All at once out of Hawthorne Street shot an engine, as if coming out of a cannon. The driver was almost doubled up and the horses were going at a two-twenty clip; where they came from or how they ever got out of that furnace alive is a mystery.

The new six story brick Young Men's Christian Association building caught first in the upper story and then all over; hose was burned at this point as fast at it was laid. An electric car of the Boston and Northern Railroad which had been stopped on Broadway, just below Bellingham, by the shutting off of the power, was pushed up the street and over the bridge to safety by fully a hundred men.

Beyond Broadway lay blocks of substantial residences. The flames were gnawing up the structures on Hawthorne Street, and the Unitarian Church and Newspaper Row on Fourth Street were quickly burned. The fury of the spreading flames was indescribable. There would be no sign of fire in a building, when all at once it would seem to fairly burst into flames and simply melt away. One large double house, which was timed, took just eight minutes to burn from the moment the flames were first seen until the building was a mass of ruins in the cellar.

All this time people were fleeing from the fire, many moving things to what they considered a place of safety, only to be obliged to move them again and eventually have them burned. Many people who lived east of Broadway went out to see the fire before it had crossed that thoroughfare, only to return and find their homes either on fire or already destroyed. No one seemed to realize how fast the fire was traveling, except those who fought it. If people had heeded the first warnings of the soldiers and the police, many could have saved something, but they waited, not wishing to appear timid, and afraid of ridicule if they started to move too soon. In the face of the great battle they had to fight, firemen and police officers could not give heed to the frantic appeals of women to save furniture.

Many people, when they realized that they had lost everything, threw themselves in the street and cried aloud in their suffering. It was no uncommon sight to see white-faced women walking aimlessly along the street, heedless of where they were going, yet carrying a frying pan or tin dipper. One man rushed into his house, at the risk of his own life, to save the family cat. After carrying it a block the cat scratched itself free and dashed back into its burning home. Hundreds of people saved canary birds, and one woman came along the street with a statue, which had no head or feet, under one arm, and a bird cage with a cat in it under the other. When asked why she was saving the broken statue she looked at it in a dazed sort of a way and threw it away in disgust, and then wonderingly inquired how her bird had got out of the cage, never realizing that the cat had eaten it. One woman, remembering that she had left a pocket-book containing $17 on her dining-room table, rushed back into her home and grabbed up what she thought was her pocket-book, but when she had gotten several blocks away she found that in her excitement she had taken a piece of cut glass instead, and it was then too late to return. Another woman was ordered out of her house by a militiaman, but would not go until she had first filled her tea-kettle with water. Afterward she couldn't explain why herself. Many people went temporarily insane. On the Washington Avenue bridge one man stood for hours making appeals for volunteers to fight the fire; his coat was off and his hair was mussed. People paid no heed to his frantic gestures, but he probably imagined he was saving the city. Another man committed suicide by shooting himself near Union Park. Some lost the power of speech, but under the circumstances the number of minds affected was small.

One woman lugged a great marble clock under one arm and a dog under the other for three quarters of a mile. The dog couldn't lay down for three days, she had held him so tight. Many people saved things of little value and left things impossible to replace. One man carried twenty-two pieces of cut glass loose and unpacked, tied up in a sheet and thrown over his shoulder, for over a mile, through all the excitement, and not one piece was smashed.

A fireman entered Freeman's drug store while it was burning and taking the reflection of himself in the long mirror at the end of the store for another fireman walked through the glass.

Two men trying to save an upright piano gave it up when the cloth in the back caught fire. One opened the lid and played "There'll be a hot time in the old town to-night," while the buildings all about him burned.

Fate was especially kind to Eli C. Bliss, who lived in what is called Chestnut Street Pocket,—a short blind end of Chestnut Street beyond Washington Avenue, ending in a steep embankment at the railroad tracks. The fire approached so rapidly that escape was impossible, except by way of the embankment. Just as Mr. Bliss was leaving his attractive home a passing freight train stopped directly at the end of the street, and the train crew rushed up the bank and announced that they had two empty box cars. Working like demons nearly everything in the house of any value, including a grand piano, a lot of old mahogany furniture, books, and paintings, was piled into the cars, until they were nearly full. The train then pulled out just as the house commenced to burn, none too soon, as the cars were smoking themselves. Mr. Bliss later located his furniture in Lynn, after it had landed in Portland and had been shipped back. . . .

Many people made a frightful mistake by thinking they were

safe in fleeing to the Garden Cemetery. Those who did were surrounded on all sides by the flames, and for hours they crouched behind tombs, fighting the burning embers and gasping for breath.

The flames fairly shot up Bellingham Street, on which were
many fine homes. Chief among them, on the very top of the hill,
was the beautiful estate of Ex-Mayor Thomas Strahan, filled with
valuable paintings, tapestries, and art treasures, collected from all
parts of the world. The house was of brick and stone with a slate
roof and plenty of land about it, and it seemed as if it could be
saved. The view from the tower of the Strahan house can never be
forgotten. As far as one could see, a seething mass of flame, like
a tidal wave, was rolling up the hill. So fast had the fire approached
that the Lynn engine, stationed halfway up Bellingham Street, was
unable to get away. The firemen did not abandon it until their
faces were burned and their hair singed. It was beyond human force
to withstand the terrific heat and suffocating smoke, and it was with
difficulty, when they finally abandoned it, that they were able to
save their lives, as the fire completely surrounded them. . . .

. . . We fled down the hill in the direction of Orient Heights.
Hundreds were going the same way; poor and rich were on equal
terms. The wind blew with such force that women were blown into
fences and trees or lost their balance and fell. Great pieces of furniture went bounding end over end down the hill, blown by the wind.
Horses were running away, and the scene was one of terrifying confusion. Escape was possible only by enduring the hostile breath of
the flames, running, tripping over abandoned furniture in the blind-
ing, sickening smoke, towards the marshes to the northeast, where,
although safe from the flames, the refugees suffered untold agony
from the hail-storm of stones and showers of blazing embers that
fell upon them, burning holes in their clothes and starting grass
fires in every direction.

One old lady's celluloid back comb caught fire and her white
hair was burned down to the scalp in back before the flames could
be smothered. The many horses set loose on the marsh also en-
dangered lives. The wails of hundreds of frantic parents vainly
searching for their children added to the excitement. One mother
fell in a dead faint when her two-year-old child, whom she had
given up as lost, was brought to her.

The two bridges to East Boston next fell and cut off this means of escape, and in this way a Boston engine was burned and a boy lost his life. Near the bridges were many fine yachts, that of Mr. Seaver being worth $50,000. This, and many other vessels, were burnt. One broke away from its moorings and drifted to the East Boston shore, setting fire to the Standard Oil Works. This was about four o'clock, but from the time the fire began to spread into the east side of Chelsea, East Boston was in peril from the shower of sparks and burning brands which the high wind swept over its roofs. More than half the residents packed their belongings and were ready to move at a moment's notice. Despite the desperate efforts of the many engines the flames spread to a one-story brick building, containing three hundred barrels of oil, and soon four other buildings of the plant were burning. Next the great oil tanks went up, the flames shooting several hundred feet into the air and sending skyward great clouds of flame and thick, black smoke. This swept down the harbor, across the bay, and out to sea, continuing to do so for two days and two nights. Reports from Scituate, Cohasset, and other places showed that showers of embers dropped from the clouds, and in places good-sized pieces of burnt shingles were picked up. Grass fires were started in Nantasket and Winthrop. The glare from the fire in the evening was seen from Portland, Me. The natives at first believed it to be York Beach,[1] it was so bright. . . .

The Public Library, a gift to the city from the Hon. Eustis C. Fitz, containing over eighty thousand volumes and many historical records and relics, caught and burned without an attempt being made to save it or its contents.

One of the best illustrations of the heat of the fire to those familiar with the burning of books, is the fact that after the fire not one scrap of paper was found. Granite will often crumble and iron melt before a book will be totally burned up. . . .

As the sky grew light and the morning mist cleared away, it disclosed a vast expanse of smoking ruins. The night had passed, and what a night! filled with vivid, awful memories of the dead and injured, the homeless and destitute. The great blackened tract over which the fire had swept, which only the day before had been

[1] Approximate distances from Chelsea, as the sparks fly: Scituate, 17 miles; Cohasset, 14; Nantasket, 12; Winthrop, 2; Portland, 90; York Beach, 65.

covered with dwellings, stores, and public buildings, was deserted, save for the soldiers, and here and there little groups of firemen, tired and worn out, but still working. As it grew lighter more people appeared. On the playground to the west soldiers were pitching tents for the homeless. As far as one could see lay nothing but a barren waste, with here and there the ragged walls of a church or school standing out against the sky, like the ruins of some old castle.

On the sides of Bellingham Hill, with the exception of the walls of the Highland School, nothing remained.

The granite curbs that edged the streets were crumbled into little piles of sand and gravel, and in the entire area there was not enough inflammable material to kindle a kitchen fire. So intense and searching had been the heat that the telegraph poles in places were burned two feet into the ground. Nowhere were there any ashes; they had all gone with the gale. It was the most complete sweep that could be imagined; hardly a brick wall stood, save those of public buildings.

BIBLIOGRAPHY

Adams, Henry. *Letters (1858–1891)*. Edited by Worthington Chauncey Ford. Boston and New York: Houghton Mifflin Company, 1930. Pp. 425–27, 451–52.

Adams, John Quincy. *Memoirs*. Edited by Charles Francis Adams. Philadelphia: J. B. Lippincott & Co., 1874–77. Vol. 4, p. 74; Vol. 6, pp. 162, 169–70, 406; Vol. 7, pp. 27–28, 35–36; Vol. 8, pp. 64–65; Vol. 12, p. 64.

Aldrich, Mrs. Thomas Bailey. *Crowding Memories*. Boston: Houghton Mifflin Co., 1920. Pp. 143–44, 146–48, 157–60.

Alleman, Tillie Pierce. *At Gettysburg*. New York: W. Lake Borland, 1889. Pp. 18–67.

Allen, James. "Diary" *The Pennsylvania Magazine*. Philadelphia: Historical Society of Pennsylvania, 1885. Vol. IX, pp. 193–96, 278, 280–82, 294–96.

Anonymous (An Officer). *The Falling Flag*. New York: E. J. Hale & Son, 1874. Pp. 7–64.

——— (An Officer). *A Narrative of the Campaigns of the British Army, at Washington, Baltimore and New Orleans*. Philadelphia: M. Carey & Sons, 1821. Pp. 131–35.

——— (A Lady). *Rural Hours*. New York: George P. Putnam, 1850. Pp. 156–59, 378–80.

Barbé-Marbois, Francois, Marquis de. *Our Revolutionary Forefathers*. Translated by Eugene Parker Chase. New York: Duffield & Co., 1929. Pp. 184–87.

Beard, Dan. *Hardly a Man Is Now Alive*. New York: Doubleday, Doran & Co., 1939. Pp. 336–38, 344–45.

Blake, John. *The Private Instructor and Young Gentlemen's Pocket Companion*. Trenton, N. J.: D. Fenton, 1815. Pp. 16–17.

Burge, Dolly S. Lunt. *A Woman's Wartime Journal*. Introduction by Julian Street. Macon, Ga.: J. W. Burke Co., 1927. Pp. 16–63.

Cartwright, Peter. *Autobiography*. Edited by W. P. Strickland. Cincinnati: Cranston & Curts, 1856; New York: Hunt and Eaton, 1856. Pp. 48–52.

Chambers, Julius. *The Book of New York*. New York: The Book of New York Co., 1912. Pp. 59–62.

Clarke, Joseph I. C. *My Life and Memories*. New York: Dodd, Mead & Co., 1925. Pp. 160–63.

Cobbett, William. *A Year's Residence in America*. London: Chapman & Dodd, n.d. Pp. 142–43.

Coke, Lt. E. T. *A Subaltern's Furlough*. Philadelphia: Waldie's Circulating Library, Adam Waldie & Co., 1833. P. 383.

Combe, George. *Notes on the United States of North America during a Phrenological Visit in 1838–9–40*. Philadelphia: Waldie's Circulating Library, Adam Waldie & Co., 1841. P. 273.

The Connecticut Journal. New Haven, Conn., 1778 and 1781.

Craven, Bvt. Lieut. Col. John J., M. D. *Prison Life of Jefferson Davis.* New York: G. W. Dillingham Co., 1905. Pp. 39–44, 47–49.

Crowninshield, Mary Boardman. *Letters, 1815–1816.* Edited by Francis B. Crowninshield. Cambridge, Mass.: Riverside Press, 1935. Pp. 23–24, 35–36, 53–58.

Dickens, Charles. *The Works of Charles Dickens.* New York: Peter Fenelon Collier, n.d. Vol. XXVII, pp. 145–46.

Dickinson, S. N. *The Boston Almanac For the Year 1838.* Boston: S. N. Dickinson, 1838. Pp. 37–44.

Dimsdale, Thomas J. *Vigilantes of Montana.* 3rd ed. Helena, Mont.: State Publishing Co., 1915. Pp. 109–11, 118, 122–24, 133, 142.

Dorsey, Anna H. *An Article in The Washington Chronicle.* Washington, D. C.: May 12, 1861.

Dow, Lorenzo. *The Dealings of God, Man, and the Devil.* 2 vols. New York: Sheldon, Lamport & Blakeman, 1856. Vol. I, pp. 85–87.

Foulke, William Dudley, LL.D. *A Hoosier Autobiography.* New York: Oxford University Press, 1922. Pp. 116–18.

Fox, Ebenezer. *The Revolutionary Adventures.* Boston: Monroe and Francis, 1838. Pp. 54–67.

Garland, Hamlin. *Roadside Meetings.* New York: Macmillan Co., 1930. Pp. 447–49.

Gerry, Elbridge, Jr. *Diary.* New York: Brentano's, 1927. Pp. 193–99.

Gilder, Richard Watson. *Grover Cleveland: A Record of Friendship.* New York: The Century Company, 1919. P. 190.

Golovin, Ivan. *Stars and Stripes.* London: W. Freeman, 1856; New York: D. Appleton & Co., 1856. P. 13.

Goodrich, S. G. *A System of Universal Geography.* New York: Collins & Hannay, 1832. Pp. 100–102.

Greeley, Horace. *Recollections of a Busy Life.* New York: J. B. Ford & Co., 1868; Chicago: J. A. Stoddard & Co., 1868. Pp. 99–101, 414–16, 424.

Hall, Francis. *Travels in Canada and the United States in 1816 and 1817.* Boston: Wells and Lilly, 1818. Pp. 197–98.

Hawthorne, Nathaniel. *American Note-Books.* Boston: James R. Osgood & Co., 1817. Vol. I, pp. 152–55.

Hayes, Rutherford B. *Diary and Letters.* Edited by C. R. Williams. Columbus, Ohio: Ohio State Archeological and Historical Society, 1925. Vol. IV, p. 304.

Hobart, Mrs. Garret A. *Memories.* Privately printed, 1930. Pp. 37–43.

Hobart, Pasha, Admiral. *Sketches from My Life.* New York: D. Appleton & Co., 1887. Pp. 89–91, 93, 96, 98–101, 108–13.

Howe, M. A. DeWolfe. *George von Lengerke Meyer: His Life and Public Services.* New York: Dodd, Mead and Company, 1920. Pp. 376, 381.

——— *Life and Letters of George Bancroft*. New York: Chas. Scribner's Sons, 1908. P. 246.

Hughes, Thomas. *A Journal*. Introduction by E. A. Benians, M.A. Cambridge, England: Cambridge University Press, 1947. Pp. 23–27.

Humphrey, Seth K. *Following the Prairie Frontier*. Minneapolis University of Minnesota Press, 1931. Pp. 95–160.

Jefferson, Joseph. *Autobiography*. New York: Century Co., 1889. Pp. 158–65.

Logan, Mrs. John A. *Reminiscences of a Soldier's Wife*. New York: Chas. Scribner's Sons, 1916. Pp. 320–24.

Maclay, William. *Sketches of Debate in the First Senate of the United States*. Edited by George W. Harris. Harrisburg, Penna.: Lane & Hart, 1880. Pp. 129–30.

Manly, William Lewis. *Death Valley in 1849*. Santa Barbara: Wallace Hebberd, 1929. Pp. 157–60, 201–10.

Marryat, Capt. *Diary in America*. Philadelphia: Carey & Hart, 1839. P. 154.

Martin, Frederick Townsend. *Things I Remember*. New York: John Lane Company, 1913. Pp. 280–85.

Martineau, Harriet. *Society in America*. New York and London: Saunders and Otley, 1837. Vol. II, p. 200.

McCullogh, Hugh. *Men and Measures of Half a Century*. New York: Charles Scribner's Sons, 1889. Pp. 373–77.

Morse, Jedidiah. *Geography Made Easy*. Boston: Thomas and Andrews, 1806. Pp. 173–74.

Nation, Carry A. *The Use and Need of the Life of Carry A. Nation*. Topeka: F. M. Steves & Sons, 1905. Pp. 69–106.

Newton, Harry J. *Yellow Gold of Cripple Creek*. Denver, Colo.: Nelson Publishing Co., 1928. Pp. 85–86.

Niles, H. (ed.). *Niles' Weekly Register*. Baltimore: Franklin Press, 1814–15. Vol. VII, pp. 17, 48, 372–73, 385.

Offenbach, Jacques. *Offenbach in America*. Indianapolis: Pratt Poster Co., 1928. Pp. 134–40.

Ogle, Charles. *The Regal Splendor of the President's Palace: A Speech Delivered in the House of Representatives, April 14, 1840*. Pp. 2–19.

Pancoast, Charles Edward. *A Quaker Forty-Niner*. Philadelphia: University of Pennsylvania Press, 1930. Pp. 123–36.

Pollard, Henry Robinson. *Memories and Sketches*. Richmond, Va.: Lewis Printing Co., 1923. Pp. 46–47.

Poore, Ben: Perley. *Perley's Reminiscences*. Philadelphia: Hubbard Bros., 1886. Pp. 349–50.

Porter, A. Toomer, D.D. *Led On!* New York: G. P. Putnam & Sons, 1898. Pp. 157–65.

Pratt, Sarah S. *The Old Crop in Indiana*. Indianapolis: Pratt Poster Co., 1928. Pp. 134–40.

Pratt, Walter Merriam. *The Burning of Chelsea*. Boston: Sampson Publishing Company, 1908. Pp. 39–85.

Pumpelly, Raphael. *Across America and Asia*. New York: Leypoldt & Holt, 1870. Pp. 1–5.

Quincy, Josiah. *Memoir of the Life of Josiah Quincy Jun*. Boston: Cummings, Hilliard, & Co., 1825. Pp. 34–39.

Revoil, Benedict. *The Hunter and Trapper in North America*. Translated by W. H. Davenport Adams. London, Edinburgh and New York: T. Nelson and Sons, 1874. Pp. 130–34.

Russell, Charles Edward. *A-Rafting on the Mississipp'*. New York: The Century Company, 1928. Pp. 120–28.

Sargent, Nathan. *Public Men and Events*. Philadelphia: J. B. Lippincott & Co., 1875. Vol. II, pp. 193–94, 231–32.

Sartain, John. *The Reminiscences of a Very Old Man, 1808–1897*. New York: D. Appleton & Co., 1899. Pp. 205–12.

Smith, Mrs. Samuel Harrison. *The First Forty Years of Washington Society*. Edited by Gaillard Hunt. New York: Chas. Scribner's Sons, 1906. Pp. 109–13, 117–18.

Stewart, Senator William M. *Reminiscences*. Edited by George Rothwell Brown. New York and Washington; Neale Publishing Co., 1908. Pp. 188–89, 193–95.

Street, Julian. *Abroad at Home*. New York: Century Co., 1920. Pp. 435–38.

Temple, J. H. *History of the First Sabbath School*. Boston: Wright & Potter, 1868. Pp. 27–28.

Towbridge, John Townsend. *My Own Story: With Recollections of Noted Persons*. Boston and New York: Houghton Mifflin and Company, 1903. Pp. 311–13.

Trollope, Frances. *Domestic Manners of Americans*. New York: Dodd, Mead & Company, 1901. Vol. I, pp. 233–45.

Twining, Thomas. *Travels in America 100 Years Ago*. New York: Harper and Bros., 1893. Pp. 99–104.

Tyler, Samuel. *Memoir of Rogers Brooke Taney*. Baltimore: John Murphy & Co., 1872. Pp. 109–17.

Winthrop, Theodore. *Life in the Open Air, and Other Papers*. Boston: Ticknor and Fields, 1863. Pp. 251, 257–63.

Wortley, Mrs. E. Stuart. *A Prime Minister and His Son*. New York: E. P. Dutton & Co., 1925. Pp. 160–61.

Young, John Russell. *Men and Memories*. Edited by May D. Russell Young. New York and London: F. Tennyson Nealy, 1901. Vol. 1, pp. 59–72.

PICTURE CREDITS

THE EDITOR wishes to thank the White House Curator for permission to reproduce the photograph on page 18; the Mariners' Museum, Newport News, Virginia, for use of the illustration on page 95; and the Nebraska State Historical Society for the photograph on page 336. Acknowledgment is also made to the following institutions for other illustrative material as listed:

Pages 5, 10, 23, 33, 34, 41, 42, 43, 49, 78, 79, 158, 164, 187, 200, 205, 206, 221, 233, 244, 245, 252, 260, 268, 279, 289, 310, 343, Library of Congress; page 58, The I. N. Phelps Stokes Collection, The New York Public Library, Astor, Lenox & Tilden Foundations; page 100, Historical Society of Pennsylvania; pages 104, 184, U. S. Signal Corps, The National Archives; pages 190, 191, 213, 230, 312, The Smithsonian Institution.

PICTURE SOURCES

Page 33, *Frank Leslie's Illustrated*; page 42, *Frank Leslie's Illustrated*, March 22, 1873; page 43, *Harper's Weekly*, March 22, 1873; page 72, *Harper's Weekly*, May 25, 1861; page 90, *Harper's Weekly*, September 29, 1860; page 100, *The Pennsylvania Magazine*, 1885; pages 120, 121, *The First Forty Years of Washington Society*; page 189, *Letters of Mary Boardman Crowninshield*; page 200, Engraving by Samuel Hallyer after Lilly M. Spencer; page 212, the Harry T. Peters *America on Stone* Lithograph Collection; page 223, *Things I Remember*; page 233, *Frank Leslie's Illustrated*, October 23, 1858; pages 244, 245, 252, *Das Illustrirte Mississippithal*, by Henry Lewis; page 260, *The Recollections of a Lifetime* by S. G. Goodrich (Peter Parley) 1857; page 268, Lithograph by Kennedy & Lucas. Drawn on stone by H. Bridport; pages 279, 310, *American Scenery* by Nathaniel P. Willis; page 297, *The Life of Bret Harte* by Henry Childs Merwin; page 315, *The New Natural History* by Richard Lydekker, 1890; page 324, *Vigilantes of Montana*; page 320, *The Autobiography of Joseph Jefferson*; page 347, *The Burning of Chelsea*. All other illustrations are from material in the editor's collection.

ABOUT THE EDITOR

BULKLEY SOUTHWORTH GRIFFIN is a veteran newspaperman who has distinguished himself as an observer of the Washington scene for more than four decades. As chief of the Griffin-Larrabee News Bureau, which he established soon after coming to the nation's capital from the Springfield, Massachusetts, *Republican,* he has covered important developments in every branch of the Government, though his attention has been given mainly to Congress. This day-by-day study over the years has convinced him that, with all its faults, "Congress is the best thing we have and is the safeguard of our freedoms."

The compilation of OFFBEAT HISTORY, he remarks, was not only an unhurried and pleasant task, but a revealing voyage of historical discovery as well, and not a costly one. During half his years as a collector Mr. Griffin operated with a self-imposed maximum of a dollar for any one book, and some of the best of these secondhand volumes were secured under this limitation. Pursuing a hobby within a hobby, he has specialized in collecting the works of Mark Twain; his library contains several hundred books by and about that author, including volumes in Russian, Arabic, Turkish, and Japanese.

Another of Mr. Griffin's interests is the phenomenon of Unidentified Flying Objects. His first newspaper series on the subject appeared in 1958, and he continues to report on the UFO mystery.

Mr. Griffin served in World War I as an Army Air Force pilot, and during World War II was for some months a war correspondent with General Patton's Third Army in Europe.